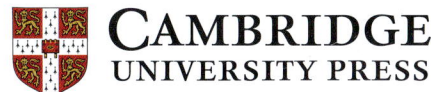

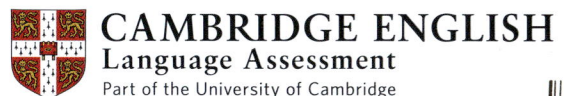

CAMBRIDGE UNIVERSITY PRESS

CAMBRIDGE ENGLISH
Language Assessment
Part of the University of Cambridge

Cambridge English

EMPOWER

COMBO B
STUDENT'S BOOK

B1+

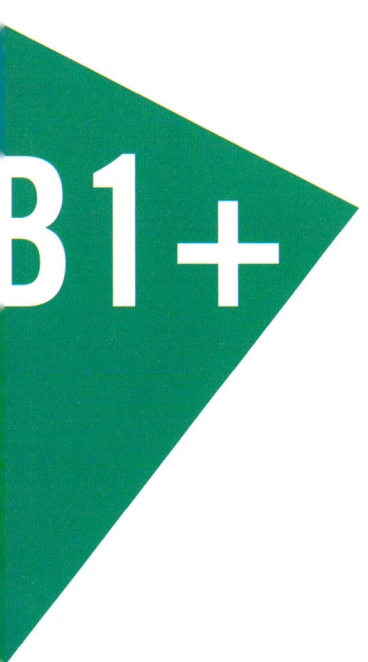

Adrian Doff, Craig Thaine
Herbert Puchta, Jeff Stranks, Peter Lewis-Jones
with Rachel Godfrey and Gareth Davies

This page is intentionally left blank

Contents

STUDENT'S BOOK

Map of Student's Book	4
Unit 6 Different cultures	67
Unit 7 House and home	79
Unit 8 Information	91
Unit 9 Entertainment	103
Unit 10 Opportunities	115
Communication Plus	129
Grammar Focus	142
Vocabulary Focus	156
Audioscripts	167
Phonemic symbols and Irregular verbs	174

WORKBOOK

Map of Workbook	2
Unit 6 Different cultures	34
Unit 7 House and home	40
Unit 8 Information	46
Unit 9 Entertainment	52
Unit 10 Opportunities	58
Vox pop video	68
Audioscripts	74
Answer key	82

Contents

Lesson and objective	Grammar	Vocabulary	Pronunciation	Everyday English
Unit 6 Different cultures				
Getting started Talk about different cultures				
6A Talk about advice and rules	Modals of obligation	Compound nouns; Multi-word verbs	Word stress: compound nouns	
6B Describe food	Comparatives and superlatives	Describing food	Sound and spelling: /ʃ/ and /tʃ/	
6C Ask for and give recommendations			Sounding interested	Asking for and giving recommendations
6D Write a review of a restaurant or café				
Review and extension More practice		WORDPOWER *go*		
Unit 7 House and home				
Getting started Talk about ideal houses				
7A Describe a building	Modals of deduction	Buildings	Modal verbs: sounding the final *t* or *d*	
7B Describe a town or city	Quantifiers	Verbs and prepositions	Sentence stress: verbs and prepositions	
7C Make offers and ask for permission			Sounding polite	Making offers and asking for permission
7D Write a note with useful information				
Review and extension More practice		WORDPOWER *over*		
Unit 8 Information				
Getting started Talk about an interesting news story				
8A Talk about the news	Reported speech	The news	Sound and spelling: /g/ and /k/	
8B Talk about what other people say	Verb patterns	Shopping; Reporting verbs	Sound and spelling: /s/ and /z/	
8C Generalise and be vague			Sound and spelling: /h/ and /w/	Generalising and being vague
8D Write an email summary of a news story				
Review and extension More practice		WORDPOWER *in/on* + noun		
Unit 9 Entertainment				
Getting started Talk about street entertainers				
9A Talk about films and TV	The passive	Cinema and TV	Auxiliary verbs in passive sentences	
9B Give extra information	Defining and non-defining relative clauses	Music; Word-building (nouns)	Relative clauses: pausing; Word stress	
9C Recommend and respond to recommendations			Showing contrast	Recommending and responding
9D Write an article				
Review and extension More practice		WORDPOWER *see, look at, watch, hear, listen to*		
Unit 10 Opportunities				
Getting started Talk about different kinds of opportunities				
10A Talk about new things you would like to do	Second conditional	Sport; Adjectives and prepositions	Sentence stress: *would*	
10B Talk about imagined past events	Third conditional	Expressions with *do*, *make* and *take*	Sentence stress: *would* and *have*	
10C Talk about possible problems and reassure someone			Sounding sure and unsure	Talking about possible problems and reassuring someone
10D Write an email with advice				
Review and extension More practice		WORDPOWER Easily confused words		
Communication Plus p.129	**Grammar Focus** p.142		**Vocabulary Focus** p.156	

Contents

Listening and Video	Reading	Speaking	Writing
Conversation: a TV programme	Article: *The Toughest Place to be a …*	Advice about living in another country	
Monologue: vending machines in Japan	Blog: *Hungry adventures*	Describing a special meal	
Planning to get married		Asking for and giving recommendations; Sounding interested	Unit Progress Test
Three monologues: special occasions	Reviews of a café	Places to go out	Two reviews Positive and negative language; adverbs
	Web page: *A more personal place to stay*	Describing buildings	
Conversation: comparing life in a town and a city	Five reasons why small towns are better than cities	Talking about where you live	
Meeting the parents		Making offers, requests and asking for permission; Imagining people's feelings	Unit Progress Test
Conversation: a holiday in Florida	Article: *Top five things to do … in and around Miami*; A note	A recent holiday	A note with useful information Offering choices
	Article: *Everyone's a journalist*	A news website	
Conversation: a fake restaurant		Describing experiences using reporting verbs	
Giving good news		Generalising; Being vague	Unit Progress Test
Monologue: a news story	A news story	Air travel	An email about a news story Summarising information
Radio discussion: CGI in films	Article: *Film-making has changed a lot in the last 100 years – or has it … ?*	Recommending a film or TV show	
Three monologues: music experiences	Article: *The three best music festivals you've probably never heard of*	A music experience	
Planning an evening out		Recommending and responding; Asking someone to wait	Unit Progress Test
Two monologues: live music	A blog about staying at home	Live music	An article about a form of entertainment Contrasting ideas; The structure of an article
Conversation: trying new sports		Taking new opportunities	
	Article: *Searching for serendipity*	A past event that made life better	
Making a marriage proposal		Talking about possible problems and reassuring someone; Changing the subject	Unit Progress Test
Monologue: volunteering	A web page about volunteering; Emails giving advice	Volunteering	An email with advice Advising someone a course of action

Audioscripts p.167   **Phonemic symbols and Irregular verbs** p.174

This page is intentionally left blank

CAN DO OBJECTIVES

- Talk about advice and rules
- Describe food
- Ask for and give recommendations
- Write a review of a restaurant or café

UNIT 6
Different cultures

GETTING STARTED

a 💬 Look at the photo. Ask and answer the questions.
1 Where do you think the photo was taken?
2 Where are the people from?
3 What do they have in common?
4 How are they different?

b 💬 Have you met people from different cultures? What did you have in common? How were you different?

6A You have to use pedestrian crossings

Learn to talk about advice and rules
- **G** Modals of obligation
- **V** Compound nouns; Multi-word verbs

1 READING AND SPEAKING

a 💬 Talk about the jobs that you do or would like to do. Which one is the most difficult?

b 💬 Read *The Toughest Place to be a …* and answer the questions.
1. Which person do you think has the most difficult job?
2. Which British worker do you think will find the change the most difficult? Why?
3. Which episode would you find most interesting? Why?

2 VOCABULARY Compound nouns

a Read about compound nouns, then underline the compound nouns in the article.

> Compound nouns combine two words. Some compound nouns are one word (e.g. *lunchtime*), others are two words (e.g. *swimming pool*). They are usually formed of:
> - noun + noun (e.g. *newspaper*)
> - verb+*ing* + noun (e.g. *washing machine*)
> - noun + verb+*ing* (e.g. *windsurfing*)

b ▶2.22 **Pronunciation** Listen to the compound nouns from the article. Which part is stressed – the first or the second word? Practise saying the words.

c Complete the compound nouns with the words in the box.

> air   cycle   hour   jam   pedestrian   traffic
>
> 1 _____ crossing   4 _____ lights
> 2 _____ conditioning   5 traffic _____
> 3 rush _____   6 _____ lane

d Complete the email with the compound nouns from 2c.

> What a stressful morning! I woke up late and my car didn't start for 30 minutes. By the time I was on the road it was ¹_____ _____ and the roads were very busy. All the ²_____ _____ in the city centre were stuck on red so everything was moving very slowly. The lights at a ³_____ _____ were broken, so lots of people were walking across the roads through the traffic. I sat in the same ⁴_____ _____ for about 45 minutes. To make things worse, the ⁵_____ _____ wasn't working in my car so I was boiling hot! I was just thinking that I really should use public transport instead of my car when suddenly I saw someone waving at me from the ⁶_____ _____. It was you, on your new bike, looking very pleased with yourself!

e 💬 Look at the picture on p.129. How many compound nouns can you find in two minutes?

The TOUGHEST place to be a …

In this TV series, workers from the UK experience what it's like to try doing their jobs in some of the most difficult conditions around the world.

 A London taxi driver tries his job on the busy streets of Mumbai.

 A nurse goes to work in the Emergency Department of a hospital in Ciudad Juárez in Mexico.

 A bus driver tries driving a jeepney in Manila, the Philippines, which is the most densely populated city in the world.

 A firefighter goes to Brazil to fight forest fires with a team in an area of the Amazon the size of England.

As well as the culture shock from moving to a workplace in a completely new country, they often have to deal with tough living conditions. But they get lots of help and support from a local host who looks after them and shows them how to do the job in a very different working environment.

UNIT 6

3 LISTENING

a Read about an episode from the TV series *The Toughest Place to be a ...* . What do you think Mason will find difficult about working in Mumbai?

In tonight's episode, London taxi driver Mason McQueen works in Mumbai, India for ten days. He is supported by local taxi driver Pradeep, and has driving lessons from a local driving instructor. But how will Mason manage when he has to go out on his own to find passengers in the Mumbai rush hour?

b ▶2.23 Listen to three friends talking about *The Toughest Place to be a ... Taxi Driver*. Tick (✓) the things that they mention.
1 ☐ The roads in Mumbai were very busy.
2 ☐ The roads were in a bad condition.
3 ☐ Mason had to drive an old car.
4 ☐ There were a lot of traffic jams.
5 ☐ Mason couldn't communicate with the local people.
6 ☐ The taxis that Mason drove had no air conditioning.
7 ☐ There weren't any traffic lights.
8 ☐ The passengers didn't like Mason.
9 ☐ It was difficult to get passengers.

c ▶2.23 Listen again and complete the sentences with one word or a number.
1 Mason spent _____ years studying maps of London.
2 He spent a _____ learning how to drive in Mumbai.
3 Mason drove _____ different taxis in Mumbai.
4 People in India call taxis with air conditioning '_____ cabs'.
5 The temperature in Mumbai was in the _____s.
6 Mason used _____ signals to indicate left and right.
7 Pradeep works _____ hours a day.
8 Pradeep earns about £_____ a day.

d 💬 Discuss the questions.
1 Do you think this was a good experience for Mason and Pradeep? Why / Why not?
2 Would you like to watch the programme?
3 Would you like to take part in the programme?

4 VOCABULARY Multi-word verbs

a ▶2.24 What are the missing multi-word verbs? Complete the sentences with the correct form of the verbs in the box. Listen and check.

get around   pick up   show around

1 He got on really well with Pradeep, the guy who _____ him _____ .
2 He learned how to _____ _____ the city pretty quickly.
3 He _____ _____ a few phrases of the local language.

b ▶ Now go to Vocabulary Focus 6A on p.156

69

UNIT 6

5 GRAMMAR
Modals of obligation

a 💬 What do you think people might find difficult when they spend some time in a different culture?

b Read *Culture shock*. Find four things people might find difficult.

c 💬 Have you ever experienced culture shock? When? Where?

d Read the text again. <u>Underline</u> the words or phrases which express obligation and advice (*must*, *have to*, etc.).

e Complete rules 1–5 with the words in the box.

> can   can't   don't have to   have to
> must   mustn't   ought to   should

1 We use _____ and _____ to give advice.
2 We use _____ to say that something is not necessary.
3 We use _____ and _____ to say that something is necessary.
4 We use _____ and _____ when we say that something is forbidden/not allowed.
5 We use _____ to talk about a choice to do something.

f ▶ Now go to Grammar Focus 6A on p.142

g Complete these rules about transport in your country. Use the verbs in the box.

> must/have to   don't have to   mustn't
> should   shouldn't   can   can't

Buses
1 You _____ buy a ticket in advance.
   You _____ buy a ticket on the bus.

Walking and cycling
2 You _____ use pedestrian crossings when you want to cross the road.
3 You _____ wear a cycle helmet.
4 You _____ cycle on the pavement.
   You _____ use cycle lanes.

Cars
5 Passengers _____ wear a seat belt.
6 You _____ drive with your lights on during the day.

Taxis
7 You _____ stop taxis in the street.
8 You _____ book taxis in advance.
9 You _____ give taxi drivers a tip.

CULTURE SHOCK

Some people choose to live in another country, other people have to move for family or work reasons. If you're going to live in a new place for some time, you ought to be prepared to experience culture shock at some point.

At first, when you're in a very different environment, everything seems exciting and new. Then, the differences start to be annoying. Life feels too fast or too slow, the food tastes strange, you miss your favourite television programmes. Laws are different – there are things you mustn't do here that you can do at home. This is culture shock.

The good news is, you don't have to spoil your experience of living abroad. Culture shock doesn't usually last very long.

h A foreign visitor is coming to live in your country for six months. Prepare to give him/her some advice. Use the ideas in the box and your own ideas to make a list of rules and tips.

> roads, pavements and cycle lanes   public transport
> eating and drinking   talking to people who are older than you
> going out at night   clothes   language   parks and public spaces

You mustn't eat or drink when walking in the street.
You should always give your seat to an older passenger on the bus.

i 💬 Take turns to read out your rules. Discuss the questions.
   1 Which rules are about safety?
   2 Which are about being polite to people?
   3 Which rules are the most important?

6 SPEAKING

a Read the questions and make notes about your answers.
   1 Which foreign country/other area would you like to study/do your job in?
   2 Why would you like to live there?

b 💬 Discuss the questions in 6a. Think of anything your partner should/must/mustn't do to prepare. What other advice would you give them?

I'd like to work in France.

You should do some French classes before you go.

Good idea!

6B It's tastier than I expected

Learn to describe food
- G Comparatives and superlatives
- V Describing food

1 VOCABULARY Describing food

a 💬 Look at photos a–e and discuss the questions.
1 Which food would you most like to eat?
2 What country do you think each dish comes from?
3 What ingredients does each dish contain?
4 Which of the dishes could a vegetarian eat?

b Match descriptions 1–5 with photos a–e.

> 1 Tasty Moroccan meatballs cooked in a tomato sauce, served with couscous and fresh herbs.
> 2 Creamy Mexican avocado and tomato dip with crunchy tortilla chips.
> 3 Japanese noodles with vegetables in a light soup served with a raw egg.
> 4 White fish cooked in a spicy Thai sauce with hot green chillies.
> 5 A slice of rich Austrian chocolate cake with a bitter orange filling.

c Which adjectives in 1b could you use to describe a salad, a soup, or a curry?

d ▶ Now go to Vocabulary Focus 6B on p.156

e ▶2.29 **Pronunciation** Listen and repeat these words. Pay attention to the pronunciation of the letters *sh* and *ch*.

/ʃ/	/tʃ/
fre<u>sh</u>	<u>ch</u>ocolate
ma<u>sh</u>	<u>ch</u>op
	ri<u>ch</u>
	crun<u>ch</u>y

f 💬 A visitor has come to your town. You're going to give advice about where to go and what typical dishes to try.
Student A: Give the visitor advice.
Student B: You are the visitor. Listen and ask further questions.

g 💬 Now change roles and have a second conversation.

2 LISTENING

a 💬 Look at the photo on the right and discuss the questions.
1 Do you have vending machines in your country? What do they sell?
2 How often do you use them?

b ▶2.30 Listen to part of a radio programme about vending machines in Japan.
1 What food and drink is mentioned?
2 What are the advantages for customers of vending machines over buying things from a shop?
3 What does the reporter think of the hot meal?

c 💬 Would you buy hot food from vending machines?

71

UNIT 6

3 GRAMMAR
Comparatives and superlatives

a ▶ 2.31 Complete the sentences with the words in the box. Then listen and check your answers.

| as good as | a bit longer than | the best |
| by far the highest | much better than | much cheaper |

1 Japan has _____ number of vending machines per person in the world.
2 It's _____ for sellers to run a vending machine than a shop.
3 But is curry and rice from a machine _____ curry and rice from a restaurant?
4 It's taking _____ I imagined.
5 It's actually _____ I expected.
6 I think it might be _____ vending machine meal I've ever eaten.

b ▶ Now go to Grammar Focus 6B on p.142

c Use the ideas below to write sentences with comparatives, superlatives and (not) as … as.

| cheap | fun | good for you | healthy |
| interesting | nice | spicy | sweet | tasty |

- dark chocolate / milk chocolate / white chocolate
- street food / food in expensive restaurants / home-made food
- Japanese food / British food / Indian food
- vegetarian food / meat dishes / fish dishes
- food from my country / food from other countries
- eating alone / eating with friends

Dark chocolate isn't as nice as white chocolate.

d 💬 Read out your sentences. Do you agree or disagree with each other?

'Have you eaten?'
May 13th

Singaporeans are my kind of people – they're passionate about food and eating!

People here eat often – they have five or six meals a day. Instead of 'Hello' or 'How are you?' they ask, 'Have you eaten?'. And it's hard to believe just how many different kinds of dishes you can get in this tiny country – Chinese, Indian, Arabic, European and many, many more.

The best meal of the day today was lunch. The main course was *muri ghonto* or fish head curry – far more delicious than it sounds! It's a southern Indian dish. You can have it with rice, but we had it the way that the Chinese do, with a soft bread roll.

Dessert was *cendol* – coconut milk, ice and green noodles. It's a typical south-east Asian dish. It wasn't as sweet as I expected, but the noodles were lovely – a bit like jelly.

There are places to eat here to suit everyone – from food stalls in shopping malls to more upmarket (and more expensive!) restaurants. My plan is to try as many as I can in the short time I'm here.

4 READING

a 💬 Look at the photo on the left. Which country do you think it is?

b Read the blog, *Hungry adventures*. Check your answer to 4a.

c Read the blog again. Find the descriptions of the dishes and match them with the food photos a–d.
1 ☐ chicken satay 3 ☐ cendol
2 ☐ muri ghonto   4 ☐ thosai

d 💬 Discuss the questions.
1 Did the blog writer enjoy the dishes in 4c?
2 Which of the dishes would you like to try?

HUNGRY ADVENTURES

UNIT 6

Travelling and eating around the world

Hawker centres – street food, but not on the streets
May 14th

Singapore is famous for its street food, but it's been illegal to sell cooked food in the streets for many years. So, if you're looking for Singapore's famous street food, hawker centres are the places to go. These are indoor food markets with stalls that sell freshly cooked food. You choose your hawker centre according to what kind of cuisine you fancy – Thai, Malay, Chinese, Indian, Middle Eastern.

I went to the Golden Mile Food Centre – it was amazing to see so many different food stalls under one roof. *Sup tulang* – a Malay-Indian dish of beef bones in a red spicy sauce – looked very tasty. But in the end I wanted something lighter, so I chose *ayam buah keluak*, a Paranakan (Chinese-Malay) dish. It's chicken with Indonesian black nuts, served with steamed rice. A good choice – one of the most unusual dishes I've ever tasted.

Little India, big appetite
May 15th

This part of Singapore was full of the sights and smells of India. I ate *thosai* – crispy Indian pancakes made from rice and lentils. They were served with rich and spicy dips and vegetable curry. The meal was light and fresh – delicious!

Still full from my Indian lunch, I explored the Arab Quarter. There was plenty of great food on offer, but sadly I wasn't hungry! I'll have to come back to Singapore. I haven't had a chance to explore Chinatown either.

By the evening I was hungry again, so I tried some of the barbecued food at Lau Pa Sat, an old market. I went for Malaysian chicken *satay*, pieces of chicken on sticks served with spicy peanut sauce. Absolutely delicious!

---

e Read the blog again and answer the questions.
1. What two habits show that the people in Singapore love food?
2. What did the blog writer eat with her fish head curry?
3. Why can't you buy food on the street in Singapore?
4. Why didn't she have *sup tulang* at the Golden Mile Food Centre?
5. Why didn't she eat anything in the Arab Quarter?
6. Which area of Singapore did she not go to?

f 💬 Imagine you are visiting Singapore. Where will you go? What will you eat?

> I'd really like to go to a big hawker centre, so we can see all the different options.

5 SPEAKING

a You are going to talk about a special meal. Make notes about one of these meals. Use the ideas in the box to help you plan what to say.
- the most special meal that you've ever made
- the most delicious meal you've ever eaten
- a meal you'll never forget

where?   when?   who with?   ingredients?
how was the food cooked?   taste, smell, colour?

b 💬 Take turns to describe your meals. Then talk about which of the meals sounds the most delicious.

> The most delicious meal I've ever eaten was in a little restaurant near my grandparents' house. I ate …

6C Everyday English
Do you think I should take her somewhere special?

Learn to ask for and give recommendations
- P Sounding interested
- S Asking for and giving recommendations

1 LISTENING

a 💬 Discuss the questions.
  1 Which of these do you think is the most romantic?
     - flowers
     - dinner at a restaurant
     - a home-made meal
     - a handwritten love letter
     - an expensive gift (e.g. jewellery)
  2 Have you ever bought/done these things for anyone?

b 💬 Look at the photo below. Where are Tom and Rachel? What are they doing? What do you think they are talking about?

c ▶ 2.33 Watch or listen to Part 1 and check.

d ▶ 2.33 Watch or listen again. Are the sentences true (T) or false (F)?
  1 Tom isn't going to ask Becky to marry him.
  2 Tom is going to take Becky to Paris.
  3 Mark asked Rachel to marry him at a special place.
  4 Becky and Tom used to work together.

e 💬 Do you agree with Rachel's advice? Where should Tom propose to Becky?

2 USEFUL LANGUAGE
Asking for and giving recommendations

a Look at the phrases in **bold** below. Which ones are asking for recommendations? Which are giving recommendations?
  1 **Do you think I should** take her somewhere special?
  2 **If I were you, I'd** take her somewhere special.
  3 **It's probably worth** asking her where she wants to go.
  4 **What would you do** about the ring?
  5 **Would you recommend** buying a very expensive ring?
  6 **It's much better to** buy something that's her style.
  7 **It's not a good idea to** ask her what she likes.

b Complete the conversations with the correct form of the verbs in brackets. Look back at the phrases in 2a to help you.

  1
  A What do you think I should [1]_____ Dad for his birthday? (get)
  B If I were you, I [2]_____ him what he wants. (ask)
  A But that will ruin the surprise.
  B It's much better [3]_____ him what he wants though. (get)
  A True, I suppose.

  2
  A Where would you recommend [1]_____ the party? (have)
  B It's probably worth [2]_____ Laura if she can recommend a restaurant. She knows lots of great places. (ask)
  A And what about the cake? What would you [3]_____? (do)
  B Get it from a bakery. And it's a good idea [4]_____ them as soon as you can. They get very busy. (contact)

74

UNIT 6

3 CONVERSATION SKILLS
Expressing surprise

a Look at the sentences about the next part of the story. Which option do you think is most likely?
1 Rachel advises Tom to buy *a huge diamond / something that's Becky's style.*
2 Tom thinks that the rings in the jewellery shop are *very expensive / cheap.*
3 Rachel and Tom see Becky and *say hello to her / hide in the shop.*

b ▶2.34 Watch or listen to Part 2 and check your answers to 3a.

c ▶2.34 Watch or listen to Part 2 again and complete the sentences.
1 **Tom** So, what about the ring? What would you buy? A big diamond, right? So she can show it to her friends?
   Rachel _____? Tom, do you know Becky at all?
2 **Rachel** It's £1500.
   Tom I _____ _____ _____! That's ridiculous.
3 **Rachel** Tom! It's Becky! Over there.
   Tom _____ _____! What should we do?

d 💬 Take it in turns to say the sentences below and express surprise.
1 I'm getting married.
2 I passed all my exams.
3 That coat costs £300.
4 I lost my phone yesterday.

4 PRONUNCIATION
Sounding interested

a ▶2.35 Listen to this extract. Is the intonation flat or not? <u>Underline</u> the correct word in the rule.

Rachel I am so excited. I still can't believe you're going to ask Becky to marry you.

Sometimes, intonation is more important than the words we use. If we use *varied / flat* intonation, we may sound as if we're bored, or don't care about the subject.

b ▶2.36 Listen to exchanges 1–3. Which of the B speakers sounds bored?
1 **A** I've got a new job.
   B Wow. That's incredible.
2 **A** I've just bought some new shoes.
   B That's amazing.
3 **A** We lost the game last night.
   B That's terrible.

c Practise saying the exchanges in 4b. Try to sound interested.

5 SPEAKING

▶ **Communication 6C** 💬 Student A: Read the instructions below. Student B: Go to p.131

Student A
1 You have been offered an amazing job. The salary is very high, and it is a great opportunity. The problem is that you need to move to New York next month! Tell your partner your news and ask for some recommendations what to do.
2 Listen to your partner's surprising news and give some recommendations.

I've been offered a new job. It's in New York!

No way! That's great.

Do you think I should take it?

Unit Progress Test

CHECK YOUR PROGRESS

You can now do the Unit Progress Test.

75

6D Skills for Writing
It's definitely worth a visit

Learn to write a review of a restaurant or café
W Positive and negative language; adverbs

1 SPEAKING AND LISTENING

a Look at situations 1–3. Where would you go for these occasions? Choose from the locations in the box.
1 to meet friends for a chat and a drink
2 a birthday or an anniversary
3 a party at the end of term or the end of a language course

> a café   a cheap restaurant   an expensive restaurant
> a venue with music or dancing (e.g. a club)

b 💬 Compare your ideas. Do you agree?

c ▶ 2.37 Listen to Jeff, Fabio and Carla. Which places in photos 1–3 are they talking about?

d ▶ 2.37 Listen again and answer the questions.
1 Why doesn't Jeff like the atmosphere at expensive restaurants?
2 What does he say about the food?
3 Does Fabio go to cafés alone, or with friends, or both?
4 Why does he like pavement cafés?
5 What does Carla do before she starts dancing?
6 What kind of music does her favourite place play?

e Think of one place to go out that you really like and one that you don't really like. Make notes about their good and bad points.

f 💬 Discuss your places. If your partner(s) know the two places you chose, do they agree?

2 READING

a Read the four reviews of a café on p.77. The first review gave five stars (= excellent). How many stars do you think the other reviews gave?

b Read reviews a–d again. <u>Underline</u> any words or phrases that are used to describe the things below.
1 the atmosphere
2 the kind of food and drinks they serve
3 the quality of the food
4 the service
5 value for money
6 the location

UNIT 6

a 'Very highly recommended. Would go back again.'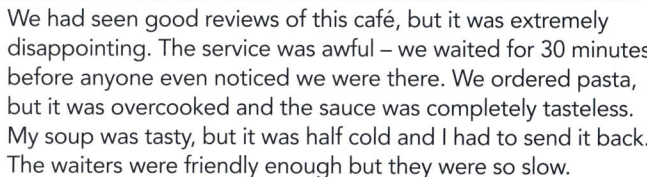

I came here on my birthday. The coffee and cakes were delicious and there was a relaxing atmosphere, with plenty of space. The staff were very friendly and gave us free birthday drinks. I can definitely recommend this café and I'll be going back.'

b 'Visited twice in 3 days!'

We had lovely food here. The fish was very fresh and they had delicious salads. It's also a great place to just sit and relax. The second time we went, we just ordered drinks and the waiters were friendly and left us alone. We stayed for three hours! It's right in the town centre, so it's a bit noisy, but it's a convenient place to meet and fairly easy to get to. It's definitely worth a visit!

c 'Completely overrated'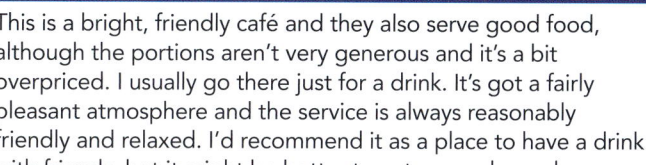

We had seen good reviews of this café, but it was extremely disappointing. The service was awful – we waited for 30 minutes before anyone even noticed we were there. We ordered pasta, but it was overcooked and the sauce was completely tasteless. My soup was tasty, but it was half cold and I had to send it back. The waiters were friendly enough but they were so slow.

d 'A nice place to meet friends'

This is a bright, friendly café and they also serve good food, although the portions aren't very generous and it's a bit overpriced. I usually go there just for a drink. It's got a fairly pleasant atmosphere and the service is always reasonably friendly and relaxed. I'd recommend it as a place to have a drink with friends, but it might be better to eat somewhere else.

3 WRITING SKILLS
Positive and negative language; adverbs

a Add the adjectives or phrases from the reviews above to the table.

positive	fairly positive
delicious	friendly enough

fairly negative	negative
a bit noisy	awful

b Compare your answers. Did you choose the same adjectives and phrases?

c The two sentences below are similar in meaning. Do you think that in sentence 1 … ?
  a the writer isn't sure what he/she thinks
  b the writer doesn't want to be too negative

1 The portions weren't very generous.
2 The portions were absolutely tiny.

d Which of the sentences are slightly negative (like sentence 1 in 3c)? Which are very negative (like sentence 2 in 3c)?
1 It was extremely disappointing.
2 The bread wasn't very fresh.
3 The sauce was completely tasteless.
4 My soup wasn't really hot enough.
5 The portions were rather small.
6 The service was awful.

e Do we use these adverbs to make adjectives or phrases stronger or weaker?

a bit   absolutely   completely   extremely   fairly   not really
not very   quite   rather   really   reasonably   terribly

f Change the strong comments in the sentences in 3d so that they sound weaker. Change the weaker comments so that they sound stronger.
1 It was a bit disappointing.   2 The bread was really old.

4 WRITING A review

a Choose two places you know (restaurants, cafés or venues with music). Think of one place you like a lot and one place you don't really like. Make notes about the points below:
- general atmosphere
- location
- how busy it is
- what they serve
- quality of food
- service
- friendliness
- prices
- value for money

b Compare your ideas with a partner.

c Write two reviews, one for each place.

d Work in pairs. Read your partner's reviews. Check that your partner has done the things below.
1 covered all the points in 4a
2 used appropriate adjectives and phrases
3 used adverbs appropriately

e Show your reviews to other students. If they know the places, do they agree?

77

UNIT 6
Review and extension

1 GRAMMAR

a Read the text and underline the best words.

Essaouira is a wonderful place to visit. You ¹*must / should / can* enjoy walking through the streets, shopping at the market or tasting local food. It's often windy in Essaouira, so you ²*don't have to / should / have to* bring warm clothes. The wind means that the beach isn't good for sunbathing but you ³*ought to / shouldn't / must* go kite-surfing – it's really exciting!
If you like history, you ⁴*don't have to / have to / should* explore the old part of town. There are lots of market stalls here. If you want to buy something, discuss the price with the stallholder. You certainly ⁵*shouldn't / ought to / must* pay the first price you hear!
Many people here speak English, Spanish or French, so you ⁶*don't have to / should / mustn't* learn Arabic, although you ⁷*should / must / have to* probably learn a few useful phrases. You ⁸*can't / don't have to / mustn't* stay in expensive hotels; there are other options, including riads, which are hotels that feel like family homes.

b Complete the sentences with the correct form of the words in brackets. Add any extra words you need.
1. A burger in China is _____ (slightly cheap) a burger in Saudi Arabia.
2. Indonesia is _____ (a bit hot) Jamaica.
3. On average, trains in Japan are _____ (much fast) trains in India.
4. Thai food is _____ (by far spicy) I've ever eaten.
5. Travelling on the Rome metro isn't _____ (quite expensive) travelling on the London Underground.

2 VOCABULARY

a Complete each pair of sentences with compound nouns made from the words in the boxes.

air   crossing   conditioning   pedestrian

1. It's safer to use a _____. There's so much traffic.
2. **A** It's so hot!
   B I'll put the _____ on.

hour   public   rush   transport

3. Let's go at ten o'clock when _____ is over.
4. Shall we drive or use _____?

jam   lights   traffic   traffic

5. Sorry I'm late. I got stuck in a _____.
6. Wait for the _____ to change from red to green.

cycle   cash   lane   machine

7. That car shouldn't be in the _____!
8. I need some money. Is there a _____ near here?

b Complete the multi-word verbs.
1. I picked _____ Spanish when I went to Mexico.
2. We'd like to show you _____ our city.
3. I like eating _____, but a lot of restaurants are expensive.
4. I waited for an hour, but Helen didn't turn _____.

3 WORDPOWER *go*

a Match questions 1–6 with responses a–f.
1. ☐ Where does that path **go**?
2. ☐ How did your trip **go**?
3. ☐ This is my new dress. Do these shoes **go** with it?
4. ☐ Where's the milk?
5. ☐ Where's the cake you were making?
6. ☐ Was there food at the party?

a Really well. I met some lovely people.
b No, they're the wrong colour.
c To the beach, I think.
d Yes, but when I got there it had all **gone**.
e It **went** off. I threw it away.
f It **went** wrong. I threw it away.

b Match the phrases with *go* in 3a with these descriptions.
We can use:
- *go* to mean *disappear* _d_
- *go* (*with*) to mean *look similar/look good together* ___
- *go* to mean *go towards* ___
- *go wrong* to mean *develop problems/not succeed* ___
- *go* + adverb to describe how things happen (e.g. *go badly*) ___
- *go* + adjective to describe a change (e.g. *go grey*) ___

c Complete each sentence with the correct form of *go* and a word or phrase from the box, if necessary.

around   orange   really well   with my eyes   wrong

1. In the autumn, the leaves _____.
2. I had a job interview yesterday. It _____. I got the job!
3. Don't worry if it _____. Just start again.
4. When I turned to speak to Fred, he had already _____.
5. The road _____ the lake. It's a nice drive.
6. The man in the shop said the scarf _____.

d 💬 Look at what the people are saying. Think of two things that each person might be talking about.

1 It went very well, thanks.
2 It went completely white.
3 It goes very well with cheese.
4 Oh no! It's gone wrong!
5 It goes over the river.
6 It's gone. Good!

⟳ REVIEW YOUR PROGRESS

How well did you do in this unit? Write 3, 2 or 1 for each objective.
3 = very well   2 = well   1 = not so well

I CAN . . .

talk about advice and rules. ☐
describe food. ☐
ask for and give recommendations. ☐
write a review of a restaurant or café. ☐

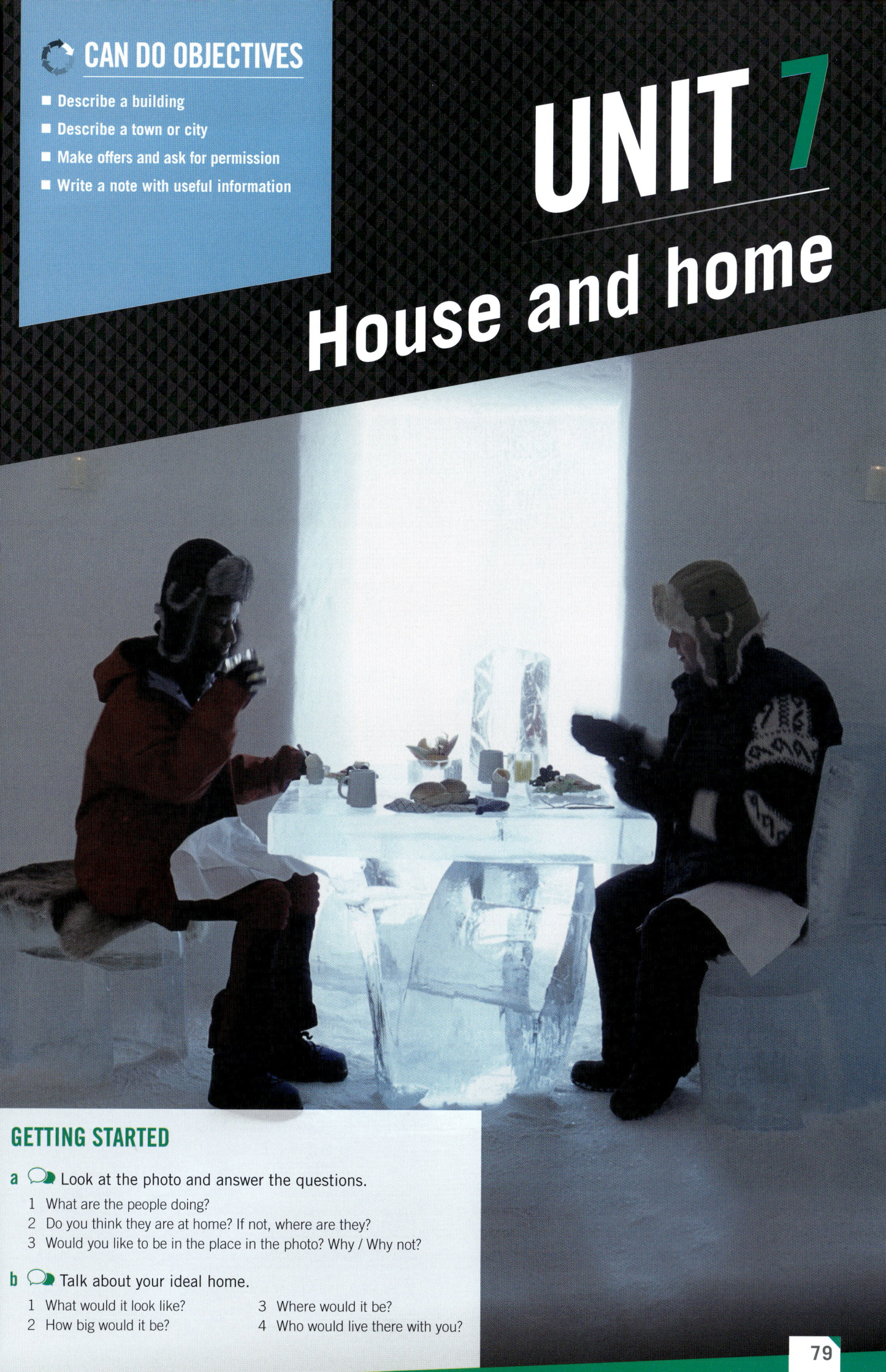

CAN DO OBJECTIVES

- Describe a building
- Describe a town or city
- Make offers and ask for permission
- Write a note with useful information

UNIT 7
House and home

GETTING STARTED

a 💬 Look at the photo and answer the questions.
1 What are the people doing?
2 Do you think they are at home? If not, where are they?
3 Would you like to be in the place in the photo? Why / Why not?

b 💬 Talk about your ideal home.
1 What would it look like?
2 How big would it be?
3 Where would it be?
4 Who would live there with you?

79

7A It might be a holiday home

Learn to describe a building
G Modals of deduction
V Buildings

1 GRAMMAR Modals of deduction

a ⃝ Look at photos a–d and discuss the questions.
1 Where do you think the buildings are? Are they in the city or the countryside? Which country? Why?
2 Who do you think lives in each building? A large family? A young couple? Why?

b ▶2.38 Listen to four people talking about photos a–d. Which photo is each person talking about?

Speaker 1 ___   Speaker 3 ___
Speaker 2 ___   Speaker 4 ___

c ▶2.38 Listen again. Where do the speakers think the buildings are? Who do they think lives there? Are their answers the same as yours in 1a?

d Do you like these buildings? Why / Why not?

e Complete each sentence with one word.
1 It's very small, so it _____ belong to a big family.
2 There _____ be much space in there!
3 It _____ belong to a single person or a couple.
4 It _____ be on the outskirts of any big city.
5 It _____ not be a house.
6 Whoever lives there _____ have children.
7 Or it _____ be a holiday home.

f ▶2.38 Listen again and check your answers.

g Match sentences 1–4 with meanings a–c. Two have the same meaning.
1 ☐ It **must** be a holiday home.
2 ☐ It **might** be a holiday home.
3 ☐ It **could** be a holiday home.
4 ☐ It **can't** be a holiday home.

a I think it's a holiday home (but I'm not sure).
b I'm sure it's a holiday home.
c I'm sure it's not a holiday home.

h Look again at the sentences in 1g. What verb form comes after *must*, *might*, *could* and *can't*?

i ▶ Now go to Grammar Focus 7A on p.144

j ▶2.40 Pronunciation Listen to the sentences in 1g. Underline the correct words in the rule.

We *pronounce / don't pronounce* the final *t* or *d* in a word when it is followed by a consonant sound.

k ▶2.41 Listen and tick (✓) the sentences where you hear the final *t* or *d*. Practise saying the sentences.
1 ☐ It can'**t** get much sun.
2 ☐ You coul**d** be right.
3 ☐ She mus**t** earn a lot of money.
4 ☐ It migh**t** be very expensive.
5 ☐ You mus**t** enjoy living here!

l ⃝ Discuss the questions.
1 What do you think it might be like to live in the homes in 1a?
2 What would you see from the windows?
3 Would you have a lot of space? Are there a lot of rooms?
4 What might the bedrooms be like?

2 VOCABULARY Buildings

I'm ¹*moving house / moving my house* next Friday, so here's my new address: Flat 4c, 82 Buckington Road, Banville, BN1 8UV. I'm ²*renting / buying* it for six months and if I like it I'll stay longer. It's on the fourth ³*level / floor* of a modern ⁴*house / block* of flats and it's got ⁵*views / sights* of the sea!

It's in a good ⁶*location / place*. The ⁷*neighbour / neighbourhood* is quiet, but there are some nice cafés and shops nearby. You'd like it – you should come and visit. If it's sunny, we can sit on the ⁸*upstairs / balcony* and look at the sea!

I've got to move out ⁹*of / to* this house on Tuesday, but I can't move ¹⁰*of / into* my new place until Friday, so I'll be staying with my parents for a few days next week. Are you going to be in the area?

a Read Amanda's email and underline the correct words.

b ▶ Now go to Vocabulary Focus 7A on p.158

UNIT 7

3 READING

a 💬 Imagine you're going to stay for three nights in a city that you don't know. Discuss the questions.

1 What are the advantages and disadvantages of staying in:
- a hotel?
- a rented apartment?
- a spare room in a local person's house?

2 Where would you prefer to stay? Why?

b Read the introduction of *A more personal place to stay* and choose the best summary.

1 Airbnb is an advertising website for hotels.
2 Airbnb is a website for travellers and people who have rooms to rent.
3 Airbnb is a travel advice website that has reviews of hotels and restaurants.

c 💬 Would you like to stay in someone else's home? What would be good or bad about it?

d Read *What the guests say …* . Answer the questions. Write A (Antonia) or K (Kumi).

1 ☐ Who could swim at the place they stayed?
2 ☐ Who felt 'at home' in the neighbourhood?
3 ☐ Who could easily get around the city?
4 ☐ Who cooked their own food?
5 ☐ Who is going to see their host(s) again?

e 💬 Which of the places would you rather stay in?

A MORE PERSONAL PLACE TO STAY

Do you find hotels too cold and unfriendly? Do you want to live like a local when you go on holiday? A new generation of websites, such as Airbnb, can help you find privately owned rooms, apartments and houses to rent.

'Hosts' create profiles of places to rent. 'Guests' can browse the profiles, read reviews written by guests and make reservations online. Prices range from about £25 to £100 per night, depending on the accommodation and the location.

But what's it like to stay at a stranger's house when you're on holiday? And if you're a host, what's it like to open your home to people you don't know? We spoke to some guests and hosts to find out.

WHAT THE GUESTS SAY …

Antonia My friend and I stayed in this amazing modern villa in California for ten days. It had eight bedrooms, a pool and the biggest kitchen I've ever seen (in which Jeff, our host, cooked fantastic breakfasts for us!). Jeff was so nice. He gave us lots of information about the local area and invited us to join him for dinner. We ended up becoming good friends – he's going to come and stay in my house when he comes to Italy next year.

Kumi I've stayed in Berlin a few times, but I've always stayed in a hotel. This experience was completely different. I had the whole of the top floor of an old house, and the rent included a bicycle too, which was great for travelling about. The hosts (Karl and Alexandra) were very kind, and we had good conversations every mealtime. They let me use the kitchen, which was great as the restaurants nearby are quite expensive. The shopkeepers in the area knew I was staying at Karl and Alexandra's and they were all very friendly. I felt like a local by the end of the week!

UNIT 7

f 💬 What might be the advantages and disadvantages of being an Airbnb host?

g Read *What the hosts say …*. Do they mention the advantages and disadvantages you talked about?

WHAT THE HOSTS SAY …

Roberto I've been an Airbnb host for three years. In that time I've met some wonderful people – musicians, families, sportspeople, professors, hikers and students – who've needed **accommodation** for different reasons. They've come from different parts of the world and it's been a **pleasure** to get to know them. The only problem is that you have to do so much washing and cleaning!

Lisa Some people worry about **theft**, but I've had more than 100 guests and no one has ever stolen anything from me. Some guests are nicer than others, of course, but on the whole they've been charming and friendly. I usually ask people why they're travelling when they make a **reservation**. It's a good way to get to know a bit about them.

Clara My family has a holiday **cottage** in Scotland. We decided to rent it out when we're not using it. It was easy to set up the profile on the website. You have to trust people to treat your **property** as if it was their own home, but we only accept reservations from guests who have good reviews.

h Read the texts above again and match the words in **bold** with the definitions.

1 a building that someone owns
2 place(s) to stay
3 a small house in the countryside
4 an enjoyable experience
5 the crime of stealing something
6 an arrangement to stay somewhere (e.g. a hotel room)

4 SPEAKING

a 💬 Look at the buildings below and discuss the questions.
1 How old is the building?
2 Where is it?
3 What do you think it's like inside?
4 Would you like to live there?

b 💬 Imagine you are going on holiday with your partner. Discuss which of the houses/flats you would like to stay in. Can you agree on one house/flat to visit?

> I'd like to stay in the New York flat in 'e'. It must be a really great city to visit.

7B There are plenty of things to do

Learn to describe a town or city
- G Quantifiers
- V Verbs and prepositions

1 LISTENING

a 💬 Where did you grow up – in a big city or a small town? Did you like it? Why / Why not?

b Read *Five reasons why small towns are better than cities*. Do you agree with the reasons in the list? Can you add any more reasons?

c 💬 Think of five reasons why cities are better places to live than small towns. Tell a partner.

d ▶2.44 Listen to Tim and Kate's conversation. Are Tim's reasons the same as yours in 1c?

e ▶2.44 Listen again. Are these statements T (true) or F (false)?
1 Kate grew up in a small town.
2 Tim wouldn't want to live in a small town.
3 Kate thinks small towns are safer.
4 More people have driving accidents in the city than in the country.
5 People who live in the country have a smaller carbon footprint.

f 💬 Discuss the questions.
1 Where do you think it's safer to live in your country – in the city or in the countryside? Think about:
   • driving   • crime   • hospitals   • other ideas
2 Is your (nearest) city designed in a way that's good for the environment? Why / Why not?
3 How could your (nearest) city be better? Think about:
   • public transport   • cycle lanes   • other ideas

Five reasons why small towns are better than cities

1 There are no traffic jams. You don't need to spend hours trying to get to work. Fantastic!

2 Everyone knows your name. And who your parents are. And they help you when times are bad.

3 EVERYTHING is cheaper – eating out, buying houses, even going to the cinema.

4 You don't have to queue for the most popular restaurant in town. You probably know the waiter, anyway.

5 You can't get lost. Who cares if you don't have any signal on your phone – you don't need GPS!

83

UNIT 7

2 VOCABULARY Verbs and prepositions

a Complete the sentences with the words in the box.

> about (x2)   on   to

1. People care _____ you.
2. It's like you belong _____ one big family.
3. That makes sense if you think _____ it.
4. You can't rely _____ public transport in the countryside like you can in the city.

b ▶2.45 **Pronunciation** Listen and check your answers to 2a. Then complete the rule.

> When we use a verb and a preposition, we *usually / don't usually* stress the verb and *stress / don't stress* the preposition.

c ▶2.45 Listen again and practise saying the sentences.

d Match the verbs in the box with the prepositions.

> apologise   argue   believe   belong   care
> complain   cope   depend   pay   rely
> succeed   think   wait   worry

1 _____ ---- with someone
2 _____ ---- with something
   think
3 _____
4 _____ ---- about something
5 _____
   pay
   wait ---- for something
6 _____
7 _____ ---- in something
8 _____ ---- in doing something
   rely
                on someone/something
9 _____
10 _____ ---- to someone

e Complete each sentence with the correct form of a verb + preposition from 2d.

1. Do I like living in the countryside? That _____ _____ the weather – when it's warm and sunny, I love it!
2. My friend has just moved from the countryside to the city and she's finding it hard to _____ _____ all the noise.
3. He moved here to look for work, but he hasn't _____ _____ finding a job yet, unfortunately.
4. I'd like to _____ _____ what I said earlier. I didn't mean to be so rude.
5. I _____ _____ the traffic warden about the parking fine for ten minutes, but in the end I had to pay.
6. People _____ _____ the traffic here, but it isn't bad compared to a big city.
7. **A** Do you _____ _____ bad luck?
   B No, not really. I think people are in control of their own lives.
8. All of the land near the river is private – it _____ _____ the university. You can't walk there.

f 💬 Complete the game instructions below with the correct prepositions. Then play the game in teams.

'TWO'
Think of two things for each category. You win a point for each answer that no other team has written.

a ways you can pay _for_ things
   1 _____ 2 _____
b things hotel guests often complain _____
   1 _____ 2 _____
c ways you can apologise _____ being late
   1 _____ 2 _____
d things people often do when they're waiting _____ a bus or train
   1 _____ 2 _____
e things that lots of adults worry _____
   1 _____ 2 _____
f things that lots of children believe _____
   1 _____ 2 _____

84

UNIT 7

3 GRAMMAR Quantifiers

a 💬 Discuss the questions.
1 Are there parks and other green spaces where you live?
2 What activities can people do there?
3 How often do you use them?

b Look at the photo of the High Line Park on p.84 and below. What's unusual about it? Read *The High Line, New York City* and check.

c Read the article again. Underline the correct words.
1 There are *lots of / enough* species of plants in the High Line park.
2 How *much / many* visitors go to the park each year?
3 There is *very little / too much* crime in the park.
4 Jen thinks there are *very few / too many* tourists there.
5 The website contains *lots of / not enough* information.
6 There's *not much / too much* rubbish in the park.

d ▶ Now go to Grammar Focus 7B on p.144

e Write sentences about each of the places below. Use quantifiers and the words in the box, and your own ideas. Don't include the name of the place.
- a city area that you know
- a country area that you know

| noise | crime | space | people | flowers | things to do |
| shops | cafés | wildlife | views | pollution | traffic |

f 💬 Read out your sentences. Can your partner guess where the places are?

> A lot of people go there at weekends, but there's enough space for everyone. There aren't many shops or cafés.

> Is it the beach?

4 SPEAKING

a You are going to talk about the area where you live. Make notes about these questions:
- Is it a healthy or safe place to live? Why / Why not?
- What do people complain about? (e.g. the noise, the roads)

b 💬 Take turns to talk about your areas. Would the places you talk about be good to live in for these people?
- a teenager who likes film and music
- a family with young children
- an elderly couple
- someone who likes sport and outdoor activities

THE HIGH LINE, NEW YORK CITY

Even the most enthusiastic city lover needs green spaces from time to time. In New York, one of the best places to find some nature is The High Line. Originally a 1930s railway bridge, this park opened in 2006 – ten metres above the street! It has more than 200 species of plants and spectacular views over the Hudson River. The park now attracts 4 million visitors a year, who escape the city streets to take a walk, take photos, and even get something to eat at one of the cafés. The High Line website (www.thehighline.org) is full of useful information about the history of the park and how they built it.

WHAT THE LOCALS SAY

I love The High Line. Calm and beautiful. It's safe too – apparently the crime rate is very low. **Pablo**

It used to be a lovely quiet place to go. Now it's full of tourists. Don't go at weekends! But one good thing is that it's quite clean and tidy – they clean up all the rubbish regularly. **Jen**

Make sure that you allow plenty of time. You need about three hours to see it properly. There's a lot to see – and you don't want to miss any of it! **Kira**

7C Everyday English
Is there anything we can do to help?

Learn to make offers and ask for permission
- **P** Sounding polite
- **S** Imagining people's feelings

1 LISTENING

a 💬 Discuss the questions.
1. Do you take presents when you visit someone's house? What might you take?
2. What should you do to be polite when visiting someone's house? (e.g. arrive on time, take your shoes off, etc.)

b 💬 Look at the photos on this page. What do you think is happening? How do you think the people feel?

c ▶️ 2.50 Watch or listen to Part 1 and check your ideas.

d ▶️ 2.50 Watch or listen again. Are the sentences true (T) or false (F)?
1. Becky hasn't met Tom's parents before.
2. Michael wants to watch a football match.
3. Becky got Charlotte's name wrong.
4. Charlotte is a teacher.
5. Tom tried to tell his parents that Becky is a vegetarian.

e Do you think that Becky has been a good guest? Has she made a good first impression?

2 USEFUL LANGUAGE Offers, requests and asking for permission

a Match questions 1–5 with responses a–e.
1. **Is there anything we can do to help**? [c]
2. **Do you think you could** give me a hand? [ ]
3. **Let me** get you something else. [ ]
4. **Is it OK if I** just have some bread and butter? [ ]
5. **I'll** get you a green salad. [ ]

a No, it's fine, really.
b Sure.
c Oh no, it's all under control!
d OK, that would be lovely. Thanks.
e No, we can do better than that.

b What phrases in **bold** in 2a do we use to …
1. offer something politely?
2. ask for help politely?
3. ask for permission?

c Match requests 1–5 with responses a–e.
1. [ ] Do you mind if I borrow some money?
2. [ ] May I sit here?
3. [ ] Do you think I could have a glass of water?
4. [ ] Can I use your phone for a moment?
5. [ ] Would you mind if I opened the window?

a Yes, of course. Let me get you one.
b Not at all. How much do you want?
c Sure. Here it is.
d Not at all. It's hot in here.
e Of course. There's plenty of space.

86

3 LISTENING

a Look at the photo. What do you think Tom and Michael are talking about?

b ▶ 2.51 Watch or listen to Part 2 and check.

c ▶ 2.51 Watch or listen again. Are the sentences true (T) or false (F)?
1 Tom thinks Becky hasn't made a good impression.
2 Michael doesn't like Becky.

4 CONVERSATION SKILLS
Imagining people's feelings

a ▶ 2.52 What word is missing in each sentence? Listen and check.
1 I _____ you're excited about the match this afternoon.
2 Tom tells me you're an architect. That _____ be very interesting.

b Read the exchanges and underline the phrases we use to imagine what someone else is feeling.
1 A I'm doing three part-time jobs at the moment.
  B You must be very tired!
2 A I'm going to meet my boyfriend's parents for the first time.
  B I imagine you're a bit nervous!

c 💬 Look at the sentences below. Respond with *must* and an appropriate adjective.
1 I'm planning a holiday to France.
2 I've just broken my tooth!
3 I've lost my smartphone – and I can't remember any of my friends' numbers.
4 I'm learning Japanese at the moment.

> I'm planning a holiday to France.

> That must be exciting!

d 💬 Tell your partner about some of the things below. Answer with a phrase from 4a or 4b.
- something you're planning on doing soon
- a hobby you have
- a problem you have at school/work

> I go to Spanish lessons at 7.30 in the morning before I go to work.

> That must be tiring.

> Yes, but I really enjoy them.

5 PRONUNCIATION Sounding polite

a ▶ 2.53 Listen to these sentences spoken twice. Which sentence sounds more polite, a or b?
1 Do you think you could give me a hand? *a / b*
2 It's lovely to meet you at last. *a / b*

b ▶ 2.54 Listen to three more pairs of sentences. Which sentences sound more polite, a or b?
1 How long are you staying? *a / b*
2 She seems really great. *a / b*
3 I'm really happy to hear that. *a / b*

c 💬 Practise saying the sentences in 5b with polite intonation.

6 SPEAKING

▶ **Communication 7C** 💬 Student A: Read the instructions below. Student B: Go to p.131.

> **Student A**
> 1 You are staying with Student B in his/her home. During the conversation, ask permission to:
>   - use the internet
>   - have a shower
>   - wash some clothes
> 2 Student B is a new colleague in your office. Ask him/her how it's going and try to sound interested (e.g. *That must be …*). He/She will ask you permission to do things. Decide whether or not to give permission.

Unit Progress Test

CHECK YOUR PROGRESS

You can now do the Unit Progress Test.

7D Skills for Writing
Make yourselves at home

Learn to write a note with useful information
W Offering choices

1 SPEAKING

💬 Talk about a recent holiday.
1 What kind of activities did you do?
2 Did the people you were with want to do the same things as you or different things?
3 Think of a holiday you would like to go on. What would you do on the holiday?

2 READING AND LISTENING

a 💬 You're going to read about Miami. Before you do, discuss the questions.
1 Where is Miami? Have you ever been there? Do you know anyone who's been there?
2 What is it like, or what do you imagine it's like? Talk about:
 • the weather
 • the people
 • buildings
 • the atmosphere
 • things to see and do

b 💬 Read about the top five things to do in and around Miami. Which would you like to do? Why? Are there any you would <u>not</u> want to do? Why not?

c ▶ 2.55 Sue is talking to a colleague. Listen to their conversation and answer the questions.
1 How many people are in Sue's family?
2 Where are they staying?
3 Which of the 'top five things' are they going to do?

d ▶ 2.55 Listen again and make notes in the table.

	Where does he/she want to go?	Why does he/she want to go there?
Sue's daughter		
Sue's son		
Sue's husband		
Sue		

e 💬 Do you think Sue is looking forward to the holiday? Why / Why not?

Top five things to do
... in and around Miami, Florida

1 Admire the architecture of Miami Beach
Wander the streets of Miami Beach and admire the art deco hotels and houses from the 1930s. The movie stars from the 1930s stayed here when they came to Miami. Many of the buildings have been repainted in their original colours.

2 Go to the beach
Miami has endless sandy beaches along the coast. You can find crowds if you want them or you can have a beach to yourself. And the water is always warm.

3 Visit the Everglades
Ninety minutes from Miami are the Everglades, a huge area of natural swamp which is home to alligators, snakes and rare birds. Take a boat through the area and get a close-up view of the wildlife.

4 Spend a day at Disney World
Disney World is just a day's drive away from Miami – a great day trip. You can find all the characters from Disney films and have hours of fun with (or without) your kids.

5 Take a trip to Cape Canaveral
North of Miami is Cape Canaveral, where the USA sends its rockets into space. You can take a tour round the Kennedy Space Center and see where they built the Apollo space rockets.

3 READING

a Read the note below which Sue's cousin left in the apartment in Miami. Underline the correct words.
1 The streets are safe *in the daytime / all the time*.
2 The apartment is *in the centre of / just outside* Miami.
3 The apartment is *right next to / far from* the sea.
4 Jutka will be away for *a week / more than a week*.

b Which adjectives in the box best describe the tone of the note? What words or phrases in the note helped you decide?

friendly   formal   funny   practical

c Match the purposes a–f with sections 1–6 in the note.
a ☐ to explain options for buying food
b ☐ to give information about going to places further away
c ☐ to finish the note
d ☐ to greet the reader and say what the note is about
e ☐ to give safety advice about the area round the apartment
f ☐ to give information about things in the apartment

d What general order are the sections in? Choose the correct answer.
1 things the reader needs to know now → things they need later
2 things which are very important → things which are less important
3 things which are less important → things which are more important

① Welcome to Miami! Hope you have a nice stay in the apartment. Here are a few things you need to know …

② Please make yourselves at home and help yourselves to anything in the kitchen. There's some chicken in the fridge, and lots of fruit and salad, so that should be enough for a couple of meals. I also got a couple of pizzas for the kids – they're in the freezer.

③ After that, you'll need to go shopping. The best place is the Sunshine Center. Go out of the main entrance of the apartment and turn left, and you'll see it about 100 metres down the road. It's got a couple of supermarkets, a good bookshop and a few good places to eat. Otherwise, there's a good place for burgers a bit further down the road. Apart from that, there are some good restaurants by the sea, but they're a bit further away.

④ By the way, if you do go out in the evening, don't walk around late at night – the streets round here are not very safe at night, though they're OK during the daytime.

⑤ Anyway, the car's in the parking lot, so you can use that for any trips. If you're going into Miami, another possibility is to take the train, but you'll find the car easier! You'll also need the car to go to the beach. The nearest one is Golden Beach, about 15 minutes' drive away. Another option is Ocean Beach, about 30 minutes further north, which is usually much less crowded. Alternatively, you could try Miami Beach nearer the centre, but it can be difficult to park.

⑥ Enjoy your stay and see you in a fortnight!
Love,
Jutka

4 WRITING SKILLS Offering choices

a What do the words in **bold** mean below?
1 The Sunshine Center has got a few good places to eat. **Otherwise**, there's a good place for burgers a bit further down the road.
  a if you don't like that idea
  b however
  c finally
2 The nearest one is Golden Beach, about 15 minutes' drive away. **Another option is** Ocean Beach, about 30 minutes further north.
  a A different direction is
  b A different choice is
  c A much better beach is

b Read the note again and find three more words or phrases that you could use instead of *Otherwise* or *Another option is …* .

c Use words or phrases from 4a and 4b in the second sentences below.
1 If you drive north, you can visit Disney World. You can also go to the Space Center at Cape Canaveral.
Another option is the Space Center at Cape Canaveral.
2 There are lots of good restaurants at Miami Beach. Or you can try the restaurants at South Beach.
3 To go to the West Coast you can get an inter-city bus. You can also hire a car for a few days.
4 You can drive through the Everglades and stop to look at the birds and alligators. You can also go round them by boat.

5 WRITING A note with useful information

a You are going to write a note for someone who will be staying in your home while you are away. Think about:
- things in the house/flat
- things he/she can and can't do
- things you want to ask him/her to do
- food and shopping
- things to do in the area.

b 💬 Compare your ideas with a partner.

c Read another student's note and answer the questions.
1 Did you understand all the information?
2 Did he/she put the information in a logical order?
3 Did he/she use words and phrases from 4a or 4b correctly?

d Write a reply.

89

UNIT 7
Review and extension

1 GRAMMAR

a Underline the correct answer.
1 There are *lots / too many / too much* stairs in this building!
2 There isn't *enough light / light enough / enough of light*. It's always dark.
3 There's too *many / few / much* noise outside.
4 It's got *lots / lots of / much* windows.
5 There are very *little / much / few* buildings in the area.
6 It hasn't got *many / much / little* floors.

b 💬 Discuss the pictures. Use *must*, *might*, *could* and *can't*.
1 Is each person a man or a woman?
2 How old are they?
3 Where are they?

2 VOCABULARY

a Complete the text with the words in the box.

| block floor location neighbourhood views |

Holiday home swap
This summer, we exchanged homes with the Acuna family from Lisbon. Our home is in a quiet ¹_____ in the Welsh countryside, with ²_____ of the hills in every direction. The Acunas live on the third ³_____ of a ⁴_____ of flats in the Portuguese capital. The flat was in a lively ⁵_____ and there were lots of places to visit nearby. Home swapping is a fantastic way to discover new places.

b Complete each sentence with a preposition.
1 Don't worry ____ the neighbours.
2 Who does that house belong ____?
3 You'll have to wait ages ____ a bus.
4 How do you cope ____ the cold winters here?
5 You can't rely ____ public transport here.
6 We succeeded ____ finding a good hotel.
7 Are you going to complain ____ the noise?

3 WORDPOWER *over*

a Match questions 1–6 with responses a–f.
1 ☐ When did you paint the house?
2 ☐ How many people live in Hong Kong?
3 ☐ How long was the meeting?
4 ☐ Can we start the test?
5 ☐ What's the matter?
6 ☐ Was the hotel room nice?

a Yes, we had a view **over** the lake.
b **Over** the summer.
c Yes, turn your papers **over** and begin.
d **Over** 7 million.
e You're getting mud all **over** the floor!
f It started at 2 and it was **over** by 3.15.

b Match the meanings of *over* 1–6 with sentences a–f in 3a.
1 ☐ finished
2 ☐ across / from one side to the other
3 ☐ more than
4 ☐ during (a period of time)
5 ☐ the other way up
6 ☐ covering

c Complete each sentence with *over* and information from the box. One sentence only needs *over*.

| 16 a lifetime someone the last few days the next few days the world your city |

1 Where can tourists go to get views _____?
2 What businesses from your country are known all _____?
3 How much work have you done _____?
4 What can you do in your country when you are _____? How about 18?
5 What kind of things do people learn _____?
6 When was the last time you were sad that something was _____?
7 Imagine you spill a drink _____ else in a restaurant. What would you do?
8 What are you going to do _____?

d 💬 Ask and answer the questions.

REVIEW YOUR PROGRESS

How well did you do in this unit? Write 3, 2 or 1 for each objective.
3 = very well   2 = well   1 = not so well

I CAN ...

describe a building.	☐
describe a town or city.	☐
make offers and ask for permission.	☐
write a note with useful information.	☐

CAN DO OBJECTIVES

- Talk about the news
- Talk about what other people say
- Generalise and be vague
- Write an email summary of a news story

UNIT 8
Information

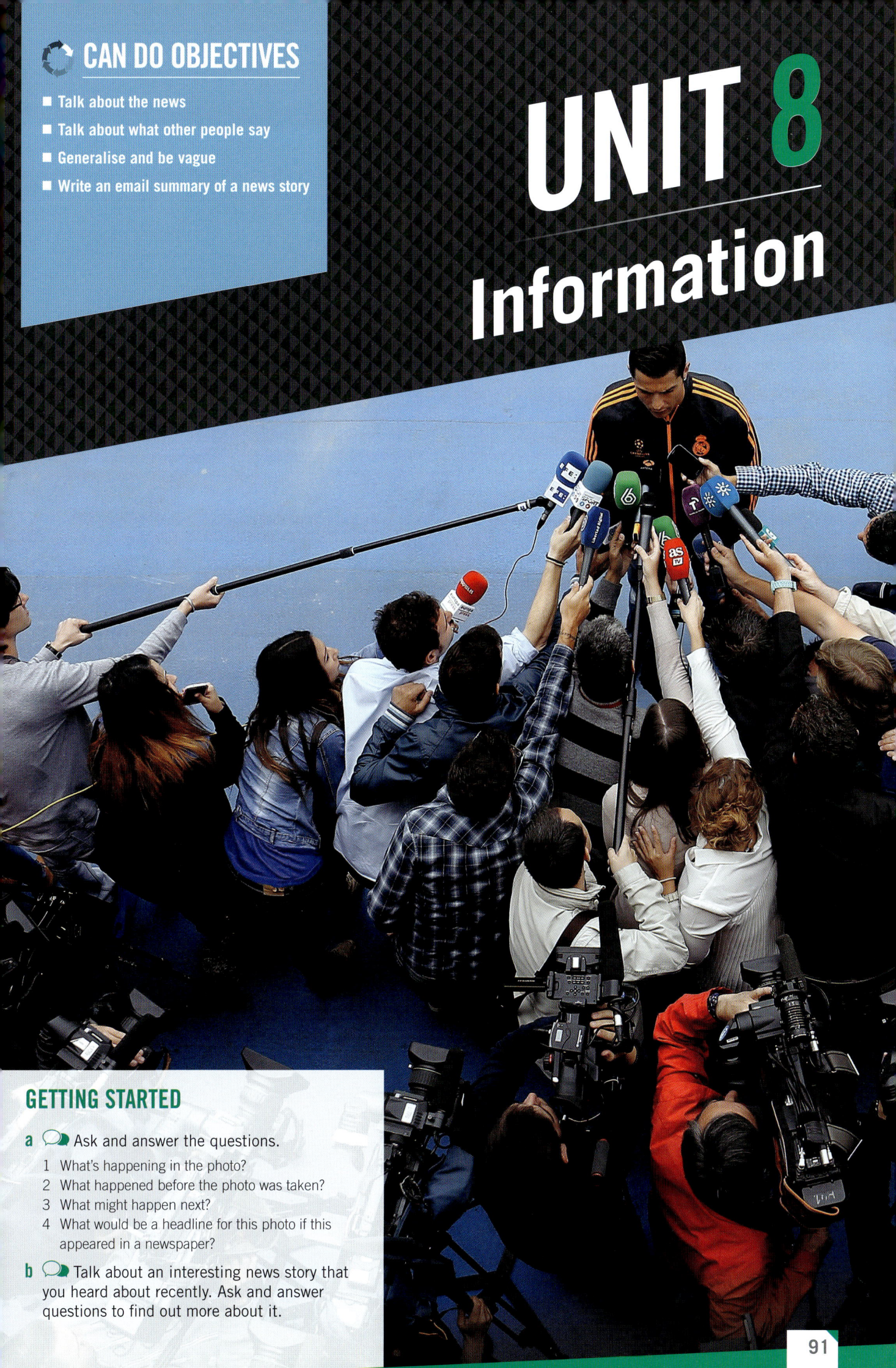

GETTING STARTED

a Ask and answer the questions.
1 What's happening in the photo?
2 What happened before the photo was taken?
3 What might happen next?
4 What would be a headline for this photo if this appeared in a newspaper?

b Talk about an interesting news story that you heard about recently. Ask and answer questions to find out more about it.

91

8A He said he'd read the news online

Learn to talk about the news
G Reported speech
V The news

1 VOCABULARY The news

a 💬 Discuss the questions.
1 When did you last read a newspaper?
2 How often do you read the news online?
3 Where do you get most of your news from? (TV? / smartphone?)

b Compare your answers in 1a with the information on the right about how people get their news. Did your group have similar results?

c Complete the blog *Too much news* with words in the box.

articles   affairs   breaking   celebrity
news feeds   headlines   the news

Too much news

The other day a friend said I was addicted to the news. I didn't know what he meant. Me? Well, yes, every day I watch ¹_____ on TV, read a few ²_____ in newspapers and magazines and I subscribe to a couple of ³_____ online. Yes, I'm interested in current ⁴_____ and I always want to keep up to date with ⁵_____ news in my country and abroad. But is it the most important thing in my life? Of course not.
Or is it?
Maybe my friend is right. I quite often go on websites to check the latest ⁶_____ gossip about TV stars and footballers.
And now I think about it, there are screens everywhere – in the streets, on my phone – so I'm surrounded by news. There are dramatic ⁷_____ everywhere I look, and I'm always checking my phone to see what's happening …
News is everywhere, and it all looks important. I think my friend is right, after all. Maybe it's time to take a break …

d 💬 Discuss the questions.
1 Look at the kinds of news in the box. Which are you interested in? Which are you not interested in? Are you interested in similar things?

business   celebrity gossip   entertainment
fashion   nature and the environment
politics and current affairs
science and technology   sport   travel   weather

2 What makes you read news stories (e.g. interesting headlines, a topic you know about, breaking news)?
3 Are we surrounded by too much news?

e ▶ Now go to Vocabulary Focus 8A on p.159

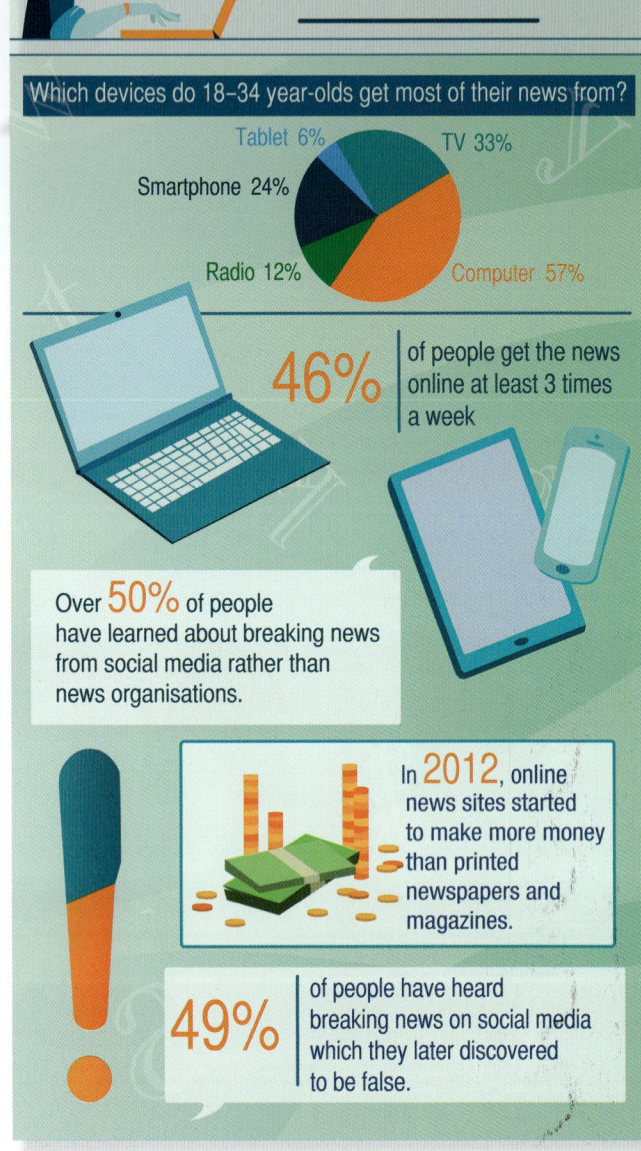

f ▶3.2 **Pronunciation** Listen to the words below. How are the underlined letters *c*, *g* and *k* pronounced?

blogger   breaking   comments
current   gossip   organisation

g Complete the rules with /g/ or /k/.

1 When you say _____, there is a sound in the throat.
2 When you say _____, there is no sound in the throat.

h ▶3.2 Listen again and repeat the words.

92

2 READING

a 💬 Look at the photos of news stories. Do you know anything about these stories?

b Read *Everyone's a journalist* and answer the questions.
1. What's the connection between social media and the photos?
2. Which news stories not shown in the photos are mentioned in the article?
3. What is the danger of relying on social media to get news?

c Read the article again and answer the questions.
1. How many people died in the Hudson River plane crash?
2. How did people spread images and videos of Chelyabinsk?
3. What did NASA tell people about on Twitter?
4. How did Carel Pedre use social media?
5. What was the problem with some of the photos of Hurricane Sandy?

d Match words in the article with the definitions below.
1. a place where something happens: s_____
2. full of action and excitement: d_____
3. found (for the first time): d_____
4. a very bad situation in which people die or are hurt: d_____
5. a person who sees an event happen: e_____
6. jokes or tricks: h_____
7. things that look real but aren't: f_____

e 💬 Discuss the questions.
1. Have you ever seen breaking news on Facebook or Twitter before it was on TV? What was it? Was it true?
2. Have you ever shared a photo or news story that you later discovered to be false?
3. Do you agree that social media can 'save lives and change the world'? Why / Why not?

EVERYONE'S A JOURNALIST

On 15 January 2009, several interesting things happened. Firstly, a plane crash-landed into the Hudson River, right in the middle of New York City. The pilot, crew and 155 passengers all escaped safely. But then, something else happened …

Jim Hanrahan was nearby and watched the event happen. He immediately tweeted that he had just seen a plane crash in the Hudson. From there the news spread quickly. People contacted him immediately and asked him what was happening, and other people on the street took photos and videos with their phones and posted them online. Ordinary people suddenly became journalists. It was 15 minutes before the news broke on official news channels.

Photos, videos and tweets from ordinary people at the scene of dramatic events now provide the words and images that describe events in the news. When a meteor exploded over the Russian city of Chelyabinsk in 2013, millions of people around the world watched videos and photos of the event on Facebook and YouTube. When NASA discovered ice on Mars, it used Twitter to spread the news. 'Are you ready to celebrate?' they tweeted. 'We have ICE!!!!! Yes, ICE, WATER ICE on Mars!' News from another planet suddenly felt personal.

Social media can also save lives. In January 2010, an earthquake hit the Caribbean island of Haiti. The government said that there had been an earthquake, but they didn't give many details at first. Meanwhile, people living in the disaster area were posting photos and eyewitness accounts on Twitter and Facebook and telling the world that it was an emergency and houses were collapsing. Carel Pedre, a local radio presenter, used this information in his reports to help people find family members, and people even phoned his programme to ask if their relatives were safe.

News travels fast on social media, but false stories spread just as quickly as the truth. Some of these are 'facts' reported in error, others are deliberate hoaxes. When Hurricane Sandy hit the east coast of the USA in 2012, many of the dramatic photos of storms and floods were real. But did you see the photos of stormy skies above the Brooklyn Bridge? Did you see the photos of seals and sharks in the streets? Or the deep-sea diver in the New York subway? These photos were all fakes – either real photos from other events or computer-generated images.

Hoaxes like these remind us that not everything people post and publish is reliable. But social media can change our lives for the better. In the words of Carel Pedre, 'May we continue to use Twitter to save lives and change the world.'

Hudson River crash

Meteor in Chelyabinsk, Russia

UNIT 8

3 GRAMMAR Reported speech (statements and questions)

a Read these sentences from the text. <u>Underline</u> the reported speech.
1 He immediately tweeted that <u>he had just seen a plane crash in the Hudson</u>.
2 People contacted him immediately and asked him what was happening.
3 The government said that there had been an earthquake.
4 Meanwhile, people living in the disaster area were posting videos and telling the world that it was an emergency and houses were collapsing.
5 People even phoned his programme to ask if their relatives were safe.

b What do you think they actually said (or tweeted)? Complete the sentences.
1 Jim Hanrahan: 'I _____ a plane crash in the Hudson.'
2 Other people (to Jim Hanrahan): 'What _____ ?'
3 The government of Haiti: 'There _____ an earthquake.'
4 People in the disaster area: 'It _____ an emergency. Houses _____ collapsing.'
5 Radio listeners: '_____ my relatives safe?'

c <u>Underline</u> the correct words in the rules.

> 1 When we report what someone has said or written, we often change the tense of the direct speech *backwards / forwards* in time.
> 2 We use *question order / normal sentence order* in reported questions.
> 3 We often don't change the tense when we report things which are *still true / no longer true*.

d Write the tense changes in reported speech.

Direct speech	Reported speech
Present simple	_____
Past simple	_____
Present perfect simple	_____
Present perfect continuous	_____
will	_____

e ▶ Now go to Grammar Focus 8A on p.146

f Work in pairs. Write a story using reported speech and questions.
1 Write the first two sentences. Begin like this and continue using reported speech.
My friend phoned me a few weeks ago with some news. He/She said …
2 Pass your sentences to another pair. Read the sentences you received and add another sentence. Begin:
I asked him/her …
3 Pass your sentences to another pair. Read the sentences you received and add another sentence. Begin:
He/She said …
4 Pass your sentences to another pair. Read the sentences and add a final sentence. Check that the reported speech is correct. Then read out the story to the class.

4 SPEAKING

a You're going to talk about a website that you often visit. It should be a news site, a blog, a forum or a social networking site. Make notes about the questions below.
1 What's the website called?
2 What kind of news or information do you get from it (e.g. sport, music, entertainment, current affairs, etc.)?
3 How often do you visit it?
4 Why do you like it? Do you find it useful?
5 What stories or other information have you found out?
6 Have you ever posted a comment there?
7 Have you made any friends through this website?
8 Why would you recommend this website to other people?

b 💬 Take turns to tell each other about your website in 4a. Try to encourage your partner to visit your website. Ask questions to find out more.

I use the MTV website for entertainment news.

Has it got current affairs?

No, not really.

8B I recommended visiting a local restaurant

Learn to talk about what other people say

G Verb patterns
V Shopping; Reporting verbs

1 VOCABULARY Shopping

a 💬 Discuss the questions.
1 Do you prefer browsing online, or in real shops?
2 Do you buy the latest products as soon as they come out?
3 Have you ever returned something or asked for a refund?
4 Where do you look for bargains?
5 What would you like to be able to afford to buy?

b ▶ Now go to Vocabulary Focus 8B on p.159

2 LISTENING

a 💬 Discuss the questions.
1 When was the last time you bought something expensive (e.g. a car, a holiday, a computer, a meal in an expensive restaurant)?
2 How did you decide to buy it? Did you read online reviews or get personal recommendations from people you know?
3 Do you trust online reviews? Why / Why not?
4 Do you ever write reviews?

⭐⭐⭐⭐⭐
'It's worth travelling 100 miles to get there!'

I enjoy going to the country's best restaurants and I've wanted to try this 'restaurant on a boat' for a long time. The location keeps changing depending on the season and making a reservation isn't easy. But we managed to get a table and had an absolutely wonderful evening. You choose your fish from the menu, then a member of staff goes fishing to catch it for you! It's easy to see why this place gets so many five-star reviews.

Dean 56, Bristol, UK

Was the review helpful? ◯ Yes ◯ No

b Read the restaurant review above.
1 Where is the restaurant?
2 What's unusual about the location?
3 What kind of food does it serve?

c 💬 Would you like to eat at this restaurant? Why / Why not?

d ▶3.6 Listen to the first part of the conversation between Harry and Erica. Why can't they go to the restaurant?

e ▶3.7 Listen to the whole conversation. Are the sentences true (T) or false (F)?
1 The restaurant had excellent reviews.
2 The person who invented Oscar's owned a hotel.
3 His friend's hotel was successful because it got lots of good reviews online.
4 Erica thinks there isn't enough control over online reviews.
5 Fake reviewers often only write one review.

f 💬 Discuss the questions.
1 Which online review websites are common where you live?
2 Which ones do you trust? Why do you trust them?

UNIT 8

3 GRAMMAR Verb patterns

a Match the verb patterns in sentences 1–4 with rules a–d.
1. ☐ **Making** a reservation isn't easy.
2. ☐ It's worth **travelling** 100 miles to get there!
3. ☐ I enjoy **going** to the country's best restaurants.
4. ☐ After many attempts, we finally succeeded in **getting** a table.

> We use verb + -ing:
> a after prepositions
> b after certain verbs (e.g. *keep, mind, love*, etc.)
> c after some expressions (e.g. *it's worth, it's no good*, etc.)
> d as the subject of a sentence

b Match the verb patterns in sentences 1–4 with rules a–d.
1. ☐ It's easy **to see** why this place gets so many five-star reviews.
2. ☐ We managed **to get** a table.
3. ☐ A member of staff goes fishing **to catch** it for you!
4. ☐ I didn't know what **to choose** from the menu.

> We use *to* + infinitive:
> a after question words
> b after certain verbs (e.g. *want, plan, seem, decide*, etc.)
> c after certain adjectives (e.g. *difficult, good, important*, etc.)
> d to show purpose

c ▶ Now go to Grammar Focus 8B on p.146

d Write the correct form of the verbs in brackets. Then choose an option or add your own idea to make it true for you.
1. I enjoy ____ (shop) *for clothes / with friends / … .*
2. I'm planning ____ (get) *a new phone / some new shoes … soon.*
3. It's difficult ____ (choose) *clothes / music / … for other people.*
4. I know how ____ (write) *a good review / blog / … .*
5. I think it's worth ____ (spend) *a lot of money on a meal in a restaurant / good haircut / … .*
6. I'm not interested in ____ (hear) about *people's problems / new shops and restaurants / … .*
7. I often *walk round the shops / look online / …* ____ (see) if there's anything I want ____ (buy).
8. ____ (go) to *language classes / the gym / …* is a good way to meet new people.

e 💬 Compare your sentences in 3d. Can you find anyone who has four or more statements which are the same as yours?

> I enjoy shopping for clothes.   Me too!

4 VOCABULARY Reporting verbs

a ▶3.9 Listen and match conversations 1–3 with pictures a–c. Is each customer happy?

b ▶3.9 Listen again. Are the sentences true (T) or false (F)?

Conversation 1
a He **suggests** changing the woman's hairstyle.
b She **warns** him not to cut her hair too short.
c He **recommends** trying a new hair product.
d She **agrees** to have the new product on her hair.

Conversation 2
a He **invites** them to stay another night.
b He **reminds** them to write a review.
c They **promise** to write a good review.
d They **advise** him to advertise the hotel more.

Conversation 3
a The woman **admits** eating the dessert.
b The woman **refuses** to pay for the dessert.
c The woman **threatens** to write a bad review.
d The waiter **offers** to get the manager.

c ▶3.10 **Pronunciation** Listen to the sentences below and the words in **bold**. Is the letter *s* pronounced as /s/ or /z/?
1 He **suggested** changing the woman's hairstyle.
2 They **promised** to write a good review.
3 They **advised** him to advertise the hotel more.
4 The woman **refused** to pay for the dessert.

d Practise saying the words in **bold** in 4c.

e Look at pictures 1–8 below. Report what the people said using the reporting verbs from the box.

| admitted | advised | offered | promised |
| refused | ~~reminded~~ | suggested | warned |

1 She _reminded_ him to read the label.
2 He _____ writing all the reviews.
3 He _____ to delete the reviews.
4 She _____ her to make a formal complaint.
5 He _____ to pay for lunch.
6 She _____ him not to sit down.
7 She _____ asking someone for directions.
8 He _____ to ask anyone for help.

5 SPEAKING

a You're going to talk about an experience you've had. Make notes about one of the following:
- a time when you recommended something to someone (e.g. a restaurant or a film) or someone recommended something to you
- a time when someone warned you not to do something
- a time when you admitted making a mistake. What had you done? How did you feel? How did other people react?
- a time when you refused to do something. What did you refuse to do? Why did you refuse to do it?
- a time you or someone else promised to do something, but didn't do it. What was it?

b 💬 Take turns to talk about your experience for at least a minute. Has anyone in your group had a similar experience?

> I suggested watching my favourite film to my best friend. I'd kept telling my friend how good it was, but as soon as it started I realised that …

1 Don't forget to read the label
2 OK, it's true. I wrote all the reviews.
3 I'll delete them. Really, I will.
4 If I were you, I'd make a formal complaint.
5 I'll pay for lunch, if you like.
6 Don't sit down!
7 Why don't we ask someone for directions?
8 No! I know where we are.

8C Everyday English
On the whole, I prefer taking action shots

Learn to generalise and be vague
- P The sounds /h/ and /w/
- S Being vague

1 LISTENING

a Discuss the questions.
1. Have you had any good news to share recently? Have you been told any good news? What was it?
2. How do you usually share your good news – by text, online, in person?

b Look at the photo. What do you think is happening? How do you think Becky is feeling?

c ▶3.11 Watch or listen to Part 1. Answer the questions.
1. What does Becky ask questions about in the interview?
2. How does Becky think the interview went?

d ▶3.11 Watch or listen to Part 1 again. Complete each sentence with one or two words.
1. Rachel is worried that there's not enough _____ in the area for two florists.
2. Becky prefers taking _____.
3. The course can include a _____ in a local gallery.
4. There are normally two _____ a year.
5. Becky found her interview more _____ than she was expecting.
6. They will tell her _____ whether she got a place.

e Discuss the questions.
1. Do you think Rachel is right to be worried about the new florist's in her area? Do you know of an area in your town/city with lots of the same types of shops/restaurants?
2. Would you like to do the photography course that Becky has applied for? Why / Why not?

2 USEFUL LANGUAGE Generalising

a ▶3.12 Listen and complete the sentences with the phrases in the box.

> generally   on the whole   normally   tends to   typically

1. But I think, _____, I prefer taking action shots.
2. It _____ either be working at a local gallery on a photography exhibition or working with a professional photographer as an assistant.
3. The placement _____ lasts two weeks.
4. Yes, _____ each class has two opportunities to go on study visits per year.
5. Well, _____ they don't tell you during the interview …

b Underline the phrases for generalising in these sentences.
1. It can be difficult to relax at the end of the day. I find my yoga class really helpful for that.
2. As a rule, I'm not very good at interviews – I get too nervous.
3. I don't usually spend much time worrying about things that haven't happened yet.

c Are the sentences in 2b true for you? If not, change them to make them true.

3 CONVERSATION SKILLS Being vague

a Replace the words in **bold** with the words in the box.

> a couple of   things   sort

1. I prefer taking action shots – sport and **stuff** like that.
2. You have **a few** portraits in your portfolio.
3. I'm not very good with that **kind** of thing.

b Complete the second sentence in each pair using vague language so that it means the same as the first sentence. More than one answer might be possible.

> a couple of   things/stuff like that
> that sort/kind of thing

1. I like swimming, playing tennis and jogging.
   I like swimming and _____.
2. Everything went well except for one or two problems.
   Everything went well except for _____ problems.
3. I'm going to the supermarket. I need some milk, eggs, bread and cheese.
   I'm going to the supermarket. I need some milk and _____.

UNIT 8

4 LISTENING

a Look at the photos. Discuss the questions.
1 What news do you think Tina has about the new shop?
   a The builders have stopped work.
   b It's going to be a clothes shop.
   c It has closed down.
2 What news do you think Becky might receive?
   a She's got a new job as a photographer.
   b She's got some money to help her do the course.
   c She's got a place on the photography course.

b ▶3.13 Watch or listen to Part 2 and check your ideas.

5 PRONUNCIATION
The sounds /h/ and /w/

a ▶3.14 Listen to these sentences. What sounds do the underlined words begin with?
1 Pretty well, I think, on the whole.
2 What was the question?
3 I was there around two hours.

b ▶3.15 Match the words in the box with the sound each word begins with. Listen and check.

white   honest   hotel   wrap   who   work

- /h/ e.g. happy:
- /w/ e.g. water:
- first letter silent:

c ▶3.16 Listen to the following sentences. Choose the word you hear.
1 You can eat / heat the food up in the microwave.
2 He wrote on the board invite / in white.
3 A few weeks ago she lost her earring / hearing.
4 The man you are looking for is the one in the west / vest.
5 I hate / ate the food that my daughter cooked.

6 SPEAKING

 Ask your partner for advice on one of these topics:
- a course you would like to do
- a local restaurant for a special occasion
- an area of your town/city to live in

I'd like to study French at university.

I've heard that it's quite difficult to get a place. But, on the whole, the teachers are very good.

Unit Progress Test

CHECK YOUR PROGRESS

You can now do the Unit Progress Test.

8D Skills for Writing
Fortunately, everything was all right

Learn to write an email summary of a news story
W Summarising information

1 LISTENING AND SPEAKING

a Look at the three photos of air travel below. What is happening in each photo?

b Think about the last time you travelled by air. What was the best/worst thing about it?

c You are going to listen to someone talking about a news story. Some of the key words from the story are in the box. What do you think happened?

| eleven | Manchester | mother | shopping |
| airport | security | plane | Rome | complained |

d Compare your stories with other students.

e 3.17 Listen to the story. How close was it to your story?

f Do we know if these statements are true? Write true (*T*), false (*F*) or don't know (*DK*).

1. The speaker read the story in a newspaper.
2. The boy was alone in the shopping centre.
3. His mother went to the airport to look for him.
4. The boy spoke to the children in the other family.
5. The boy didn't have a boarding pass.
6. They didn't count the passengers before they took off.
7. The airline offered the mother free flights in the future.
8. It's the first time something like this has ever happened.

g 3.17 Listen again and check your answers.

h Discuss the questions.

1. Do you think something like this could happen in your country?
2. Do you think airport security in your country is:
   a too strict
   b not strict enough
   c about right?

2 READING

a Look at the headline of a similar news story below. What do you think happened? Choose a or b.

1. a He drove the car himself.
   b He was a passenger in the car.
2. a He flew the plane himself.
   b He was a passenger on the plane.

b Read the story quickly and check your answers to 2a.

c Read the story again. Note down things that are the same as in the story you listened to.

13-YEAR-OLD BOY DRIVES TO AIRPORT AND FLIES ACROSS USA

Kenton Weaver is 13 years old and has no photo ID. But that didn't stop him from stealing his father's car in the middle of the night, driving more than 20 miles to a Florida airport and taking two connecting flights to San José, California. 'I really enjoyed it,' said Kenton.

Kenton's mother, Kim Casey, lives just half an hour from San José airport in Fresno, California, but the boy's father, Dean Weaver, thinks it was the journey itself that interested the boy. According to Dean, his son is fascinated by airplanes. 'He'll do anything to go to an airport,' Dean said. 'He wants to be a pilot.'

Kenton did not own a credit card, passport, driver's licence, or photo ID of any kind. Yet he was able somehow to buy a plane ticket, go through airport security, fly to Chicago and catch his connecting flight to San José without any problems. His father said it is possible Kenton used the numbers from one of his own credit cards to buy the ticket online.

UNIT 8

3 WRITING SKILLS
Summarising information

a Read a summary of the news story. Which words or phrase in **bold** tell us … ?
1 that the person is reporting a story he/she read or heard about somewhere
2 that the person is commenting on what happened

> There was an **incredible** story in the newspaper last week. **Apparently, a boy of 13 stole his father's car, drove it to the airport and then took two flights from Florida to California to see his mother, who lives there.** **Amazingly**, he did all this without a credit card, ID or driver's licence. **It seems that** he used his father's credit card number to buy the plane ticket online and no-one asked him any questions. **Fortunately**, they found the car and everything was all right in the end.

b Look at audioscript 3.17 on p.171. Find more words used to comment on the story.

c Compare the sentences below with the highlighted sentence in the summary in 3a. Answer questions 1–4.

> A boy of 13 stole his father's car. The boy drove it to the airport. The boy took two flights from Florida to California. The boy flew there to see his mother. His mother lives in California.

1 How many sentences are in this part of the summary?
2 What words are added to join the sentences together in 3a?
3 What words are left out or changed in the summary in 3a? Why?
4 Why is the summary in 3a better than the sentences in 3c?

d Here is a different summary of the same news story. Join the sentences together to make four or five sentences. Use the words in the box to help you (you can use the words more than once).

> and   before   but   who   with

> I read an incredible news story about a boy.
> Apparently he flew alone from Florida to California.
> He was only 13.
> He managed to fly alone across America.
> He even changed planes in Chicago.
> He bought a ticket online.
> He used his father's credit card number.
> No one at the airport asked him any questions.
> He even took his father's car.
> He parked it in the airport car park.
> He got on the plane.

e Work in pairs and compare your summaries. Are they the same?

4 WRITING

a Work in pairs. Choose one of the news headlines below or a story in the news at the moment. Discuss and make notes about what happened.

POLICE FIND MISSING GIRL

Tiger escapes from zoo

MAN JUMPS FROM PLANE – AND SURVIVES

SURFER ESCAPES SHARK ATTACK

b Work in pairs. Write an email to a friend, summarising the story in a few sentences. Include words or phrases to comment on the story.

c Work with another pair. Read each other's emails and answer the questions.
1 Is the information clear and in a logical order?
2 Is the amount of information right?
3 Are there too many or too few sentences? Are they connected in the best way?
4 Can you improve the summary?

d Tell another pair about the news story you read.

UNIT 8
Review and extension

1 GRAMMAR

a Read the text and underline the correct answers.

'Internet users worry about ¹*to lose / losing* private information online, but they don't mind ²*to see / seeing* advertisements that are personally directed at them.' That's what the Digital Advertising Alliance discovered when they conducted a survey ³*to find out / finding out* how consumers feel about targeted advertising. Only 4% said they didn't like the idea of ⁴*to get / getting* targeted advertising.

Consumers seem ⁵*to understand / understanding* that adverts make it possible ⁶*to have / having* free websites: 75% of people said that they didn't want ⁷*to pay / paying* for websites with no advertising on them.

b Complete the reported speech.
1 'I'll never go to that hairdresser again,' you said.
   You said _____ to that hairdresser again.
2 Kate asked John, 'What are you going to buy?'
   Kate asked John _____ to buy.
3 The editor said to me, 'Rewrite this story.'
   The editor told _____ this story.
4 The interviewer asked me, 'Have you ever written a blog?'.
   The interviewer asked me _____ a blog.

2 VOCABULARY

a Replace the words in **bold** with a word or phrase from the box that means the same. There are three words and phrases that you don't need.

| article | bargain | browsing | came out | can't afford |
| current affairs | an editor | a journalist | spread |

1 A new version of this software **was first available to buy** six months ago. _____
2 The news will **pass from person to person** very quickly and then everyone will know about it. _____
3 She's training to become **someone who is involved in communicating news to the public**. _____
4 I might buy something, but at the moment I'm just **looking to see what there is**. _____
5 Dan **hasn't got enough money for** a new phone. _____
6 He's interested in **political, social and economic events**. _____

b Complete the reporting verbs. Write a sentence with each one.
1 a _ _ i _ _
2 w _ _ n
3 t h _ _ _ _ e _
4 r _ c _ m m _ _ _
5 p _ o _ i _ e

3 WORDPOWER *in/on* + noun

a Look at the phrases in the box and underline the correct words in the rules.

on the label   on a website   in capital letters
in cash   in the photo   in a magazine

1 We use *in / on* + flat surfaces like *wall*, *page* and *screen*.
2 We use *in / on* + *film*, *photo* and *picture* (when we talk about what they contain).
3 We use *in / on* + *the internet*, *the radio*, *TV*, *Facebook* and *Twitter*.
4 We use *in / on* + written and printed material (e.g. *the newspaper, a sentence, an email, an attachment*).
5 We use *in / on* with sizes (e.g. *39, medium*), currencies (e.g. *pounds, yen, dollars*) and before *stock*.

b Complete the sentences with *in* or *on*.
1 What can you see _____ the picture?
2 I've got some photos of Paul _____ my phone.
3 The answer was _____ the first paragraph.
4 Was it strange to see your name _____ print?
5 The full article is _____ page 4.
6 They were talking about his new film _____ the radio.
7 Did you pay _____ cash?
8 How much is £30 _____ euros?
9 The words 'Not for sale' were _____ the sign.
10 A I'm looking for these shoes _____ size 9.
    B I'm afraid we don't have them _____ stock at the moment.
11 Your seat number is _____ the ticket.
12 If you write _____ pencil, it doesn't matter if you make a mistake.

c 💬 Take turns to test each other on the phrases.

> The internet.
> On the internet.

REVIEW YOUR PROGRESS

How well did you do in this unit? Write 3, 2 or 1 for each objective.
3 = very well   2 = well   1 = not so well

I CAN ...

talk about the news.   ☐
talk about what other people say.   ☐
generalise and be vague.   ☐
write an email summary of a news story.   ☐

CAN DO OBJECTIVES

- Talk about films and TV
- Give extra information
- Recommend and respond to recommendations
- Write an article

UNIT 9
Entertainment

GETTING STARTED

a 💬 Look at the photo and answer the questions.
1 Where are these people?
2 What are they doing and why?
3 What do you think the passers-by are thinking?

b 🔊 3.18 Listen and check your answers.

c 💬 Are there similar street entertainers in your area? Do you like them?

d 💬 What other kinds of street entertainers can you think of? Which ones do you like best?

103

9A The film is still loved today

Learn to talk about films and TV

G The passive
V Cinema and TV

1 VOCABULARY Cinema and TV

a 💬 Discuss the questions.
1 What kinds of TV programmes and films do you like? Why?
2 What are the most popular TV shows in your country at the moment? Do you watch them? Why / Why not?

b ▶ Now go to Vocabulary Focus 9A on p.160

2 LISTENING

a 💬 Look at the four film posters and discuss the questions.
1 What do you know about these films?
2 Did they use CGI (computer-generated imagery) and special effects?

b 💬 Look at the information below about a radio programme. What do you think the presenters will say about CGI?

The Big View
Ellie and Nick exchange views on art and entertainment.
Tonight's show
'Has CGI taken the heart out of modern film-making?'

c ▶ 3.21 Listen to the programme. Do both presenters think there is too much CGI in modern films?

d ▶ 3.21 Listen again. Are the sentences true (T) or false (F)?
1 Ellie says that directors seem to be more focused on special effects than the story.
2 *Casablanca* was filmed in Paris.
3 The fight scene in *Inception* was made using CGI.
4 Nick thinks that good directors should be able to use technology well.

e 💬 Discuss the questions.
1 Can you think of other examples of … ?
 • films that have no CGI or special effects
 • films that use CGI and other special effects
2 Have you seen these films? Did you like them?
3 Who do you agree with most – Nick or Ellie? Why?

3 READING

a 💬 Look at the two film posters on the right and discuss the questions.
1 Have you seen these films? If not, would you like to?
2 How are the two films similar? How are they different?

b Read *Film-making has changed a lot in the last 100 years* and check your ideas. Does the writer prefer traditional animated films, or films made with modern technology?

c Read the article again. What do these numbers refer to?

33   1,500,000   4   24   10,318   1937   525   3

d 💬 Discuss the questions.
1 What animated films like this have you seen? What did you think of them?
2 Do you agree with the last sentence of the article?

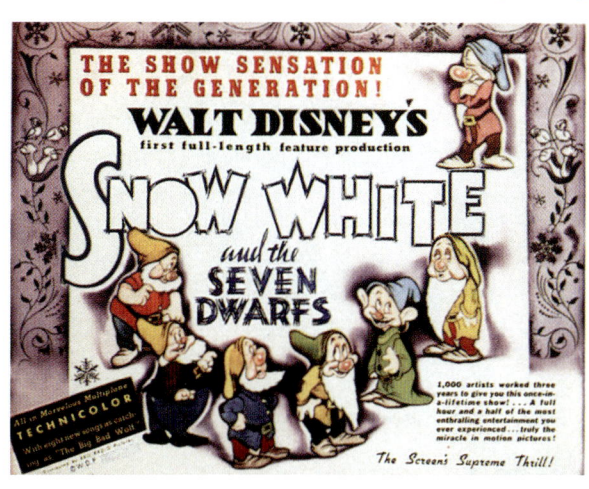

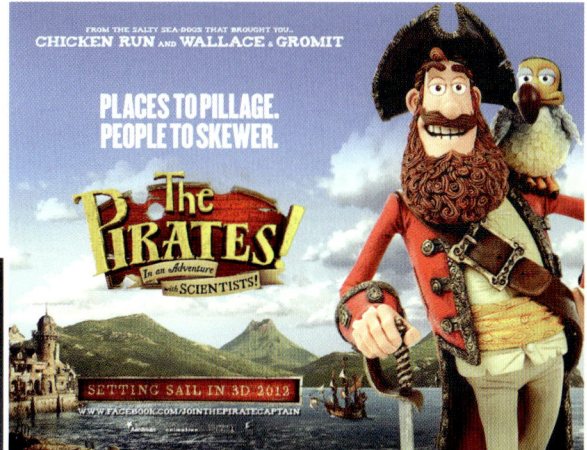

FILM-MAKING
HAS CHANGED A LOT
IN THE LAST 100 YEARS – OR HAS IT …?

They're slow. They're boring. They don't have any special effects. That's the opinion many people have about old movies. But some film directors continue to use film-making techniques that have not changed in nearly a hundred years, and the results can be charming and fun.

The Pirates! In an Adventure with Scientists!, created by British company Aardman Animations, is one example. It took five years to make this extremely ambitious film, using the 'stop-frame' filming technique. For every second of finished film, the puppets and models in each scene were moved up to 24 times. On average, it took a whole day to make just four seconds of screen action. A total of 525 people – including 33 animators – worked on the production. This kind of film-making requires great attention to detail. For example, pins were used to make tiny changes to the models. In total, 10,318 puppet mouths were used during filming to create realistic face movements.

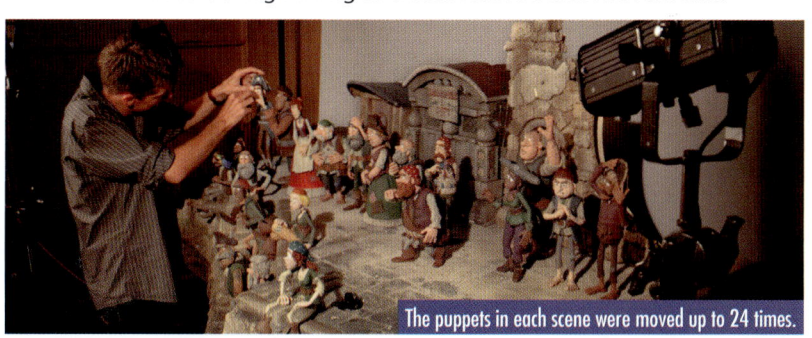

Here, a pin is being used to move the puppet's eyes.

The puppets in each scene were moved up to 24 times.

However, nearly a hundred years ago, Walt Disney was doing something very similar. Back in 1937, his team made the first ever full-length animated feature film, *Snow White and the Seven Dwarfs*. He also used the stop-frame technique. In this case, each frame was drawn by hand. More than 1,500,000 frames were used in total. The film took three years to make and cost six times more to make than Disney had planned.

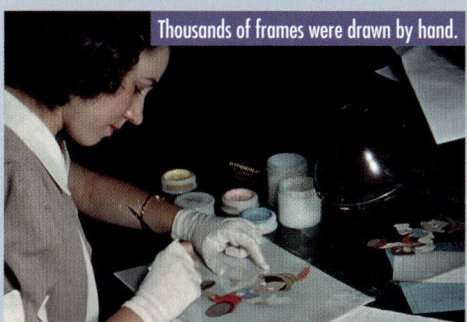

Thousands of frames were drawn by hand.

Snow White was hugely successful and it is still loved today by children around the world. There is no doubt that Aardman Animations' films will be enjoyed in the same way for many years to come. Films that use modern technology may be dramatic and exciting, but handmade films will always be more impressive and fun to watch.

UNIT 9

4 GRAMMAR The passive

a We use *be* + a past participle to make a passive verb form. Are the underlined verbs active (A) or passive (P)?
1 They don't have any special effects.
2 It took five years to make this extremely ambitious film.
3 Here, a pin is being used to move the puppet's eyes.
4 Thousands of frames were drawn by hand.
5 The film cost six times more to make than Disney had planned.
6 *Snow White* is still loved today by children.
7 Aardman Animations' films will be enjoyed in the same way for many years to come.

b ▶3.22 **Pronunciation** Listen to the passive sentences in 4a. Is the auxiliary verb *be* stressed in these sentences?

c ▶3.22 Listen again to the passive sentences in 4a and practise saying them.

d Underline the correct words in the rules.

> We can use the passive when:
> 1 we *know* / *don't know* who did an action
> 2 it's *obvious* / *not obvious* who did an action
> 3 it's *important* / *not important* who did an action.

> *Thousands of frames were drawn by hand.*
> *Small changes to the puppets were made with a pin.*
> 4 We can use *by* / *with* + noun after a passive verb when we say what is used to do the action.
> 5 We can use *by* / *with* + noun after a passive verb when we say what/who does the action.

e ▶ Now go to Grammar Focus 9A on p.148

f ▶ **Communication 9A** 💬 You are going to do a quiz about films. Student A: Look at the questions below. Student B: Look at the questions on p.130.

5 SPEAKING

a You are going to recommend a film or TV show that you like. Make notes on the questions.
• What kind of film or show is it?
• What is it called?
• When and where was it made?
• Who directed it?
• Is it based on a book or a true story?
• Who is in it? Any famous actors or celebrities?
• Does it have special effects or CGI?
• What happens? Who are the main characters?

b Write three reasons why you like this film or TV show.

c 💬 Take turns to recommend your film or TV show. Have you watched the films or TV shows you hear about? If so, do you like them too? If not, would you like to watch them? Why / Why not?

> You've got to watch this new Swedish crime show …

> Oh no! I hate detective shows. They're all the same.

> No, this is different. It's got …

HOW MUCH DO YOU KNOW ABOUT FILMS?

Complete the questions with the correct form of the verbs in brackets. Then test your partner!

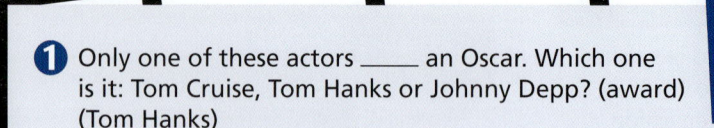

1. Only one of these actors _____ an Oscar. Which one is it: Tom Cruise, Tom Hanks or Johnny Depp? (award) (Tom Hanks)

2. True or False? 60% of the 2009 science-fiction film *Avatar* _____ with computer graphics. The other 40% showed real people. (make) (True: the director, James Cameron, wanted it to be 100%, but he didn't have enough money.)

3. Which character from a book _____ in more films: Harry Potter or Dracula? (see) (Dracula. The book, written by Bram Stoker in 1897, is one of the most filmed stories in movie history.)

4. Which actor _____ the most: Brad Pitt, Robert Downey Jr. or Leonardo di Caprio? (pay) (Robert Downey Jr. According to *Forbes* magazine, he made around $75 million from films like *The Avengers* and *Iron Man 3*.)

5. In the future, most films _____ with computer graphics. We won't need real actors. (make) (No one knows! What do you think?)

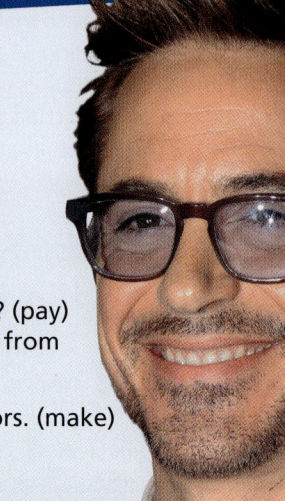

9B I went to a concert which changed my life

Learn to give extra information
- **G** Defining and non-defining relative clauses
- **V** Music; Word-building (nouns)

1 VOCABULARY Music

a 💬 What's happening in the photos below? Which words can you use to describe them?

audience   choir   DJ   play   live
festival   musician   orchestra   perform

① ② ③

b ▶ 3.24 Listen to four clips of music and underline the correct words.
1 They are playing *live / in a recording studio*.
2 You can hear a *DJ / musician*.
3 Someone is *performing / enjoying* a piece of music.
4 You can hear *a choir / an orchestra*.

c 💬 Discuss the questions. Check that you understand the words in **bold**.
1 When and where did you last listen to a **song**?
2 What are your favourite **albums**? And your favourite **tracks**?
3 Do you like making **playlists**?
4 When and where did you last sing or play a musical **instrument**?

2 LISTENING

a 💬 How many different musical experiences can you think of? Write a list.

going to concerts, singing in a choir …

b 💬 Compare your lists. Which of these experiences do you like taking part in or going to? Why?

c ▶ 3.25 Listen to three people talk about a music experience which changed their life. Match each speaker with photos a–c.

Annie _____   Jeff _____   Erica _____

d ▶ 3.25 Listen again and make notes in the table.

	What sort of music do they talk about?	Where was the event?	How did it change his/her life?
Annie			
Jeff			
Erica			

e 💬 Talk about which of the musical experiences you would like to have. Say why.

107

UNIT 9

3 GRAMMAR
Defining and non-defining relative clauses

a Look at the underlined relative clauses. Circle the noun phrase which each relative clause gives more information about.
1 It was my grandmother who started it.
2 It's a drum you play with your hands.
3 I was sitting next to one of the people who was in my group.
4 It's the kind of place where you could sit and chat all night.

b Look at the two sentences below and underline the correct answer in the rule.
1 It's a drum (which/that) you play with your hands.
2 It was my grandmother who/that started it.

> In defining relative clauses, we need to / don't need to use who, which or that when the noun is the object of the relative clause.

c ▶ 3.26 **Pronunciation** Listen to the sentences. In which sentence do you hear a pause before and after the relative pronoun in **bold**?
1 People **who** sing a lot always seem happy.
2 Carly, **who**'s a fantastic singer, works in a café during the day.

d ▶ Now go to Grammar Focus 9B on p.148

e 💬 Take turns to describe the words in the box using a sentence with a defining relative clause. Say which word your partner is describing.

| album | audience | choir | concert | DJ | festival |
| musician | orchestra | playlist | track | guitarist |

It's something which you can download.
An album?
No, it's something that you can find on an album.
A track!
Yes.

4 READING AND VOCABULARY
Word-building (nouns)

a 💬 Discuss the questions.
1 Have you ever been to a music festival?
2 If so, what kind of music was there? Did you enjoy it? Why / Why not?
3 If not, do you know of any music festivals you would like to go to? What are they like?

b Read *The three best music festivals you've probably never heard of*. Which festival would you rather go to? Why?

The three best music festivals you've probably never heard of

Fuji Rock Festival, Japan

Enjoy rock and electronic music at the foot of Mount Fuji

This is Japan's largest outdoor music event. It's held every year at the Naeba Ski Resort. You can enjoy the beauty of the forests and rivers as you walk (often quite a long way!) from one stage to another. This is one of the world's safest and most environmentally friendly festivals, which is probably why everyone's happiness levels are so high!

Past performers include: Radiohead, Coldplay, Massive Attack

Roskilde, Denmark

A rock festival that gives all its profits to charity

Here, you can enjoy rock, punk, heavy metal, hip hop, indie and music from around the world. The organisers donate all the money they make to projects for social and cultural development.
Don't forget that summer days are long in Denmark. It doesn't get dark until 11 pm, and it starts getting light at 3.30 am.

Past performers include: Metallica, Bruce Springsteen, Rihanna

UNIT 9

c Read the article again and match the comments with the festivals. Write F (Fuji Rock Festival), R (Roskilde) or C (Coachella).
1 ☐ 'Even the toilet paper is made from recycled cups from last year's festival!'
2 ☐ 'I'm glad I took a good pair of walking boots with me.'
3 ☐ 'The nights were so short!'
4 ☐ 'There was a huge wooden butterfly.'
5 ☐ 'It's really good to know that all the money goes to good causes.'
6 ☐ 'The second weekend was great.'

d Complete the table with words from the article.

adjective	noun	verb
artistic	1_____ (person)	
beautiful	2_____	
	3_____	celebrate
charitable	4_____	
creative	5_____	create
cultural	6_____	
	7_____	develop
happy	8_____	
musical	9_____ (person)	
organised	10_____ (person)	organise
	11_____ (person) 12_____	perform

Coachella, California, USA

Music and sculpture in the Californian desert

This annual music and arts festival, which takes place over two long weekends, is a celebration of creativity and culture. Live performances of rock, indie, hip hop and electronic music take place continuously.
As you walk around the grounds, you can also enjoy sculptures and other modern art installations by artists from around the world.

Past performers include: Red Hot Chili Peppers, Florence and the Machine, Kanye West

e ▶3.28 **Pronunciation** Listen to the words in 4d. Notice how the stress sometimes changes position as we change the form of the word. Mark the stress on each word.

f ▶3.28 Listen again and practise saying the words.

g Write the noun forms of the words. Use one suffix from the box for each pair of words and make spelling changes if necessary.

-ance/-ence -(a)tion -er/-or
-ity -ist -ness -ty

1 loyal, honest: loyalty _____
2 fit, sad: _____ _____
3 able, responsible: _____ _____
4 design, write: _____ _____
5 intelligent, patient: _____ _____
6 piano, guitar: _____ _____
7 locate, relax: _____ _____

h 💬 Talk about which of the qualities in the box are important for the people 1–4. Which qualities are not needed? Say why.

beauty creativity honesty intelligence
kindness musical ability responsibility

1 a pop singer
2 a friend
3 a teacher
4 a politician

5 SPEAKING

a You are going to talk about an interesting or exciting experience in your life which involved music. Make notes on the questions below.
1 What happened?
2 When was it?
3 Who was with you?
4 Why was it important?
5 Why have you remembered it?

b 💬 Take turns to talk about your experiences and ask follow-up questions.

> I went to see a band I've been a fan of for years …

9C Everyday English
It's meant to be excellent

Learn to recommend and respond to recommendations
- **P** Showing contrast
- **S** Asking someone to wait

1 LISTENING

a Discuss the questions.
1. How often do you have an evening out with friends? What do you usually do?
2. How easy is it to organise an evening out with your friends? Do you all have the same interests? Do you ever disagree on what you want to do?
3. Which of the activities in the box do you enjoy?

a meal in a restaurant   a horror film
a meal at a friend's house   a pop concert
a play at the theatre

b ▶3.29 Watch or listen to Part 1. Which activities are mentioned? What do they decide to do in the end?

c ▶3.29 Watch or listen to Part 1 again. Who …
1. suggests going to a jazz club? *Becky / Mark*
2. suggests going to a classical music festival? *Becky / Rachel*
3. doesn't like classical music? *Becky / Tom*
4. suggests a local rock band? *Tom / Rachel*
5. hasn't seen a rock band for 10 years? *Rachel / Mark*

2 USEFUL LANGUAGE
Recommending and responding

a ▶3.29 Listen to Part 1 again and tick (✓) the phrases you hear.
1. ☐ That's a great idea!
2. ☐ It's meant to be excellent.
3. ☐ It was highly recommended by …
4. ☐ It's supposed to be really good.
5. ☐ I'm not a big fan of classical music.
6. ☐ Why don't we go and see that local band?
7. ☐ They've had great reviews.
8. ☐ I think you'd love it.
9. ☐ I doubt Mark would be interested.
10. ☐ It sounds really interesting, but …

b Which phrases in 2a … ?
1. give a recommendation or opinion
2. respond to a recommendation

c Work in groups of three. Use the diagram below to have a conversation.

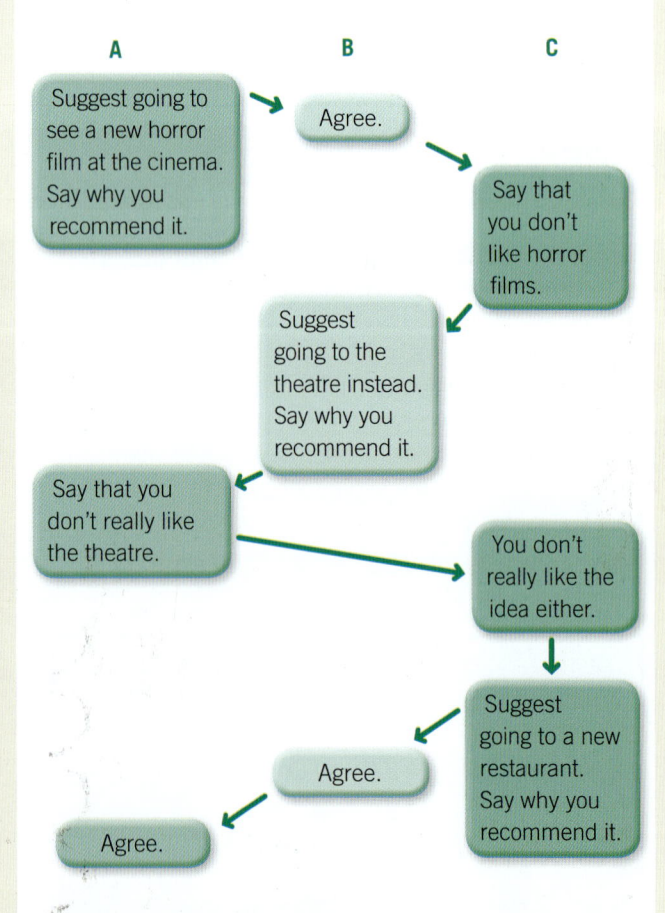

A: Suggest going to see a new horror film at the cinema. Say why you recommend it.
B: Agree.
C: Say that you don't like horror films.
B: Suggest going to the theatre instead. Say why you recommend it.
A: Say that you don't really like the theatre.
C: You don't really like the idea either.
A: Suggest going to a new restaurant. Say why you recommend it.
B: Agree.
C: Agree.

110

3 PRONUNCIATION Showing contrast

a ▶3.30 Listen to the following sentence. Which word is stressed?

Tom likes classical music.

b ▶3.31 Listen to these conversations. Decide which word is stressed more in each sentence.

1 **A** You like classical music, don't you?
  B No. Tom likes classical music. I like rock music.
     (= It's Tom who likes classical music, not me.)
2 **A** Does Tom like pop music?
  B No, Tom likes classical music.
     (= It's classical music that Tom likes, not pop.)

When we want to show a contrast (emphasise that something is different), we stress that word more.

c Work in pairs. Take it in turns to ask the questions and reply, showing contrast by stressing a word.

1 Did you buy the red shoes? (blue)
2 Did you go to the cinema with John? (theatre)
3 Did you see John? (Chris)

4 CONVERSATION SKILLS
Asking someone to wait

a ▶3.32 Listen to part of the conversation between Rachel and Becky. Complete the sentences.

1 **Rachel** Wait a _____, I'll just ask Mark.
2 **Becky** _____ on, Tom wants to say something.

b Complete the table with the words in the box.

check   hang   please   second   wait

¹ _____ on	
Just ² _____	a minute / a ³ _____ / a moment.
One moment, ⁴ _____.	
Let me ⁵ _____ (for you).	

c Which expression is more formal?

d Work in pairs. Follow the instructions and have a conversation.

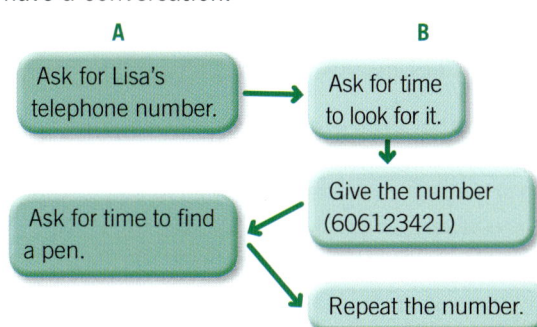

A: Ask for Lisa's telephone number.
B: Ask for time to look for it.
A: Ask for time to find a pen.
B: Give the number (606123421)
B: Repeat the number.

5 LISTENING

a Tom told Mark to wear something cool. Look at the clothes below.

Which do you think is the coolest? Which do you think Mark will wear?

b ▶3.33 Watch or listen to Part 2 and check your ideas. What do the others think of Mark's clothes?

c Discuss the questions.

1 Do you usually spend a lot of time choosing what to wear when you go out? Why / Why not?
2 What kind of clothes do people in your area wear when they go out for the evening (e.g. to a restaurant, to the cinema, to the theatre)?

6 SPEAKING

▶ **Communication 9C** You're going to have a conversation about what to do today.
Student A: Read the information below. Student B: Go to p.130.

Student A
- You would like to go to an exhibition of modern art.
- You've just eaten, so you don't want to go out for a meal.
- Someone gave you an advert for a photography exhibition. You have the advert in your bag.

We could go to the modern art exhibition. It's meant to be really interesting.

That sounds OK, but I'm not a big fan of modern art.

Unit Progress Test

CHECK YOUR PROGRESS

You can now do the Unit Progress Test.

UNIT 9

111

9D Skills for Writing
I like going out, but …

Learn to write an article
Contrasting ideas; the structure of an article

1 SPEAKING AND LISTENING

a Look at photos a–e. If you could win free tickets to go to one of the events, which would you choose? Why?

b ▶3.34 Listen to Anna and her friend, Camila. Answer the questions.
1 Who has tickets to the Kanye West concert?
2 Who doesn't want to go?
3 Why doesn't she want to go?

c Make notes on the positive and negative points of these things:
- live performances (plays, concerts, etc.)
- recorded performances (albums, films, etc.)

d Do you agree with Camila, or do you like going to live concerts?

2 READING

a Read Julia's blog, *Why I prefer to stay at home*. What is her main point?
1 Films are too expensive and it's cheaper to stay at home.
2 It's more comfortable and convenient to watch films and TV series at home.
3 Films are less satisfying than TV programmes.

b Read the blog again and answer the questions.
1 What annoys Julia about cinema audiences?
2 Why were the couple sitting behind her rude?
3 What does she do if she finds a film boring?
4 Why is the length of a TV series sometimes a good thing?

Why I prefer to stay at home

① What was your last cinema experience like? I remember the expensive tickets, the long queues and the uncomfortable seats. Does this sound familiar? I love going out to see my friends, going to parties or clubs. I like having fun. However, I don't really enjoy going to the cinema any more.

② The other problem for me is the audience at cinemas. Although many people say that seeing a film at a cinema is a good chance to go out and be sociable, I really hate listening to other people's comments. The last time I went to the cinema, there was a couple who commented loudly on everything in the film. They laughed at everything in the film, really loudly – even at things which weren't funny! I politely asked them to be quiet. Despite this, they continued as if they were watching their own TV. If I watch something at home, I can invite my friends and spend time with people I know and like rather than sitting near noisy strangers.

③ Another reason for staying at home is convenience. I like to watch films or TV shows when I want to watch them, not at specific times. In spite of my love of films and TV shows, I don't enjoy all of them. If I'm at home, I can stop the film and watch something else or I can fast-forward through the boring bits. For example, I was really disappointed with a film I saw last night – so I just switched it off!

④ While I watch a lot of films, I also watch a lot of TV shows online now. I really enjoy watching a whole series. It gives characters time to develop in interesting and unexpected ways. In fact, there are so many great TV shows to watch, I've hardly got time to go to the cinema.

⑤ So these days, when my friends invite me to the cinema, I usually say, 'No thanks'. I really do prefer to watch films and TV series at home. I can choose what I want to watch, I can choose the time when I want to watch it and I can choose who I watch it with. The question really is: why should I go out?

3 WRITING SKILLS Contrasting ideas; the structure of an article

a In the example below, *however* introduces a contrast. Find more examples of words used to contrast ideas in the blog in 2a.

I like having fun. **However**, I don't really enjoy going to the cinema any more.

b Complete the rules and examples with the words in the box. Use each word twice.

although   despite   however   in spite of   while

- *I enjoy films.* [1]_____, *I think I prefer TV series.*
  We can use [2]_____ at the beginning of a sentence. It contrasts with an idea in the previous sentence.
- [3]_____ / [4]_____ *cinemas have become more comfortable, they're not as comfortable as my sofa.*
  We can use [5]_____ and [6]_____ at the beginning of a sentence to introduce a contrasting idea. They are followed by a clause with a verb.
- *The price of cinema tickets has gone up recently.*
  [7]_____ / [8]_____ *the cost, I still love the movies.*
  We can use [9]_____ and [10]_____ at the beginning of the sentence to introduce a contrasting idea. They are followed by a noun or pronoun.

c Match ideas 1–6 with a contrasting idea a–f. Join the ideas using the words in brackets. Write only one sentence, if possible.

1. ☐ I was given two free tickets to a jazz concert (However)
2. ☐ music is something we normally listen to (Although)
3. ☐ TV screens have got bigger and bigger (Although)
4. ☐ the beat is very important in hip-hop music (While)
5. ☐ the convenience of watching a film at home (In spite of)
6. ☐ my love of special effects (Despite)

a singers still have to know how to sing a tune.
b I don't like that kind of music, so I'll give them away.
c there's nothing like the big screen at the cinema.
d I still want films to have a good story and good acting.
e it's always interesting to watch musicians perform.
f I prefer to see films at a cinema.

d Look at paragraphs 2–4 in the blog on p.112. What is the main idea of each paragraph? Choose a or b.

Paragraph 2:
a cinema audiences   b being polite in cinemas
Paragraph 3:
a boring films   b the convenience of staying at home
Paragraph 4:
a the length of TV series   b an alternative to watching films

e Discuss the questions.

1. Is the main idea mentioned at the beginning or in the middle of the paragraph?
2. Does the writer sometimes use examples?
3. How does the writer get the reader's attention in paragraph 1, the introduction?
4. In paragraph 5, the conclusion, does the writer introduce new ideas? Why / Why not?

4 WRITING An article

a You are going to write an article about a kind of entertainment you love or hate. Choose one of the topics below or your own idea. Then make notes about questions 1–4.

- music concerts in stadiums or in small clubs
- watching sport in a stadium or live on TV
- classical music or pop music

1. What's your opinion on this topic?
2. What experience do you have of it?
3. What other things do you know about it?
4. What do other people often say about it?

b Compare your ideas with a partner.

c Plan your article. Follow these instructions:

1. Write down the main ideas of the article.
2. Write down different points for each idea.
3. Think of any examples from your experience.

d Write your article. Make sure you write an introduction and conclusion. Remember to use words or phrases to show contrast.

UNIT 9
Review and extension

1 GRAMMAR

a Read the text and underline the correct words.

Can you imagine a film ¹*who / which* had no music? It would be very boring. Here are two talented film composers ²*what / that* everyone should know about.

John Williams ³*sees / is seen* as one of the greatest film composers of all time. He ⁴*has nominated / has been nominated* for more awards than anyone else, apart from Walt Disney. Williams, ⁵*whose / who* music can be heard in the Harry Potter and *Star Wars* films, is most famous for working with director Steven Spielberg on many of his films.

The music for *Titanic*, *The Amazing Spider-Man* and more than 100 other films was written ⁶*with / by* pianist and composer James Horner. In his compositions, Horner often uses Celtic music, ⁷*which / that* is traditional music from Western Europe.

b Complete the second sentence so that it means the same as the first sentence (or pair of sentences). Use three words in each gap.
1 The film was based on a book. I loved it when I was a child.
   The film was based on a _____ when I was a child.
2 That's the place. The final scene was filmed there.
   That's the place _____ scene was filmed.
3 *Catching Fire* is the second film in the *Hunger Games* series. *Catching Fire* came out in 2013.
   Catching Fire, _____ in 2013, is the second film in the *Hunger Games* series.
4 People are forgetting many traditional folk songs
   Many traditional folk songs _____.
5 They were recording the concert when I was there.
   The concert _____ when I was there.

2 VOCABULARY

a Read the text and underline the correct words.

The epic historical film, *Les Misérables*, is based ¹*on / at* the book in which the different ²*characters / performers* fight for social change in 19th-century France. ³*Character / Director* Tom Hooper successfully combines big dramatic ⁴*frames / scenes* with quieter moments. What makes the film so powerful is that the songs weren't recorded in a ⁵*scene / studio*: all the actors sang ⁶*live / tune* as they were filmed. Music played by ⁷*an orchestra / a performance* was added after filming had finished.

b Complete the sentences with noun forms of the words in brackets.
1 The festival is a _____ of music from different cultures. (celebrate)
2 We'd like to thank the _____ for all their hard work in preparing the show. (organise)
3 This film shows the _____ of the Pacific Islands. (beautiful)
4 The _____ are preparing for their _____ this evening. (music; perform)

3 WORDPOWER see, look at, watch, hear, listen to

a Match questions 1–8 with responses a–h.
1 ☐ Amy! Amy! Why isn't she answering?
2 ☐ What's that noise?
3 ☐ Have you found another painting?
4 ☐ Are they dancing?
5 ☐ What's that light in the sky?
6 ☐ Do you **see** what I mean?
7 ☐ Are you going to **see** the doctor?
8 ☐ Have you **seen** *Iron Man 3*?

a Yes, I've got an appointment tomorrow.
b I can't **see** anything.
c No, I don't understand.
d Yes, I **watched** it with Brendan.
e I can't **hear** anything.
f She's **listening to** music.
g Yes, come and **look at** it! It's amazing!
h Yes, come and **watch**.

b Add the words in **bold** in 3a to the table.

1 _____	pay attention to something because of its appearance (e.g. a photo, a flower)
2 _____	pay attention to something because of the movement (e.g. a film)
3 _____	be able to recognise sights
	go and watch something that's moving
	understand
	visit
4 _____	be able to recognise sounds
5 _____	pay attention to sounds

c 💬 Underline the correct words. Then discuss the questions.
1 How often do you *watch / look at* old photos of yourself?
2 When did you last *see / watch* the dentist?
3 What music do you *listen to / hear* when you're in a bad mood?
4 *Watch / Look* out of the window. What can you *see / look at*?
5 *Listen / Hear*. What can you *listen / hear*?
6 If you *listened to / heard* a strange noise in the night, would you go and *watch / see* what it was?
7 What is the worst film you've ever *seen / looked at*?

⟳ REVIEW YOUR PROGRESS

How well did you do in this unit? Write 3, 2 or 1 for each objective.
3 = very well 2 = well 1 = not so well

I CAN . . .

talk about films and TV.	☐
give extra information.	☐
recommend and respond to recommendations.	☐
write an article.	☐

CAN DO OBJECTIVES

- Talk about new things you would like to do
- Talk about imagined past events
- Talk about possible problems and reassure someone
- Write an email with advice

UNIT 10
Opportunities

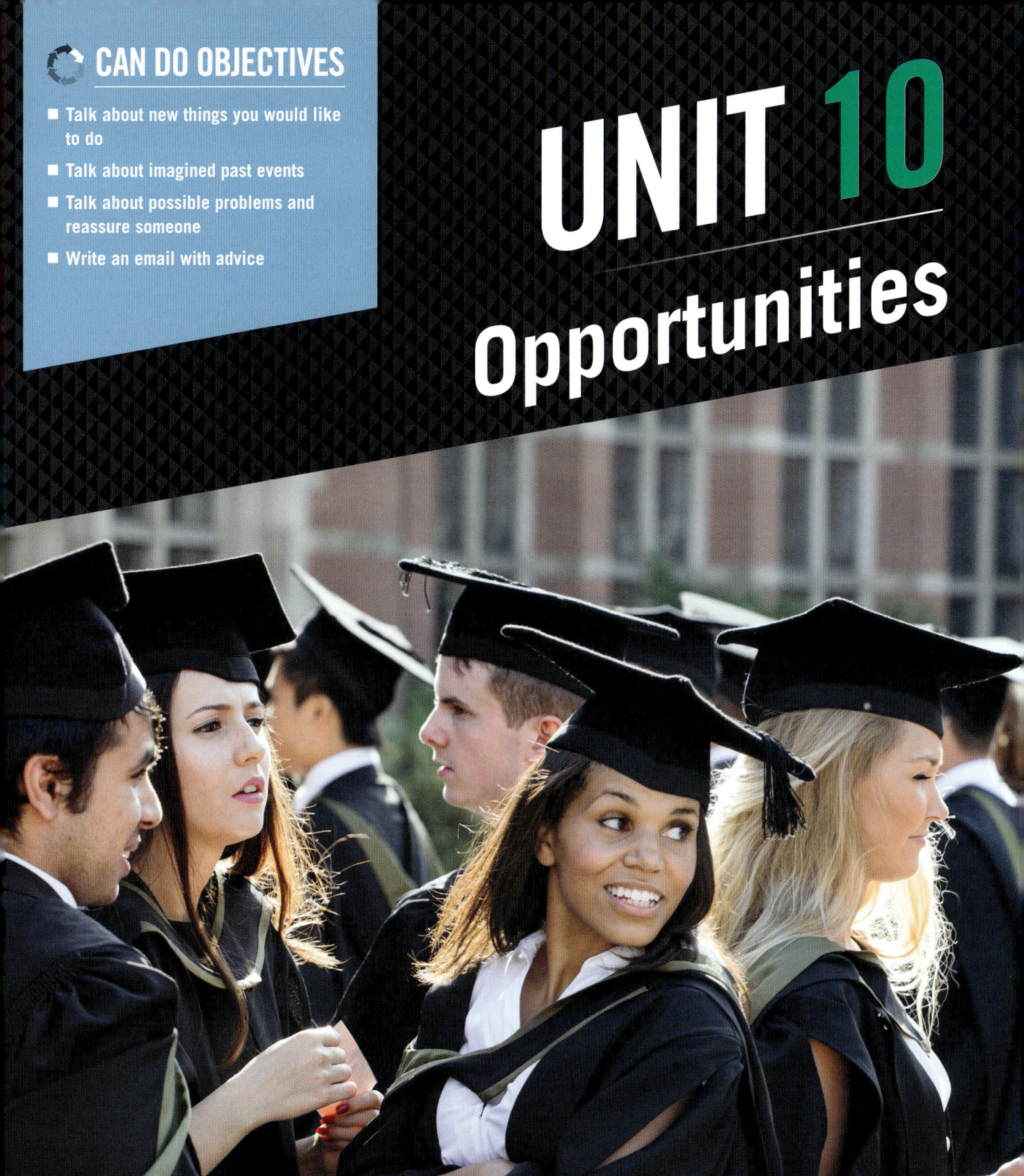

GETTING STARTED

a   What do you think is happening in the photo?

b   What do you think happens next? Think of three ideas.

c   Ask and answer the questions.
1 What opportunities can studying at university give you?
2 What opportunities have you had in your life? For example, think about education, travel, meeting people, work.
3 Have you ever taken the opportunity to do something very scary or difficult (for example, sky-diving, talking in public or doing a performance)? If not, would you like to have one of those opportunities?

115

10A If I was fitter, I'd do it!

Learn to talk about new things you would like to do

G Second conditional
V Sport; Adjectives and prepositions

1 SPEAKING

a Look at photos a–c.
1 What is happening (or going to happen) in each photo?
2 How are the people in each photo feeling?

b Add more sports to the lists.
- winter sports: skiing, …
- ball sports: tennis, …
- water sports: surfing, …

c Discuss the questions.
1 Which of the sports on your lists in 1b have you tried?
2 Which do you think are the most …?
   - fun
   - exciting
   - dangerous
   - difficult
3 Would you like to try any new sports? Which would you like to try?

2 VOCABULARY Sport

a Check that you understand the words in **bold**. Match the sports in the pictures below with sentences 1–5. There is more than one possible answer.
1 It's an **extreme** sport.
2 It's a really good **workout**.
3 You win **points** when your partner **misses** the ball.
4 If you like surfing, you should **have a go** at this.
5 The **training** is very difficult.

b Now go to Vocabulary Focus 10A on p.161

a ski jumping

b tennis

c surfing

table tennis

snowboarding

volleyball

wrestling

diving

116

3 LISTENING

a Look at the photos below and discuss the questions.
1 Have you tried these sports, or seen them in action?
2 What do you think looks most fun about them?

b 3.36 Listen to Gina and Libby talking about scuba diving and the Colour Run and answer the questions.
1 Why do they like each sport?
2 What do they agree to do at the end?

c 3.36 Listen again and discuss the questions.
1 Where did Gina try scuba diving?
2 How much training did she do?
3 Why was she scared at first?
4 How long is the run that Libby's going to do?
5 Why is it different from normal runs?

d Which of the two sports sounds more exciting/dangerous? Which would you rather try? Why?

e Write down all the reasons why you like your favourite sport. Work with someone who likes a different sport and tell them why you like yours.

> Of course, football is the greatest game in the world. People in every country love it and …

4 GRAMMAR Second conditional

a Look at these second conditional sentences and answer the questions.
- Was it scary? I think if I went, I'd be terrified!
- If I was a bit fitter, I would definitely do it.
1 When do we use the second conditional? Choose a or b.
   a to talk about things we will probably do in the future
   b to talk about things we imagine, but are not real
2 What verb form do we use after *if*?

b 3.37 **Pronunciation** Listen to the pronunciation of *would* in each of the sentences. Is it strong (stressed) or weak (not stressed)? Write S (strong) or W (weak).
1 If you went, you would absolutely love it.
2 I wouldn't do a full marathon – I'm not fit enough.
3 It would be great if there was a big group of us going.
4 Would you like to try?
5 Yes, I would, but …
6 If I was a bit fitter, I would definitely do it.

c 3.37 Listen again and repeat the sentences.

d ▶ Now go to Grammar Focus 10A on p.150

e Tick (✓) the sentences that are true for you. Then write second conditional sentences saying what you would or might do if things were different.
☐ I can't run long distances.
☐ I'm not very tall.
☐ I don't live in a country that gets lots of snow.
☐ I can't afford a personal fitness trainer.
☐ I'm scared of heights.
☐ I'm not very fit.
☐ I'm not an Olympic champion.

If I could run long distances, I'd enter a big marathon and raise money for charity.

f Compare your sentences in 4e.

UNIT 10

5 VOCABULARY
Adjectives and prepositions

a Some adjectives are followed by a preposition. Complete each sentence with a preposition.

1 I was a bit worried _____ it before we went into the water for the first time.
2 It sounds perfect _____ me!
3 And it's popular _____ all kinds of people.

b ▶3.39 Listen and check your answers.

c Underline the correct prepositions.

1 I don't like extreme sports – I'm afraid *about* / *of* hurting myself.
2 I'm not scared *of* / *to* spiders.
3 I am very proud *of* / *about* my little sister.
4 I think that having lots of friends is essential *in* / *for* a happy, healthy life.
5 I'm very interested *in* / *about* health and fitness.
6 I'm worried *of* / *about* my football team's performance at the moment.
7 I'll never get tired *in* / *of* visiting new places.
8 I've found a sport which is right *for* / *in* me.
9 American football is similar *to* / *from* rugby.

d Tick (✓) the sentences in 5c that are true for you. Change the others so that they are true for you.

e In adverts a–c below, eight prepositions are missing. Add them in the correct places.

6 SPEAKING

a Make notes about what you would do if you had one of the opportunities below.

learn a new skill or sport
• What would you learn? Why?

a free holiday to anywhere in the world with a friend
• Where would you go? Why?
• Who would you take?

meet a famous person
• Who would you choose?
• What would you say or ask?

travel in time
• What year would you travel to? Why?
• What would you do when you were there?

b Compare your ideas. Would you like to do the things your partner would like to do?

a DANCE YOURSELF FIT

Are you worried getting unfit, but afraid joining a gym? Fitness is essential good health and happiness – but what can you do if you don't like sport? That's simple – get dancing!

We're very proud our team of qualified dance instructors.

b BECOME A GUIDE RUNNER

If you want to keep fit and you're interested helping people too, why not become a guide runner? Running is popular blind people, but many of them need a guide runner for support. Just let us know your level of fitness and where you live. You'll even get automatic entry into any races!

c Body Training Adventure Programme

Are you tired the usual exercise classes? Do you need something more exciting and challenging?

Join our intensive fitness training programme for all ages and abilities. It's similar an Army-style Boot Camp but with an added emphasis on fun and team-work.

Activities include rock-climbing, mountain biking and boxing.

10B Making the most of opportunities

Learn to talk about imagined past events
G Third conditional
V Expressions with *do*, *make* and *take*

1 SPEAKING

a Think of a time when something good happened to you (e.g. you met a friend for the first time, you got a new job, you found a new hobby, etc.). Make notes about the questions.
1 What happened?
2 Why would you describe it as a good experience?
3 Why do you think it happened? Were you lucky, or did you do something to make it happen?

b 💬 Tell each other your stories.

2 READING

a 💬 Look at the photos, which show details of three true stories about good luck. Can you guess what the three stories might be about?

b 💬 Compare your ideas with other students. Are your ideas the same or different?

UNIT 10

c Read *Searching for serendipity* quickly. Were your ideas correct in 2a?

Searching for serendipity

HOME   NEWS   YOUR STORIES   LOGIN

Are you making the most of life's opportunities?

ANNA

I had my own business, but needed a website. My friend Wendy gave me the email address of a designer called Mark. Unfortunately, Wendy's handwriting is awful, so I sent the email to the wrong person. Someone called Matt replied. Obviously, there had been a mistake. He said he wasn't actually a designer – he was a primary school teacher – but he could help me if I wanted!

Matt seemed nice. And anyway, I didn't have anyone else to help me, so I decided to write back to him. In the end, Matt worked on my website for free. He did a great job and my business started to go really well. Meanwhile, we got to know each other via email. And ten months later, we met. We fell in love immediately, and a year later, we got married. If Wendy had had better handwriting, my business wouldn't have been such a success, and I certainly wouldn't have met Matt!

Two years ago, Anna Frances had some very good luck when her colleague gave her some wrong information.

So was Anna just lucky? Or did she make her own luck? Why do these lucky accidents seem to happen to some people and not to others? And is there any way to make yourself more lucky? Well, it seems that the secret of happiness is to make the most of the opportunities that life gives us. We need to be open to serendipity – the random events that lead to happy, sometimes life-changing, results.

Dr Stephann Makri is working on a project about serendipity at University College, London. He thinks that serendipity is more than an accident and that we can all have more 'luck' if we learn to pay attention to life's opportunities. He has noticed that many people's good-luck stories share the same basic pattern. First, people notice that there is an opportunity. Then, they take action to make the most of it. For example, if you imagine meeting an old friend in the street who will later introduce you to the love of your life, several things have to happen. First, you have to notice the friend. Then you have to stop and talk to them, even though you might be busy. Finally, you need to be ready to follow up on whatever comes out of the conversation. So, it might be luck that leads you to walk past the friend on the street – but the rest is up to you!

More serendipity stories...

TOM

After university, I didn't have a job. I subscribed to a job website and got lots of emails from them every day. I usually deleted them. One day, I was feeling particularly annoyed by all the emails, so I opened one of them to click on the 'unsubscribe' link. But I spotted an interesting job. It was in the USA and I didn't really have the experience they wanted, but I decided to try. I didn't get the job, but they emailed me two weeks later to say they had another job I could apply for. I got it, and I ended up working in New York City, where I met my girlfriend Paula. None of it would have happened if I had deleted the email.

CARLA

My mum Betty is 71. There's a café in town that I like and I persuaded my mum to come with me, just to get out of the house. She didn't want to come at first, but when we got there she really liked the café. While we were there, she started chatting to some bikers. My mum said she had always wanted to ride a motorbike! I was shocked! Kenny, one of the bikers, offered to take us both out with the rest of the group. To my amazement, my mother said 'yes'! I was really worried, but actually, my mum loved the experience!

---

d Complete the sentences with the names in the box.

| Anna | Betty | Carla | Kenny | Matt | Tom |

1 _____ failed at first, but was right to take a chance.
2 _____ did an activity she'd always wanted to do.
3 _____ was surprised by someone else's behaviour.
4 _____ did some work for someone, even though it wasn't his job.
5 _____ made contact with the wrong person.
6 _____ did something kind for someone the first time he met her.

e Discuss the questions.

1 Which person do you think was the 'luckiest'?
2 Do you agree that people make their own luck? Why / Why not?
3 Do you think that you are a lucky person? Do you make the most of life's opportunities in a similar way to the people in the stories?

120

UNIT 10

3 VOCABULARY
Expressions with *do*, *make* and *take*

a Underline the correct answers to complete the summary of Dr Makri's ideas.

> Can we ¹*take / make / do* our own luck? Dr Makri has been ²*doing / making / taking* research into serendipity and he believes we can. The secret lies in ³*doing / taking / making* advantage of opportunity when it comes our way. If you see an opportunity in a chance event, you should ⁴*take / make / do* action and ⁵*take / have / make* the most of that opportunity.
>
> Everyone can be 'luckier'. If you get out and meet people you'll have more chance encounters. Be brave and ⁶*take / make / do* risks in order to act freely when an opportunity comes your way.

b ▶ Now go to Vocabulary Focus 10B on p.161

4 GRAMMAR Third conditional

a Underline the correct words. Then check your answers in the article on p.120.

If Wendy ¹*had / had had / would have had* better handwriting, my business ²*wasn't / hadn't been / wouldn't have been* such a success, and I certainly ³*didn't meet / hadn't met / wouldn't have met* Matt.

b Answer the questions.
  1 Did Wendy have good handwriting? Was Anna's business successful? Did she meet Matt?
  2 When do we use the third conditional? Choose a or b.
     a to talk about real results of real past events
     b to imagine an alternative to a past event and imagine an alternative result
  3 What verb form do we use after *if*? What form of the verb do we use in the other part of the sentence?

c ▶3.40 Listen and match speakers 1–4 with pictures a–d below.

Speaker 1 ☐   Speaker 3 ☐
Speaker 2 ☐   Speaker 4 ☐

d ▶3.41 **Pronunciation** Listen to the sentences below. Which words are stressed in each sentence?
  1 I would have won easily if I hadn't hurt my arm.
  2 I wouldn't have bought it if I'd known it was in such bad condition.
  3 If you hadn't pushed me, that car would have hit me!
  4 I wouldn't have discovered the truth if I hadn't read her letters.

e ▶3.41 Listen again and practise saying the sentences.

f ▶ Now go to Grammar Focus 10B on p.150

g Write third conditional sentences about the people in the box from the article on p.120.

Anna   Wendy   Matt   Tom   Betty   Carla   Kenny

If Anna's friend had given her the correct email address, she might have fallen in love with a different person instead of Matt.

h 💬 Compare your sentences.

5 SPEAKING

a You're going to tell the story of a past event that made your life better. Make notes about one of these topics:
  • a good friend, and how you met him or her
  • a sport or hobby, and how you started doing it
  • an accident, and how it happened
  • a job, and how you got it
  • a school, and why you went there
  • a big decision, and how you made it

Think about the important events in your story. What were the consequences of what happened? How would your life have been different if you had done something differently?

b 💬 Take turns to tell your stories. Ask each other questions to find out more about what might have happened if things had been different.

> What would have been different if you hadn't gone to that school?

> I wouldn't have met my best friend, Gabriela.

10C Everyday English
You've got nothing to worry about

Learn to talk about possible problems and reassure someone

- **P** Sounding sure and unsure
- **S** Changing the subject

1 LISTENING

a 💬 Discuss the questions.
1. When was the last time you were very nervous?
2. What situations make you nervous (e.g. public speaking, flying, starting a new job)? What do you do to calm down?

b ▶3.43 Watch or listen to Part 1. What do you think Tom and Mark are talking about?

c ▶3.44 Watch or listen to Part 2 to check.

2 USEFUL LANGUAGE
Talking about possible problems and reassuring someone

a ▶3.44 Watch or listen to Part 2 again and complete the sentences.
1. You've got _____ to worry about.
2. I'm _____ it'll be OK.
3. You don't _____ it's a bit boring?
4. I'm still _____ that something will go wrong.
5. What _____ she says no?
6. She's _____ not going to say no.

b Add the sentences in 2a to the table.

Talking about a problem	Reassuring someone
	You've got nothing to worry about.

c 💬 Think of (real or invented) worries you might have about these situations. Talk to your partner. Reassure them about their worries.
- do badly in an exam
- public speaking
- a stressful day at work
- a difficult journey

> I'm worried that I will forget what to say.
>
> You'll be fine!

3 PRONUNCIATION
Sounding sure and unsure

a ▶3.45 Listen to this extract from the conversation. Does Tom sound sure or unsure?

Mark So, where are you taking her?
Tom I've booked a table at *Bella Vita*. It's the place where we went on our first date.

b ▶3.44 Now listen to Part 2 again. Does Tom sound sure or unsure all the way through?

c ▶3.46 Listen to the following sentences. Do you think the speaker is sure or unsure?
1. **A** Do you think Rachel wants to go to a restaurant?
   B I think so, yes.
2. **A** Does Rachel like pizza?
   B I think so, yes.
3. **A** When did you meet her?
   B About two years ago.
4. **A** Where did you go on your first date?
   B We went to *Bella Vita*.

122

UNIT 10

4 LISTENING

a 💬 Tom and Becky are in the restaurant. What might happen? Talk about the ideas below. Which one do you think is most likely? Why?
1 Tom is too nervous and doesn't ask Becky to marry him.
2 Becky asks Tom to marry her before he can ask her.
3 Becky is very surprised and says yes.

b ▶3.47 Watch or listen to Part 3 and check.

c Are the statements true (T) or false (F)?
1 Becky and Tom both think that they went to this restaurant for their first date.
2 Tom tried to phone Becky earlier.
3 Becky wants to talk to Tom about their plans for the weekend.
4 Becky was expecting Tom to ask her to marry him.
5 Becky says she will marry Tom.

5 CONVERSATION SKILLS
Changing the subject

a ▶3.48 Listen and complete the sentences.
1 **Becky** That _____ me, I need to book the restaurant for the office party.
2 **Tom** So, anyway, as I was _____ , you've really changed my life.

b Look again at the sentences in 5a. Who is starting a completely new subject, and who is returning to a previous subject?

c Look at the phrases in **bold**. Are they ways to change the subject or return to a previous subject?
1 **Speaking of** cafés, have I told you about the place we found last week?
2 **By the way,** did you see that new comedy programme last night?

d 💬 Work in pairs.
Student A: You want to talk about your weekend. Talk to Student B. Can you keep the conversation on the same subject?
Student B: You don't want to hear about Student A's weekend. Try to change the subject and talk about other things (e.g. a film you've seen recently, someone you saw today, etc.).

> I went to see a film this weekend.

> Oh, speaking of films, did you see that *The Hobbit* is on TV tonight?

6 SPEAKING

▶ **Communication 10C** 💬 Student A: Read the information below. Student B: Go to p.131.

> **Student A**
> You want to talk to Student B about a trip abroad you are going to take (where are you going?).
> You are worried because:
> • you are scared of flying (what might happen?)
> • you are nervous about communicating in a different language (what problems might this cause?)
> • you are not very good at trying new food (what food might you have to try?).
> Have the conversation. Reassure Student B when he/she tries to talk about a big presentation he/she has to give, but try to bring the conversation back to your trip.

> Anyway, as I was saying, I'm really nervous about what might happen.

Unit Progress Test

CHECK YOUR PROGRESS

You can now do the Unit Progress Test.

123

10D Skills for Writing
I think you should go for it

Learn to write an email with advice
W Advising a course of action

1 SPEAKING AND READING

a 💬 Read the advert on the right for an organisation called *NowVolunteer* and discuss the questions.
1. What kind of organisation do you think *NowVolunteer* is? What kinds of programmes do you think they offer, and where?
2. What kinds of people do you think do a *NowVolunteer* programme, and why?
3. Do you think volunteers have to pay money to work on a programme?

b Read the web page below quickly and check.

NowVolunteer

Join one of our programmes.
See the world, help other people, develop new skills.

NowVolunteer

HOME | PROJECTS | JOIN US

Volunteering. Adventure. Experience.

Do you want to have the adventure of a lifetime and make new friends from around the world? *NowVolunteer* is a volunteering organisation that gives you everything you need for your gap year between university and settling into a job.

Companies want to know about your experience, not just about your qualifications. So join us to improve your CV.

See our Volunteer profiles to see what people say about their experience.

Unique, award-winning programmes

We organise specialist programmes in 50 countries. You can work with children, help local communities, work on environmental projects, learn a new skill … and at the same time have a great travel experience.

We arrange everything for you

Just choose a programme and we'll take care of the details. All you need to do is raise up to $500 for our programmes before you go. We'll provide free accommodation while you're volunteering.

2 LISTENING AND SPEAKING

a You're going to hear Greg talking about his experience of working with *NowVolunteer*. Look at the photos below. What do you think he might say about his trip?

Greg from Auckland, New Zealand worked on a community health project in Madagascar.

b ▶3.49 Listen to Greg. Does he mention any of your ideas from 2a?

c ▶3.49 Listen again and make notes in the table.

1	What he studied	
2	Reason for going	
3	How he raised money	
4	What he did	
5	What happened next	

d 💬 Discuss the questions.
1. Would you like to do the same programme as Greg? Why / Why not?
2. Do you know anyone who has done volunteer work like this? If so, what was their experience of it?
3. Have you ever worked for no money? If so, did you enjoy it?

3 READING

a Vicky is in her last year at university, studying marketing. She emailed her friends asking for advice. Read her email, and answer the questions.
1 What two programmes is Vicky interested in?
2 What might be a problem for her?

Hi everyone!
I've been thinking about what to do next year, and I thought I'd take a year out and do some voluntary work. It could be my only chance and it would look good on my CV!
There's a site called *NowVolunteer* and they've got some amazing things you can do, like looking after elephants in Thailand or teaching English in China. The only problem is you have to raise about $500 for them first, but then they give you training and they pay for your accommodation.
What do you all think? Am I on to a brilliant idea here or should I just forget it and start looking round for jobs?
Replies please ;-)
Vicky

b 💬 Work in pairs. Student A: Go to p.130 and read Amanda's reply. Student B: Go to p.131 and read Laura's reply. Do they think Vicky should do voluntary work? What reasons do they give?

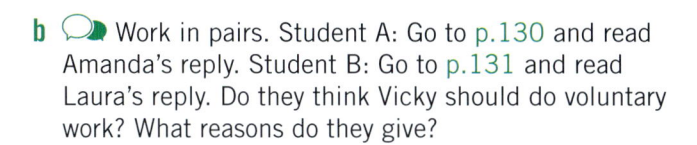

c 💬 Tell your partner about the reply that you read. Who do you agree with?

4 WRITING SKILLS
Advising a course of action

a Who uses these expressions in their replies to Vicky's email? Write A (Amanda) or L (Laura).
1 ☐ I think you should …
2 ☐ I expect you'd have a good time, but …
3 ☐ I'm pretty sure you'd …
4 ☐ I'm just suggesting that …
5 ☐ It would definitely …
6 ☐ If I were you, I'd …
7 ☐ Maybe it would be better to …

b Answer the questions.
1 Which expressions in 4a … ?
 • only give advice
 • also imagine what would (or wouldn't) happen
2 Compare Amanda's and Laura's emails. Who uses more 'careful' language? Why?
 a because she's advising a friend to do something they want to do
 b because she's advising a friend not to do something they want to do
3 Which of these does Laura use?
 a adverbs to express uncertainty (*maybe, perhaps*)
 b modal verbs to express obligation (*should, must*)
 c modal verbs to express uncertainty (*might, could, would*)
 d expressions of certainty (*I'm sure, definitely*)
 e expressions of uncertainty (*I expect, I'm not sure*)

c Rewrite these sentences using the words in brackets and make any other changes necessary.
1 Write to them and ask where they spend the money. (If I)
2 Look for a job with a marketing company in Thailand. (better)
3 It wouldn't be very interesting. (not sure)
4 You'd meet a lot of interesting people. (expect)
5 Look at other alternatives. (suggesting)

5 WRITING An email with advice

a Think of an alternative to your present lifestyle or job – something you'd like to do for a year. Write an email asking other students if they think it's a good idea.

b Work in pairs. Read your partner's email and write a reply. It can be positive and enthusiastic (like Amanda's) or more careful (like Laura's).

c 💬 Read your partner's reply to your email. Do you think it's good advice? Why / Why not? Does the advice use appropriate expressions?

UNIT 10
Review and extension

1 GRAMMAR

Underline the correct words.

1. **A** We lost so badly.
   B I know. We'd *scored / have scored* a lot more points if we *did / 'd done* more training over the last few weeks.
2. **A** Are you going to accept the offer?
   B I can't decide. What *would / did* you do if you *were / had been* me?
3. **A** If I *didn't miss / hadn't missed* the train, I'd never *met / have met* my wife, Jasmine.
   B That's so romantic!
4. **A** Hey! Was that a golf ball? Where did it come from?
   B I don't know, but you were very lucky. It *could have / could* hit you!
5. **A** James gets so disappointed when he doesn't win.
   B If he *wasn't / couldn't be* such a competitive person, he wouldn't play as well as he does.
6. **A** Why didn't you call me?
   B Well, I *would / wouldn't* have done if my phone *had / hadn't* been broken.

2 VOCABULARY

a Complete the sentences with the words in the box.

| beat | lose | net | pass | point | track | workout |

1. It's a fun game and a great _____ too.
2. He'll win the match if he scores one more _____!
3. We mustn't _____ this game! We have to win!
4. You must hit the ball over the _____.
5. You won last time, but this time I'm going to _____ you!
6. How many times did you run round the _____?
7. Helen was running behind me, but she didn't _____ me at any point.

b Complete the questions with the correct form of *make*, *do* or *take*.

1. What hobbies do you _____?
2. Do you know anyone who _____ a lot of risks?
3. How often do you _____ a break when you're studying?
4. Do you _____ the most of your free time? Why / Why not?
5. Should scientists _____ more research into medicine or space travel?
6. Have you ever _____ friends with someone from a different country? Who?
7. Have you ever had to _____ an important decision?

c 💬 Ask and answer the questions in 2b.

3 WORDPOWER Easily confused words

a Match the sentence halves.

| 1 ☐ If you need money, | a I can **lend** you some. |
| 2 ☐ If I need money, | b please can I **borrow** some? |

| 3 ☐ Go on! You mustn't **miss** | a points if you run with the ball. |
| 4 ☐ You'll **lose** | b this opportunity! It'll change your life! |

| 5 ☐ **Take** some water | a when you come to the gym. |
| 6 ☐ **Bring** some energy drinks | b when you go running. |

| 7 ☐ If you want to take part, | a **raise** your hands. |
| 8 ☐ If you have work experience, | b your chances of getting a job will **rise**. |

| 9 ☐ They **robbed** | a the money from a bank. |
| 10 ☐ They **stole** | b a bank. |

| 11 ☐ Where are you working? | a I'm **currently** working at home. |
| 12 ☐ Do you work at a bank? | b **Actually**, I work at a school. |

b Underline the correct words.

1. a borrow = *take / give*
   b lend = *take / give*
2. a miss = *not win / not take*
   b lose = *not win / not take*
3. a take = *move to here / move away from here*
   b bring = *move to here / move away from here*
4. a raise = *lift something / go up*
   b rise = *lift something / go up*
5. a rob = *take from a person or place / take something*
   b steal = *take from a person or place / take something*
6. a currently = *at the moment / in fact*
   b actually = *at the moment / in fact*

c Write down three …
- places that can be robbed.
- things that are difficult to steal.
- things that you would only lend to a good friend.
- things you sometimes borrow.
- things you always take with you when you go out.
- things people often bring back from holiday.

d 💬 Compare your answers for c. Are they the same or different?

REVIEW YOUR PROGRESS

How well did you do in this unit? Write 3, 2 or 1 for each objective.
3 = very well   2 = well   1 = not so well

I CAN …

talk about new things you would like to do. ☐
talk about imagined past events. ☐
talk about possible problems and reassure someone. ☐
write an email with advice. ☐

Communication Plus

6A VOCABULARY

1 How many compound nouns can you find in the picture in two minutes?

▶ Now go back to p.68

9A GRAMMAR Student B

HOW MUCH DO YOU KNOW ABOUT FILMS?

Complete the questions with the correct form of the verbs in brackets. Then test your partner!

1 Which city _____ in the movies more than any other? (destroy)
(New York. It was attacked by ghosts in *Ghostbusters*, aliens in *Independence Day*, a giant gorilla in *King Kong*, and in many other films.)

2 True or False? The first *Lord of the Rings* movie _____ in 1978. (make)
(True: it was an animated feature film. It was not very successful – only Part 1 was ever finished.)

3 In which country _____ most films _____: the US, India or China? (produce)
(India. 'Bollywood' makes nearly 1,000 films every year.)

4 Which fictional character _____ by more actors than any other: Sherlock Holmes or James Bond? (play)
(Sherlock Holmes. More than 75 different actors have taken on the role of this character in the cinema. Many more versions of Sherlock Holmes have been seen on TV.)

5 True or False? In the future, most films _____ on the internet, not in cinemas. (watch)
(No one knows! What do you think?)

▶ Now go back to p.106

9C SPEAKING Student B

You want to arrange an afternoon with Student A.
- You don't really like modern art.
- You are hungry. You've heard about a new café that does good food and great coffee. You can't remember what it is called, but you have the details on your phone.
- There is an exhibition of photography on across town, but you don't know where.

▶ Now go back to p.111

10D READING Student A

Hi Vicky,

No wonder you don't want to go straight into an office job next year. Looking after elephants in Thailand sounds much more exciting! I think you should definitely go for it. You've got nothing much to lose (except a bit of money) and if it didn't work out you could always come back. But anyway, I'm pretty sure you'd enjoy it and have a great time – you always have been good with animals. It would definitely look good on your CV too. It would show that you're an adventurous person and you're interested in different things, not just studying and jobs. Pity I've got a job already or I'd come with you ;-)

Let me know what you decide.

Love

Amanda

▶ Now go back to p.125

10D READING Student B

Hi Vicky,

I'm not sure what I think about your idea of doing a gap year abroad. I can see that it might be exciting to go off to somewhere like Thailand or China for a year, but if I were you, I'd think very carefully about it before you make a decision.

I expect you'd have a good time, but you also need to think about getting a job after you come back. While you're away in Thailand everyone else will be going for jobs. Maybe it would be better to do something more closely connected with marketing. I'm not sure experience with elephants would help much in getting you a marketing job!

Anyway, I don't want to sound negative, but I'm just suggesting that you think about it first and make sure it's what you really want to do.

We could meet up and talk about it if you like.

Love,

Laura

▶ Now go back to p.125

10C SPEAKING Student B

You want to talk to Student A about a big presentation you have to do (where? what is it about?).
You're worried because:
- you don't have much time to prepare (when is it?)
- you don't have any experience of public speaking (what problems might you have?)
- you are worried people might ask difficult questions (what might they ask?).

Have the conversation. Reassure Student A when he/she talks about a trip he/she is going on, but try to bring the conversation back to your presentation.

▶ Now go back to p.123

7C SPEAKING Student B

1. Student A is staying in your home. He/She will ask you for permission to do things. Decide whether or not to give permission.
2. You have started a new job and Student A is your colleague. Ask permission to:
   - play music at your desk while you're working
   - turn the air conditioning up
   - move your desk closer to the window.

▶ Now go back to p.87

6C SPEAKING Student B

1. Your partner will tell you some surprising news. Listen to the news and give some recommendations.
2. You found an old ring in your house. You think it belonged to your great-grandmother, but you aren't sure. You cleaned it and showed it to a friend, who said it was very valuable. You could sell it for about $1,000,000.

▶ Now go back to p.75

Communication Plus

Grammar Focus

6A Modals of obligation

▶ 2.25 *must* and *have to*

We use *must* when we make the rules:
*I **must get** a good night's sleep tonight.*
We use *have to* when we talk about other people's rules:
*You **have to buy** a ticket before you get on the train.*
There is no past or future form of *must*. When we talk about rules in the past or future, we always use the correct form of *have to*:
*When you go to India, you'**ll have to** get a visa.*
*I **had to** wear a uniform at school.*

> 💡 **Tip**
>
> Don't use contractions with *have to*:
> *I have to go.* NOT *I've to go.*

> 💡 **Tip**
>
> - Often there is not much difference in meaning between *must* or *have to*. *Have to* is much more common than *must*, especially in spoken English.
> - *have got to* is also used in spoken English and means the same as *have to*.
> - Questions with *must* are very rare.

▶ 2.26 *mustn't*, *can't* and *don't have to*

We use *mustn't* or *can't* to say that something is not allowed. We often use *mustn't* when we make the rules and *can't* to talk about other people's rules:
*I **mustn't** forget to email my mum.*
*We **can't** cross the road yet – the light's still red.*
For things which were not allowed in the past, use *couldn't*:
*I **couldn't** work in India because I only had a tourist visa.*

We use *don't have to* when there is no obligation. It means it's not necessary to do something:
*University students **don't have to wear** a uniform.*
*I **didn't have to** call a taxi. Robert drove me home.*

▶ 2.27 *should* and *ought to*

We use *should* or *ought to* to give advice and recommendations. They have the same meaning, but *should* is much more common:
*We **should see** as much as possible. We **shouldn't waste** time.*
*We **ought to see** as much as possible. We **ought not to waste** time.*

6B Comparatives and superlatives

	Adjectives	Adverbs
One syllable	rich → rich**er**, the rich**est**	fast → fast**er**, the fast**est**
Two or more syllables	**Ending in -y:** easy → eas**ier**, the eas**iest** friendly → friend**lier**, the friend**liest** **Other:** careful → **more** careful, **the most** careful	**All:** often → **more** often, **the most** often carefully → **more** carefully, **the most** carefully
Exceptions	good → better, the best bad → worse, the worst far → further, the furthest more / the most bored / tired / ill clever → clever**er** / the clever**est***	well → better, the best badly → worse, the worst far → further, the furthest early → earl**ier**, the earl**iest**

*Some two-syllable adjectives can follow the rules for one-syllable adjectives: clever, narrow, shallow, quiet, simple.

▶ 2.32 Comparison

We can use comparative adjectives and adverbs to compare two things, situations, times, actions, etc. usually with *than*. We can change the degree of comparison with words like *a lot, much, far, even, slightly, a bit, a little*:
*Life's **a lot more interesting than** before.*
*She's **a bit happier than** she used to be.*
*He's speaking **much more slowly than** usual today.*

The opposite of *more* is *less*. We can use it with all adjectives and adverbs:
*The car's **slightly less clean than** it was.*
*I drive **less quickly than** he does.*

as + adjective/adverb + *as* shows that two things are equal; *not as … as* means *less than*:
*They're **as wealthy as** the royal family.*
*She does**n't** listen **as carefully as** she should.*
Some common adverbs can change the degree of the comparison:
*You're **just as pretty as** your sister!* (= exactly equal)
*My brother is**n't nearly as hard-working as** me.* (= very different)
*She does**n't** sleep **quite as well as** I do.* (= slightly different)

Extremes

We use superlative adjectives and adverbs to talk about extremes:
*It's **the worst** hotel in the world!*
*I got **the lowest** score possible.*
We often use the present perfect with *ever* with superlatives:
*This is **the best** meal I'**ve ever eaten**.*
*It was **the least interesting** film I'**ve ever seen**.*
We can use the expression *by far* to say an extreme is very different from all others:
*That's **by far the highest** mountain I've ever climbed.*

142

Grammar Focus

6A Modals of obligation

a Complete the sentences with the correct form of *must* or *have to*.

1. In my country, you ___have to___ cross the road at a pedestrian crossing – it's illegal to cross anywhere else.
2. When I lived in Moscow, I _____ leave home two hours before work, because the rush hour traffic was so bad.
3. _____ Alex _____ wear a tie to work?
4. I'll tell you a secret, but you _____ tell anyone. I don't want anyone else to know.
5. We took plenty of money, but in the end, we _____ pay – everything was free.
6. The sign says all visitors _____ report to reception
7. If you want to be there on time, you'll _____ leave here very soon.
8. Your brother can borrow my books tonight but he _____ forget to bring them back tomorrow. I need them for my class.

b Look at the signs. Then complete the advice using the verbs in brackets and a modal verb. Sometimes more than one form is possible.

You ¹ ___mustn't / can't park___ (park) here.
You ² _____ (pay) for the bus to the shopping centre. 
You ³ _____ (leave) your car unlocked. It might get stolen. 
You ⁴ _____ (use) that door – it's for emergencies only. 
You ⁵ _____ (only use) the official taxis. 

c ▶ Now go back to p.70

6B Comparatives and superlatives

a Complete the sentences with the comparative or superlative form of the words in brackets. Add *than* or *the* where necessary.

1. Indian food is ___spicier than___ French food. (spicy)
2. This is _____ meal I've ever eaten. (delicious)
3. The weather was _____ I expected. (hot)
4. She's a _____ driver _____ me. (slow)
5. Are you _____ person in your class? (clever)
6. I didn't have a good holiday. The _____ thing was the hotel. It was terrible. (bad)
7. Your English is _____ mine. (good)
8. I'm sorry, I can't come on Friday. That's my _____ day. (busy)

b Complete the sentences so that they mean the same as the sentences in **a**. Use two to five words.

1. French food isn't ___as spicy as Indian food___.
2. I've never eaten a _____ meal than this.
3. I didn't expect the weather to be _____ it was.
4. She drives _____ I do.
5. Is anybody in your class _____ you?
6. I didn't have a good holiday. The hotel was _____ everything else.
7. You speak English _____ I do.
8. I'm sorry, I can't come on Friday. It's _____ the other days.

c Complete the sentences with one word from the box in each space. Use each word once only.

| ~~a~~ | as | bit | by | ever | expected | in | just | ~~more~~ |
| most | nearly | one | slightly | than | the | | | |

1. Today's lesson was ___a___ lot ___more___ interesting than usual – it was excellent.
2. That's _____ worst joke I've _____ heard!
3. The exam went really well. It wasn't _____ as difficult as I _____.
4. I think she's _____ of the _____ innovative designers in the world.
5. Our holiday was a _____ more expensive _____ we thought, but it was still good value.
6. They started _____ later than usual, but they still finished on time.
7. _____ far the oldest person _____ my family is my great-grandmother.
8. Our new TV is fantastic – the picture quality is _____ as good _____ in the cinema, or maybe even better.

d ▶ Now go back to p.72

143

7A Modals of deduction

We can use modal verbs to show that we are making a deduction using evidence, not stating a fact:

▶ 2.39

We **must be** early. Nobody else has arrived yet.
They work at the same office so they **may know** each other.
She **might not be** in. The lights are all out.
That **can't be** Mark's car. He told me his was in the garage.

Different modal verbs tell us how sure about a deduction we are:

It's cold in that house.	Fact: *I **know** it is.*
It **must** be cold in that house.	Deduction: *I'm **sure** it is.*
It **may / might / could** be cold in that house.	Deduction: *It's **possible** that it is.*
It **may / might not** be cold in that house.	Deduction: *It's **possible** that it isn't.*
It **can't** be cold in that house.	Deduction: *I'm **sure** it isn't.*
It isn't cold in that house.	Fact: *I know it isn't.*

- The opposite of *must* for deductions is *can't*. Don't use *mustn't*, *can* or *couldn't* for deductions:
  *This bill **can't** be right. I only ordered a salad.*
  NOT *This bill couldn't / mustn't be right.*
  *There **must** be a mistake.*
  NOT *There can be a mistake.*
- There is no difference between *may*, *might* and *could*. All three mean that something is possible.
- To make deductions about actions happening now, use a modal + *be* + verb + *-ing*:
  *She isn't answering the phone. She **might be listening** to music.*

7B Quantifiers

▶ 2.46 *some*, *any* and *no*

We usually use *some* in positive statements and *any* in negatives and questions:
*There are **some** nice views from the hotel.*
*He does**n't** have **any** good music.*

We can also use *no* in positive sentences to talk about zero quantity:
*There's **no** crime around here.*

To talk about zero quantity, we can use *none of* + plural or *none*:
***None of** my friends could help.*
A How many holidays have you been on this year?
B ***None** at all.*

▶ 2.47 Large quantities

We use *lots of* / *a lot of* in positive sentences, *not many* / *not much* / *not a lot of* in negative sentences and *many* / *much* / *a lot of* in questions:
*There are quite **a lot of** cars on the roads today.*
*I have**n't** got **much** money with me.*
*Did **many** people come to the concert?*
*We do**n't** need **a lot of** time to finish this work.*

In positive sentences, we can use *plenty of* to show we are happy with the amount:
*Don't worry – we've got **plenty of** food.*

▶ 2.48 Small quantities

We use *a few* / *a little* to talk about an amount. We use *few* / *little* to talk about a negative amount (i.e. there is not a lot):
*We have **a little** time before the show starts.*
*There are **a few** things I need from the shops.*
*I have **very little** time to finish this work.*
*This dish has **very few** ingredients.*

We can say *quite a few* / *very few* / *very little* to increase / decrease the amount.

▶ 2.49 *too / not enough*

We use *too much* / *too many* + noun to say there is more than the right amount. We use *not enough* to say that there is less than the right amount:

*I have **too much** furniture. There is**n't enough room** for all of it!*
*I couldn't move at the concert because there were **too many people**.*

We also use *too* + adjective / adverb and *not* + adjective / adverb *enough*:
*This suitcase is **too heavy**. They won't let you on the plane.*
*You're walking **too quickly**, I can't keep up!*
*The meeting room is**n't big enough** for all of us. There aren't enough chairs.*
*You're **not** walking **fast enough**. Hurry up!*

Grammar Focus

7A Modals of deduction

a Match the deductions 1–8 with the best sentences a–h.

1. [f] That man must be a doctor.
2. [ ] That man might be a doctor.
3. [ ] That man might not be a doctor.
4. [ ] That man can't be a doctor.
5. [ ] They must be eating dinner now.
6. [ ] They could well be eating dinner now.
7. [ ] They may not be eating dinner now.
8. [ ] They can't be eating dinner now.

a He doesn't know anything about medicine.
b They finished their dinner an hour ago.
c He's wearing a white coat.
d I remember they booked a table at a restaurant for around now.
e Perhaps they've finished.
f Look – he's listening to that man's heart.
g They usually eat around this time.
h It's possible that he's a nurse.

b Complete the sentences using an appropriate modal of deduction. Sometimes more than one modal is possible.

1. It's impossible that she's in the office – she flew to Beijing yesterday.
   She _can't be in the office – she flew to Beijing yesterday._
2. I'm sure you're right.
   You _____
3. It's possible that they want to sell their flat.
   They _____
4. I'm sure he isn't speaking Russian – it sounds more like Spanish to me.
   He _____ – it sounds more like Spanish to me.
5. It's possible that you're the perfect person for the job.
   You _____
6. There's a possibility that he doesn't know the answer.
   He _____
7. I'm sure you don't need that coat today – it's 30 degrees!
   It's 30 degrees! You _____
8. They're probably building a new shopping centre.
   They _____

c ▶ Now go back to p.80

7B Quantifiers

a Underline the correct quantifier in each sentence.

1. We had *any* / *no* / *none* problems.
2. My parents read *a lot* / *a lot of* / *much* books.
3. I'm not tall *enough* / *too* / *plenty* to be a police officer.
4. There's too *little* / *many* / *much* noise in my block of flats. I can't sleep.
5. You don't go out *little* / *many* / *enough*. You should go out more.
6. I watch *much* / *many* / *a lot of* television.
7. **A** Did you get much work done?
   B Yes, *a lot of* / *a lot* / *none*.
8. **A** Have you got any potatoes left?
   B No, I've got *some* / *any* / *none*.
9. I've been to quite *many* / *few* / *a few* countries.
10. It's *too much* / *too* / *enough* hot in here. Can I open a window?

b Complete the second sentence so that it means the same as the first sentence.

1. **a** I want no visitors for the next 30 minutes.
   b I don't _want any visitors for the next 30 minutes._
2. **a** There aren't enough chairs for everyone.
   b There are too _____
3. **a** I wanted a biscuit, but there weren't any left.
   b I wanted a biscuit, but there were _____
4. **a** Make sure you take plenty of money.
   b Make sure you take a _____
5. **a** They gave us too little information.
   b They didn't _____
6. **a** I didn't see many people.
   b I saw very _____
7. **a** We didn't have any money.
   b We had _____
8. **a** She's got plenty of time tomorrow.
   b She's got a _____

c ▶ Now go back to p.85

145

8A Reported speech

Reported speech and direct speech
When we talk about what somebody said or thought, we can use direct speech or reported speech:
- *Direct speech:* He said, 'I don't want to talk to you.'
- *Reported speech:* He said he didn't want to talk to me.

▶ 3.3
Direct speech		Reported speech
'I **don't want** to talk to you.'	→	He said he **didn't want** to talk to me.
'I'm **planning** to resign.'	→	She said she **was planning** to resign.
'I've already **told** you.'	→	He said **he had** already **told** me.
'I **saw** you break it.'	→	I told him I **had seen** him break it.
'I'm **going to cook** tonight.'	→	You said you **were going to cook** tonight.
'I'**ll** see you soon.'	→	He said he **would** see me soon.
'I **can't** hear you.'	→	She said she **couldn't** hear me.
'You **may** be right.'	→	He said I **might** be right.

Some modal verbs (*would, could, should, might*) stay the same in reported speech:
I'**d** like to go. → He said he'**d** like to go.
It **might** be difficult → She said it **might** be difficult.

▶ 3.4 **Reported questions**
When you report a *Wh-* question, put the subject before the verb. Don't use the auxiliary *do / does / did*:
'Where **are you** from?' → She asked me where **I was** from.
'Why **did she say** that?' → He asked me why **you had said** that.
For *Yes/No* questions, use *if/whether*. *Whether* is more formal than *if*:
'Are you going to help?' → We asked them **if** they were going to help.
'Did you visit the London Eye?' → She asked us **whether** we had visited the London Eye.

Other changes
When we report speech, we usually need to change the pronouns (e.g. *I, he*) and possessives (e.g. *my*), depending on who is talking to whom. Time and place words may also need to change:
'I want **you** to give **this** message to **your** boss **tonight**.'
→ She said **she** wanted **me** to give **a / the** message to **my** boss **that night**.

💡 **Tip**
You don't need to change the tense when you want to show that the speaker's words are still true now:
I **told** you yesterday that I **don't** want to talk to you.
(= I still don't want to talk to you today.)

say and *tell* have different patterns. Always use a person or pronoun after *tell*:
Tom **said** he had a new car. NOT ~~Tom said me he had a new car.~~
Tom **told me** he had a new car. NOT ~~Tom told he had a new car.~~

8B Verb patterns

▶ 3.8 **verb + -ing or to + infinitive**
- Some verbs (e.g. *enjoy, mind, keep, admit, recommend, suggest*) are followed by a verb + *-ing*:
  She **didn't mind working** late.
  The negative form is *not* + verb + *-ing*:
  I **enjoyed not cooking** for a change.
- Other verbs (e.g. *want, hope, agree, offer, promise, need, refuse, threaten, plan*) are followed by *to* + infinitive:
  They **threatened to tell** the police.
  The negative form is *not* + *to* + infinitive:
  I **promise not to break** anything.
- Some verbs (e.g. *start, begin, continue*) can be followed by both patterns, with no change of meaning:
  People **started arriving** an hour ago.
  He **started to feel** angry.
- Some verbs (e.g. *try, forget, remember*) can be followed by both patterns, but the meaning changes:
  I **tried reading** some reviews online, but they didn't help much. (= I read them as an experiment)
  I **tried to read** some reviews online, but my internet connection wasn't working. (= I attempted to read them)
  I **remember going** there for the first time. (= I'm looking back at an earlier experience.)
  Please **remember to book** a table. (= keep the plan in your memory)

- Some verbs (e.g. *advise, ask, invite, remind, tell, warn*) need an object before *to* + infinitive:
  They **warned** me not **to** tell anyone.
  I've **invited** your parents **to** visit us.
  make (= 'force') and *let* (= 'allow') are followed by an object and a bare infinitive:
  My boss **made me work** late.
  He **let me drive** his car.

Other uses of verb + -ing
- When a verb comes after a preposition (e.g. *about, of, by*), the verb is always in the *-ing* form:
  I'm worried **about** not be**ing** good enough.
  They escaped **by** break**ing** a window.
- When a verb is the subject of a sentence, it is usually in the *-ing* form:
  Eating in a restaurant is more expensive than at home.

Other uses of to + infinitive
- Infinitive of purpose:
  I went online **to read** the news.
- adjective + *to* + infinitive:
  I was relieved **to see** I wasn't late.
- verb + question word + *to* + infinitive:
  I don't know where **to go** or who **to ask**.

Grammar Focus

8A Reported speech

a Complete the reported speech with the correct verb form. Change the tense where possible.

1 It's going to be a lovely day. — He said it _was going to be_ a lovely day.
2 I don't want to go out this evening. — She told me she _____ that evening.
3 We're waiting for you. — They said they _____ for us.
4 My sister can't drive. — She said her sister _____.
5 I've lost my car keys. — She told me she _____ her car keys.
6 Lucy might have a new job. — He said Lucy _____ a new job.
7 I'll help you with those bags. — He said he _____ with my bags.
8 Mark bought a new car. — You told me that Mark _____ a new car.

b Read Harry's conversation with Andy. Then choose the best word or phrase to complete Andy's conversation with Harry's sister, Lucy.

> **HARRY** Hi. I'm trying to buy a present for my sister, Lucy. It's her birthday tomorrow.
> **ANDY** What sort of books does she like?
> **HARRY** I'm not sure. She reads a lot of history books.
> **ANDY** This is really good, *A Short History of the World*. I read it a few months ago.
> **HARRY** No, I think she's already read that. She didn't like it. No, I'm going to get her this one, *A History of Amazing Buildings*.

Two days later, Andy sees Lucy in the street …

> **ANDY** Hi Lucy. I met your brother a few days ago – he said it was ¹*my / your / her* birthday ²*tomorrow / the previous day / yesterday*.
> **LUCY** Yes, that's right. Where did you meet him?
> **ANDY** In the bookshop. When I asked him what he was doing ³*here / there / near*, he said ⁴*he was / he's / I'm* looking for a present for ⁵*me / you / her*.
> **LUCY** Really?
> **ANDY** Yes. I asked him what books ⁶*you liked / do you like / does she like*, and he said he wasn't sure. He said ⁷*she reads / you read / I read* history books. So I showed him *A Short History of the World* – I said it was really good. I told him ⁸*you've / I've / I'd* read it a few months ⁹*earlier / ago / later*. But he said ¹⁰*you'd / she's / I'd* already read it, and you hadn't liked it.
> **LUCY** What? I thought it was brilliant!
> **ANDY** Yeah. Anyway, he said ¹¹*I'm / he's / he was* going to get *A History of Amazing Buildings*.
> **LUCY** Yes – and he did. It's really cool.
> **ANDY** Great – I knew ¹²*you'd love it / she'll love that / you'll love that*.

c ▶ Now go back to p.94

8B Verb patterns

a Underline the correct option.

1 I agreed *going / to go* to the hospital.
2 He admitted *to take / taking* the money.
3 Remember *to collect / collecting* the dry cleaning on your way home.
4 We tried *making / to make* some cakes but the oven wasn't working.
5 I made the dog *sit / sitting* down.
6 Maria refused *watching / to watch* the scary film.
7 It's important *making / to make* a reservation in advance.
8 They don't mind *walking / to walk* home tonight.
9 We advised *to have / them to have* a short holiday.
10 My mum always let me *stay / to stay* up late.

b Complete the conversation.

A I want ¹ _to get_ (get) my laptop fixed. I don't know where ² _____ (go).
B Have you tried ³ _____ (look) online? It's easy ⁴ _____ (find) repair shops, and you can read reviews ⁵ _____ (see) if they're good.
A Er … no. ⁶ _____ (check) the internet is going to be pretty difficult because my computer's broken.
B Oh yes, sorry, I keep ⁷ _____ (forget). Listen, I think I know who ⁸ _____ (ask). My neighbour's a computer engineer. I'll phone him now ⁹ _____ (ask) him what ¹⁰ _____ (do).

Five minutes later …

B OK, so he says he doesn't mind ¹¹ _____ (help) but he's a bit busy. He suggests ¹² _____ (switch) it off and back on again ¹³ _____ (see) what happens. He says that usually works.
A Yes, I remember ¹⁴ _____ (do) that last time I had a problem, and it did work. But now my computer just refuses ¹⁵ _____ (start) up.
B Hmmm. I think I know how ¹⁶ _____ (fix) it, but I need ¹⁷ _____ (take) the back off. I promise not ¹⁸ _____ (break) it …

c ▶ Now go back to p.96

9A The passive

We form the passive using *be* + past participle.

Active	▶ 3.23 Passive
They **make** a lot of films in Hollywood.	A lot of films **are made** in Hollywood.
The scriptwriters **are writing** a new script this week.	A new script **is being written** this week.
The estate agent **sold** the house for £1 million.	The house **has been sold** for £1 million.
There was an accident while they **were building** the bridge.	There was an accident while the bridge **was being built**.
A film studio **will make** a film from the book.	A film **will be made** from the book.
Somebody **stole** our car in the night.	Our car **was stolen** in the night.
An expert **should do** the work.	The work **should be done** by an expert.

We use passive verb forms:
- when the main thing we are talking about is the object of the verb.
  *A film **will be made** from the book.*
  *The work **should be done** by an expert.* (We are talking about the work, not the expert.)
- when the agent (the doer) isn't important.
  *The house **has been sold** for £1 million.* (We don't care about the estate agent.)
- when the agent (the doer) is very obvious.
  *A new script **is being written** this week.* (by scriptwriters)
- when we don't know who did something / what caused something.
  *Our car **was stolen** in the night.*

Negatives and questions are made in the same way as other uses of *be*:
*Films **aren't** made here. **Is** a film **being** made here?*

We use *by* to introduce the person or thing that did the action (the agent):
*This frame was drawn **by** one of the animators.*
We usually use *with* to introduce a tool, instrument or technique that was used by the agent:
*The pirate's beard was controlled **with** a wire.*

> 💡 **Tip**
> We can say something was made by hand or by machine:
> *This jumper was made **by hand** in Scotland.*

9B Defining and non-defining relative clauses

▶ 3.27 **Defining and non-defining relative clauses**
Defining relative clauses define a noun or make it more specific. They tell us which particular thing or what kind of thing. In defining relative clauses, we can also use *that* instead of *who* or *which*:
*I love **music that makes people dance**.*
*I hate **books which don't have happy endings**.*
*My dad met **the woman who reads the news on TV** yesterday!*
*They're **the couple that I told you about**.*

Non-defining relative clauses give extra information about a noun, but they are not necessary for the sentence to make sense:
The DJ was playing hip hop. (This sentence is complete.)
*The DJ was playing hip hop, **which is my favourite kind of music**.* (This relative clause adds more information.)

In writing, we need a comma before and after a non-defining relative clause. Don't use commas in defining relative clauses:
*We visited the market on a **Sunday, when they sell clothes and jewellery**.*
*I met **Lucy, who was staying with relatives nearby**, for a coffee.*

In both types of relative clause, we can use *who, which, whose, where* and *when*:
*Have you been to **that restaurant where you cook your own food at the table**?*
*Did you meet **the girl whose father climbed Mt. Everest**?*

Omitting relative pronouns
We can often leave out *who/which/that* or *when* from defining relative clauses:
*He likes the cheese (**which/that**) I bought.*
(I bought the cheese. *cheese* = object.)

Don't leave out the relative pronoun if it's the subject of the relative clause (*who, which* or *that*):
*He likes the cheese **that** comes from Turkey.* (The cheese comes from Turkey. *cheese* = subject.)
Never leave out the relative pronoun from a non-defining relative clause:
This cheese, which Greg really likes, comes from Turkey.
NOT ~~This cheese, Greg really likes, ...~~

Grammar Focus

9A The passive

a Complete the passive sentences. Don't include any agents that are inside brackets.

1 James Cameron directed *Avatar*.   *Avatar* ___ was directed by James Cameron.
2 (People) still make these shoes by hand.   These shoes ___ are still made by hand.
3 (They) will build a new bridge next year.   A new ___
4 My grandfather gave me this watch.   I ___
5 (We)'ve told everybody to be here on time.   Everybody ___
6 (People) will laugh at you if you wear that hat.   You ___
7 A computer program creates the special effects.   The special effects ___
8 My parents are looking after our dog this week.   Our dog ___
9 (They) offered me £1,000 for my painting.   I ___
10 (Somebody) was repairing my car at the time.   My car ___

b Rewrite the sentences as either *Yes/No* questions (?) or negatives (–).

1 We were picked up at the airport.   (–) We weren't picked up at the airport.
2 The painting's already been sold.   (?) Has the painting already been sold?
3 The work will be finished by Saturday.   (–) ___
4 The film's being made in Brazil.   (?) ___
5 Tomatoes are grown in Spain.   (?) ___
6 The car was being driven too fast.   (–) ___
7 The costumes were made by hand.   (?) ___
8 The sculpture has been taken to the piazza.   (–) ___

c ▶ Now turn to p.106

9B Defining and non-defining relative clauses

a Complete the sentences with a word from the box.

which (x3)   who   where   when   whose (x2)

1 I love people ___ can make me laugh.
2 I told Paula my secret, ___ she then told everyone!
3 The film ___ I saw was really good.
4 I usually listen to music ___ I feel sad.
5 This album, ___ came out in 1967, has some great songs.
6 Mark is the person ___ father used to be a singer.
7 The shop ___ I bought this T-shirt has closed now.
8 I met Sara, ___ husband I work with, yesterday.

b Rewrite the sentences adding the information in brackets as a non-defining relative clause. Use relative pronouns which refer to the underlined words.

1 Radiohead performed 'Creep'. (They wrote it in 1992.)
   Radiohead performed 'Creep', which they wrote in 1992.
2 Plácido Domingo studied music in Mexico. (He is a well-known opera singer and conductor.)
   ___
3 We're going to Cuba. (Mambo music comes from there.)
   ___
4 Glastonbury Festival also has theatre, comedy and circus performances. (It's most famous as a music festival.)
   ___
5 My favourite singer is Adele. (Her album '21' is one of the most successful albums of all time.)
   ___
6 The best day of the festival is the last day. (There's a big firework display then.)
   ___

c Rewrite the sentences adding the information in brackets as a defining relative clause. Leave out *who*, *which* or *that* if possible.

1 I like the tune. (You were singing it.)
   I like the tune you were singing.
2 That's the DJ. (He was here two weeks ago.)
   ___
3 We need music. (It makes you want to dance.)
   ___
4 That's the stage. (We're going to perform there.)
   ___
5 I've got a CD. (You'll like it.)
   ___
6 What did you think of the music? (I chose it.)
   ___
7 What's the name of your friend? (You borrowed his CD.)
   ___
8 The song changed my life. (It's playing on the radio.)
   ___

d Are the sentences below correct or incorrect? Put a tick (✓) or a cross (✗). Sometimes both sentences in each pair are correct.

1 a I like music which makes me dance. ✓
   b I like music makes me dance. ✗
2 a It's a drum which you play with your hands.
   b It's a drum you play with your hands.
3 a My father, that is a dentist, looks after my teeth.
   b My father, who is a dentist, looks after my teeth.
4 a This album, I bought last week, is really good.
   b This album, which I bought last week, is really good.

e ▶ Now turn to p.108

149

10A Second conditional

We use the second conditional to talk about imagined events or states and their consequences. They can be about the unreal present or the unlikely future.

Real present		▶ 3.38 Unreal present and consequence
I don't know the answer.	→	If I **knew** the answer, I**'d tell** you.
Likely future		**Unlikely / imagined future and consequence**
She won't find out that you lied.	→	She **would be** angry if she **found** out you had lied.

We usually use the past simple in the *if*-clause and *would* in the main clause. We can also use *could* or *might* instead of *would*:
You **could afford** to go on holiday if you **were** more careful with your money.
If you **tried** harder, you **might win** a medal.

The verb *be* has a special form in the second conditional. We can use *were* for all persons (*if I were, if you were, if she were,* etc.):
If **I were** taller, I'd be better at basketball.

We use the phrase *If I were you* to give advice:
If I were you, I wouldn't eat that fish. It doesn't smell fresh.

We don't always need to include the *if*-clause if the meaning is clear:
Look at that house! That **would** be a great place to live. (… if I moved there)
I'm sure Jack **would** help you. (… if you asked)

> 💡 **Tip**
> The contracted form of *would* (*'d*), is the same as the contracted form of *had*. You can tell the difference by looking at the verb that comes next.
> - *'d* + past participle: He**'d won** (= had won) *the match.*
> - *'d* + infinitive: He**'d win** (= would win) *the match.*

> 💡 **Tip**
> When talking about the future, you can usually choose between the first and second conditional. Use the first conditional if you think a future event is likely, use the second conditional if you think it is unlikely.
> - If we **score** one more point, we**'ll** win.
>   (I think there's a good chance of this.)
> - If we **scored** four more points, we**'d** win (but we probably won't.)

10B Third conditional

▶ 3.42

We use the third conditional to talk about imagined past events or states and their consequences:
If you**'d told** me about your birthday, I **would have** bought you a present.

We use the past perfect in the *if*-clause and *would have* + past participle in the main clause.

We can also use *could have* or *might have* instead of *would have*:
We **could have saved** some money **if** we**'d known** about the offer.
If I **had done** more work, I **might have passed** the exam.

Common uses of third conditionals
1. Regrets about things that happened or didn't happen in the past:
   If I**'d sold** my house two years ago, I**'d have made** a fortune.
2. Relief about avoiding a past problem:
   I **might have missed** the flight if you **hadn't woken** me up.
3. Surprise about how things were different from expected:
   If you**'d told** me five years ago I'd have my own company one day, I **wouldn't have believed** you.

> 💡 **Tip**
> Be especially careful with the contraction *'d*. In the *if*-clause, it's a contraction of *had*. In the main clause, it's a contraction of *would*.

If you'd told me about your birthday, I'd have bought you a present.

Grammar Focus

10A Second conditional

a Match the sentence beginnings 1–8 with the most logical endings a–h.

1. If I had more money, — c
2. I'd be grateful
3. If I were you,
4. If you asked her again nicely,
5. I wouldn't be so relaxed
6. If he weren't so rude,
7. I could get a better job
8. Angela would be really sad

a. she might change her mind.
b. more people would like him.
c. I could eat in restaurants more often.
d. if I spoke better English.
e. if we didn't invite her.
f. I'd complain to your boss.
g. if you didn't tell anybody my secret.
h. if I had an exam tomorrow!

b Underline the correct options.

1. *I'd go* / *I went* swimming more if *I'd have* / *I had* time.
2. If *I'd know* / *I knew* his number, *I'd call* / *I called* him.
3. *Would* / *Did* you mind if *I'd ask* / *I asked* you a question?
4. If you *wouldn't* / *didn't* have a car, how *would* / *did* you get around?
5. *You'd be* / *You were* a lot healthier if you *wouldn't* / *didn't* eat so much.
6. If *I'd be* / *I were* you, *I'd get* / *I got* some new shoes.
7. What *would* / *did* you do if *you'd see* / *you saw* a fire?
8. If someone *would treat* / *treated* you like that, how *would* / *did* you feel?

c Decide if the first or second conditional is more suitable for each situation. Then complete the sentences with the correct form of the verbs in brackets.

1. I think I'll probably leave my job soon. But if I ___leave___ (leave) my job, it ___'ll be___ (be) difficult to get a new one.
2. I think it's going to be a nice day. We _____ (can) have a picnic if the weather _____ (stay) nice.
3. I'm not very good at football. If I _____ (can) play better, I _____ (join) a football club.
4. If I _____ (win) the lottery, I _____ (buy) a new house. But I know it's never going to happen.
5. I think we're the best team. If we _____ (win) the competition, I _____ (not be) surprised.
6. You drink too much coffee. If you _____ (not drink) so much coffee, you _____ (not be) so stressed.
7. She goes shopping all the time! She _____ (not have) any money left if she _____ (not stop) spending it!
8. I don't like my house in the city. If I _____ (live) in the countryside, I _____ (be) much happier.

d ▶ Now go back to p.117

10B Third conditional

a What does *'d* mean in each sentence? Write *had* or *would*.

1. If you'd (_had_) told me earlier, we'd (_would_) have saved a lot of time.
2. I don't know what I'd (_____) have done if you hadn't helped me.
3. We might have got seriously hurt if you'd (_____) crashed.
4. She'd (_____) have got the job if she'd (_____) applied for it.
5. I'd (_____) have loved to go to the party, but I wasn't invited.

b Write third conditional sentences about the situations.

1. Real past: I didn't win the competition because I made a stupid mistake.
   Unreal past: If _I hadn't made a stupid mistake, I would have won the competition._
2. Real past: He went to live in Japan. While he was there, he met his wife.
   Unreal past: If he _____
3. Real past: The car was broken so we couldn't go to the concert.
   Unreal past: We _____
4. Real past: I didn't go to see the film because I didn't know it was so good.
   Unreal past: I _____
5. Real past: You didn't take my advice so you got lost.
   Unreal past: If _____
6. Real past: You helped me so much. That's why I was so successful.
   Unreal past: I'd never _____

c Correct the mistakes.

1. If you'd been there too, you (would enjoy) yourself.
   would have enjoyed
2. We couldn't have bought the house if they wouldn't have lent us the money.
   _____
3. If they hadn't noticed the fire, the whole house could burned down.
   _____
4. If I know it was dangerous, I'd never have gone there.
   _____
5. What you would have done if I hadn't helped you?
   _____
6. He could have been an opera singer if he'd have some training.
   _____
7. If they'd arrive a few minutes later, they might have missed you.
   _____

d ▶ Now go back to p.121

151

Vocabulary Focus

6A Multi-word verbs

a Look at the multi-word verbs in **bold**. Match them with definitions a–h.
1. ☐ When I **eat out**, I generally prefer *Chinese / Italian / _____* food.
2. ☐ I try to **pick up** new English vocabulary by *watching TV / reading online newspapers / _____*.
3. ☐ I'd be a good person to **show someone around** *my local neighbourhood / my nearest big city / _____*. I know all the best places to go.
4. ☐ The quickest way to **get around** my home town is *on foot / by bus / _____*.
5. ☐ I was the *first / last / _____* person to **turn up** to class today.
6. ☐ When I get the chance, I really enjoy **looking around** *art galleries / science museums / _____*.
7. ☐ I loved my visit to *the beach / my country's capital city / _____* and I'd like to **go back** soon.
8. ☐ Next time I **go away** with my family, I'd like to go to *Spain / the USA / _____*.

a explore
b arrive (informal)
c give someone a tour
d travel or move from place to place
e have food in a café or restaurant
f learn (a language or skill) by practising, not by having lessons
g leave your home to spend time somewhere else
h return

b Complete the sentences in **a** so they are true for you. Use one of the options given or write your own answer.

c 💬 Talk about your sentences.

d ▶ Now turn to p.70

6B Describing food

a ▶2.28 Label the pictures using the pairs of adjectives in the box. Then listen and check.

creamy /ˈkriːmiː/ / crunchy /ˈkrʌntʃiː/   fresh /freʃ/ / dried /draɪd/
cooked /kʊkt/ / raw /rɔː/   heavy /ˈhevi/ / light /laɪt/   sweet /swiːt/ / sour /ˈsaʊə/

1a _____
1b _____
2a _____
2b _____
3a _____
3b _____
4a _____
4b _____
5a _____
5b _____

156

Vocabulary Focus

b Complete the two recipes with the words in the box.

add /æd/   chop /tʃɒp/ (x2)   fry /fraɪ/   heat up /hiːt ʌp/
mash /mæʃ/   mix /mɪks/   serve /sɜːv/   squeeze /skwiːz/   stir /stɜː/

Guacamole

1 _____ four chilies, two tomatoes, one onion and a bunch of coriander.

2 _____ three avocados in a bowl.

3 _____ all the ingredients together.

4 _____ the juice of half a lime into the mixture.

5 _____ with tortilla chips.

Meatballs in tomato sauce

1 _____ one onion and two cloves of garlic.

2 _____ 500g minced lamb to the onions, with salt, pepper and spices. Make the mixture into balls.

3 _____ one tablespoon of olive oil in a pan.

4 _____ the meatballs in the oil.

5 Add two tins of tomatoes and 200ml of water. Cook for 30 minutes. _____ occasionally.

c Prepare a simple recipe for a dish you like. Make notes about the ingredients you need and how you make it.

d 💬 Take turns to talk about your recipes. Would you like to eat each other's dishes?

e ▶ Now go back to p.71

157

7A Describing houses and buildings

a ▶2.42 Use the words in the box to label the pictures. Then listen and check.

attic /ˈætɪk/   balcony /ˈbælkəniː/   basement /ˈbeɪsmənt/   block /blɒk/ of flats   doorbell /ˈdɔːbel/   first floor /flɔː/
flat /flæt/   front /frʌnt/ door   ground /ɡraʊnd/ floor   landing /ˈlændɪŋ/   lock /lɒk/   steps /steps/   terrace /ˈterəs/

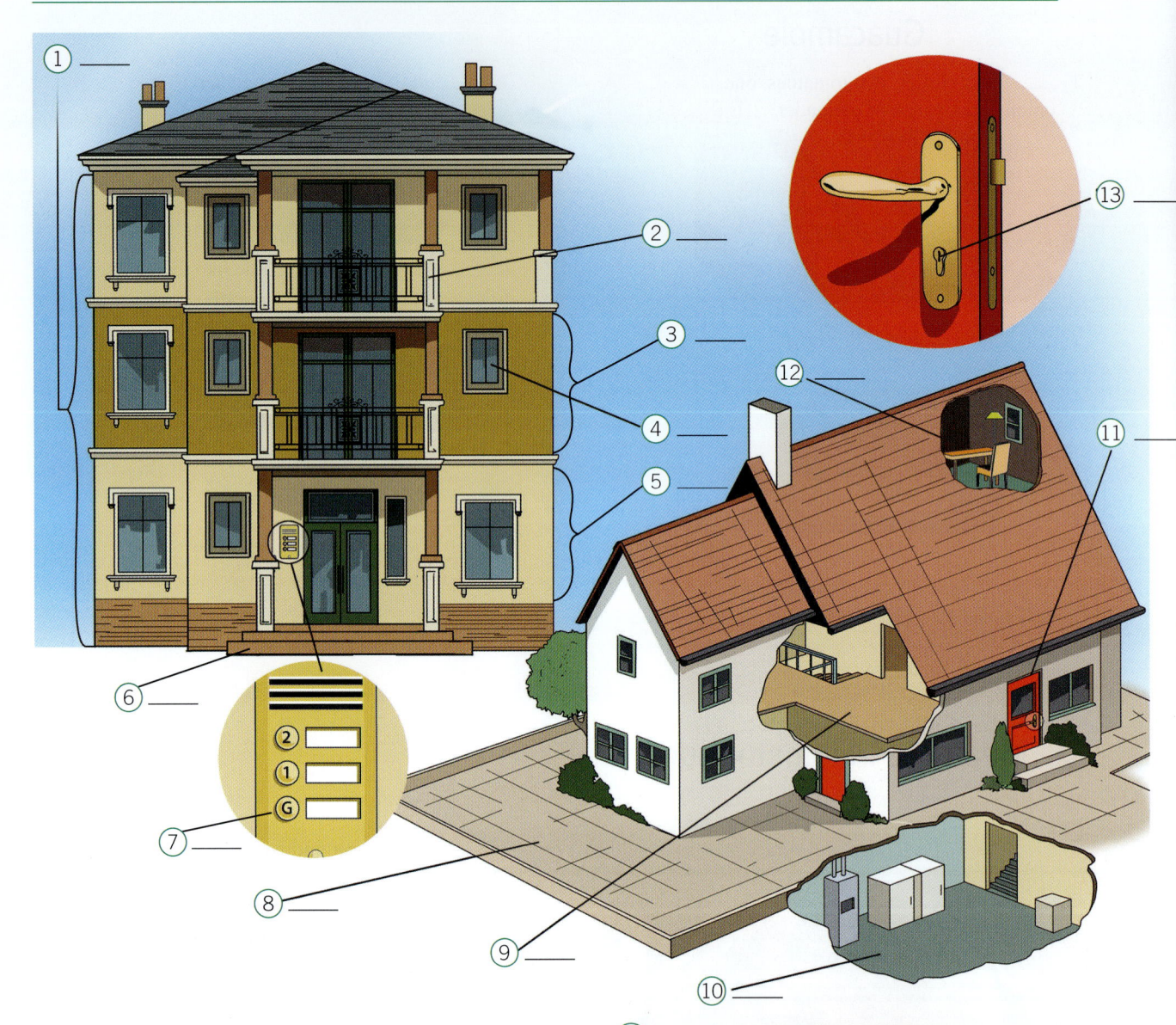

1 ____
2 ____
3 ____
4 ____
5 ____
6 ____
7 ____
8 ____
9 ____
10 ____
11 ____
12 ____
13 ____

b ▶2.43 Complete the sentences with the words in the box. Then listen and check.

attic   balcony   floor   location /ləʊˈkeɪʃən/   moved
neighbourhood /ˈneɪbəhʊd/   rent /rent/   view /vjuː/

1 I don't have my own house, so I ____ the house I'm living in.
2 I've ____ house a lot of times, so I've had lots of different addresses.
3 I live in a very busy ____. There are lots of shops, cafés and cars.
4 We don't have a garden or a terrace, but we do have a ____ where we can sit outside.
5 My home is in a good ____ because it's near the train station.
6 I put all the stuff I don't use in the ____.
7 Our flat is on the third ____ of our building.
8 The ____ from my bedroom is nothing special – just a street and more houses.

c 💬 Discuss the sentences in **b** which are true for you.

> The second sentence isn't true for me. I've only moved house once in my life.

d 💬 Imagine you are going to buy or rent a new home. What kind of house or flat would you choose and why? Which of these things are most important?
- price
- views
- location
- number of rooms
- garden
- something else

e ▶ Now turn to p.81

Vocabulary Focus

8A The news

a Match headlines 1–4 with the different kinds of news a–d.

1. HOSPITALS TO GET MORE NURSES
2. THREE BIG BANKS ANNOUNCE PROFITS
3. CAN THIS FILM WIN ANY MORE AWARDS?
4. FOOTBALLER TO MARRY POP STAR

a celebrity news
b current affairs
c entertainment news
d business news

b Complete the sentences with the words in the box.

bloggers /ˈblɒgəz/   presenters /prɪˈzentəz/
editors /ˈedɪtəz/   reporters /rɪˈpɔːtəz/

1. _____ introduce TV and radio shows.
2. _____ write online articles giving their opinions and feelings.
3. _____ often travel to places where events are happening. They conduct interviews and present news stories.
4. _____ make decisions about what appears in magazines and newspapers.

c Underline the correct words.

1. People often express their opinions about news stories on *social / sociable* media like Facebook and Twitter.
2. Young adults prefer news websites where they can *post / publish* comments about articles.
3. How much do governments influence news *sources / organisations* like Sky News and the BBC?
4. Breaking news *posts / spreads* quickly online.
5. A *journal / journalist* is someone whose job is to collect news and prepare it for the public.

d Discuss the questions below.

1. What blogs do you read?
2. What qualities do you need to be a good journalist or reporter?
3. Do you post comments on news stories or share news stories online?

e ▶ Now go back to p.92

8B Shopping

a Are the phrases in the box talking about things customers do, or talking about products?

be able to afford /əˈfɔːd/ something
be in stock /stɒk/
be on sale /ˈseɪəl/
come out
get a refund /ˈriːfʌnd/
good value /ˈvæljuː/ for money
have a guarantee /gærənˈtiː/
look for a bargain /ˈbɑːgɪn/
reasonably priced /ˈriːzənəbli praɪst/
take/send something back

b ▶3.5 Underline the correct words. Then listen and check.

A That new game came ¹*out / on* last Sunday, so I had to get it for Max, of course!
B Was it very expensive?
A No, it ²*had / was* reasonably priced, luckily!
C I've been looking for ³*bargains / good value* at the clothes market.
D Did you get anything?
C Well, there were some boots I really liked, but I ⁴*couldn't afford / afforded* them. I got these shoes instead. They were very good value ⁵*for / in* money – only £17.
E I bought this tablet online six months ago. It's already broken!
F You should ⁶*take / send* it back.
E Do you think I'll ⁷*get / send* a refund?
F ⁸*Was it on sale / Did it have a guarantee* when you bought it?
E Yes.
F That's OK, then. They'll have to give you your money back.

c 💬 Take turns to talk about something:

- you bought recently which was reasonably priced or in a sale
- you would like to buy but cannot afford
- you bought that is good value for money
- you're waiting to come out so that you can buy it

d ▶ Now go back to p.95

159

9A Cinema and TV

a ▶3.19 Match the words in the box with photos 1–12. Then listen and check.

action /ˈækʃn/   animation /ˌænɪˈmeɪʃn/   chat show /ˈtʃæt ʃəʊ/   comedy /ˈkɒmɪdiː/
documentary /ˌdɒkjuˈmentriː/   drama /ˈdrɑːmə/   game show /ˈɡeɪm ʃəʊ/   horror /ˈhɒrə/
romance /ˈrəʊmæns/   science fiction /ˈsaɪəns ˈfɪkʃən/   soap opera /ˈsəʊp ɒprə/   thriller /ˈθrɪlə/

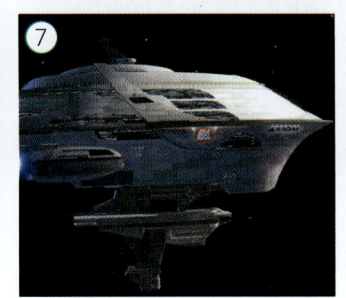

b ▶3.20 Complete the sentences with the words in the box. Then listen and check.

based on /ˈbeɪst ɒn/   character /ˈkærəktə/   director /dɪˈrektə/   film /fɪlm/   scene /siːn/   studio /ˈstjuːdiəʊ/

1 I like Christopher Nolan and Steven Spielberg, but my favourite ____ is Sofia Coppola.
2 The final ____ of the film was amazing – it looked so real!
3 They used some outdoor locations, but most of the filming was done in the ____.
4 I was very surprised when I discovered that this film is ____ a true story.
5 **A** Did you ____ the race?
   B Yes, and I caught the moment when Tom won! I'll show you later.
6 In these films, George Clooney plays a ____ who wants to steal money from a casino.

c Write notes on three of these topics.
- a famous director from your country
- a famous movie scene that many people remember
- a film based on a book
- a popular character from a film
- a big event that was filmed recently

d 💬 Take turns to talk about the topics in **c**. What else do you know about these things or people?

e ▶ Now go back to p.104

Vocabulary Focus

10A Sport

a ▶3.35 Label the pictures with the words in the box. Then listen and check.

competitor /kɒmˈpetɪtə/   court /kɔːt/   net /net/   opponents /əˈpəʊnənts/   referee /refəˈriː/   track /træk/

1 _____   2 _____   4 _____

3 _____   5 _____   6 _____

b Underline the word in each group which is not possible.

You can …
1 *win* / *lose* / *beat* / *score* a point.
2 *beat* / *attack* / *score* your opponent.
3 win a *game* / *point* / *match* / *competitor*.
4 *compete for* / *win* / *score* a prize.

c 💬 Discuss the questions.
1 When did you last play in a game or sports match? What happened? Did you win?
2 Do you prefer playing in a team or individually?
3 Are you a competitive person?

d Think of a sport and make notes on these questions.
1 Is it a team sport or an individual sport?
2 How do you play it?
3 Do you need a special place or special equipment?
4 Are there any special rules?
5 Is it a popular sport?

e 💬 Describe your sport but do not say its name. Try to guess your partner's sport.

f ▶ Now turn to p.117

10B Expressions with *do*, *make* and *take*

a Write *do*, *make* or *take* for each group of words.
1 _____ money, a decision, a mistake, progress
2 _____ a risk, advantage of something, a chance
3 _____ sense, a difference, the most of something
4 _____ your homework, (some) research
5 _____ well/badly (e.g. in an exam), your best
6 _____ part in something, care of someone, action
7 _____ a break, a nap, it easy
8 _____ a phone call, new friends easily

b Complete the topics with *do*, *make* or *take*. Then choose five topics and write short answers for each one.

When was the last time you … ?
1 _____ a big risk
2 _____ a difficult decision
3 _____ the most of something
4 _____ it easy
5 _____ an important phone call
6 _____ a new friend
7 _____ well in an exam
8 _____ a stupid mistake
9 _____ advantage of something
10 _____ your best at something

c 💬 Take turns to talk about what happened in each situation in **b**.

d ▶ Now go back to p.121

This page is intentionally left blank

Audioscripts

Unit 6

▶ 2.23

HARRY Hi, Mel!
MEL Ah, There you are! Hi.
GEMMA We were just talking about that programme last night – that *Toughest Place to Be*… Did you see it?
M No, why?
H It was about this London taxi driver …
G Mason something.
H … and he went to Mumbai. It looks like a nightmare – really, really busy roads, and people and cars all over the place! And people – even little kids – walking through the traffic.
M So, what? Did the guy have to be a taxi driver in Mumbai? I've seen some of that series. It's such a culture shock for the people when they discover how different their job is somewhere else.
G Yeah. This one was good. Mason was a very likeable guy, you know, and he got on really well with Pradeep, the guy who showed him around. You really wanted him to do OK, and he did in the end. He didn't find it easy, though. He'd spent about three years in London learning all the street names and where everything was. And then he only had a week in Mumbai to learn the job. And apart from anything else, it was so hot.
M Yeah, I can imagine.
H He drove two different cars and neither of them were 'cool cabs' – that's what they call the taxis there with air conditioning – and the temperature was over 40°, so he was finding it really difficult. And in the old car he had to use hand signals instead of lights to indicate left and right.
M Bit different from London! And did he manage on his own OK?
H Yes, it was amazing, actually. He learned how to get around the city pretty quickly, and he did all right when he went out on his own. He picked up a few phrases of the local language and of course a lot of people in India speak English.
M Mm-hmm.
H But there's a lot of competition, so he had to work really hard to get passengers.
M I guess that's true for all taxi drivers in Mumbai.
G Well, yeah. It was clear that taxi drivers in Mumbai have to work very hard and don't earn much money. Pradeep works 15 hours a day to support his family and his brother's family, and only earns about £10 a day. When Mason went back to London, he collected money to send to Pradeep and his family.
M Wow, that's really good of him.
H Yeah, so, anyway, I guess we should check out the menu …

▶ 2.30

PRESENTER Japan has by far the highest number of vending machines per person in the world. In fact it has 5.6 million – that's one vending machine for every 20 people. These machines sell all sorts of things, from coffee to bananas, flowers and umbrellas. In a busy society, they play an important role. It's much cheaper for sellers to run a vending machine than a shop. And customers can buy things more quickly and easily from a machine than in a shop.
And we're not talking here just about drinks and cold snacks. Japan also has vending machines that serve hot food, like instant noodles. Japanese students love curry and rice, it's one of the most popular meals there, and, sure enough, you can get it from a machine. The meal comes out of the machine hot and ready to eat. It's more convenient than cooking at home. But is curry and rice from a machine as good as curry and rice from a restaurant? Our reporter Luke went to central Tokyo to find out.
LUKE OK, I've just put my 300 yen into the vending machine and I'm waiting for my curry and rice to appear. Hmm, it's taking a bit longer than I imagined. OK, so my meal is here. I just have to open the packet of steamed rice. Hmm … the curry smells, well, it smells OK, like a lot of instant curries. Right, let me go and find somewhere to sit down and try it. OK, this will do. Well, this is fine. It's actually much better than I expected. What can I say? I think it might be the best vending machine meal I've ever eaten – just not the best curry I've ever eaten! For 300 yen – that's less than two pounds – I can't really complain. But I think next time I'll spend a bit more and go to a proper restaurant!

▶ 2.33 **PART 1**

RACHEL Hi, am I late?
TOM No, you're right on time.
R So, are you ready to go shopping? I am so excited! I still can't believe you're going to ask Becky to marry you.
T Well, I've been thinking about that.
R Oh no! Don't tell me that you've changed your mind!
T Oh no, not at all. I just don't know how to do it.
R What do you mean?
T Well, do you think I should take her somewhere special?
R Um, yes!
T Maybe Paris? I was thinking I could propose at the top of the Eiffel Tower.
R Wow! Just like in the movies!
T Do you think that's too much?
R No, but is it what Becky would really like?
T Um, I just don't know. What do you suggest?
R Well, if I were you, I'd take her somewhere special.
T Exactly, like Paris.
R I mean special for the two of you! Like Mark took me to the place where we first met. It was really romantic, because he'd clearly thought about it. Where did you two first meet?
T At the office where we both worked.
R Oh OK, but there must be somewhere special.
T Hmm, maybe. How about the restaurant where we had our first date?
R Now that sounds like a possibility. Anyway, let's go and look for this ring.

▶ 2.34 **PART 2**

TOM So what about the ring? What would you buy? A big diamond, right? So she can show it to her friends?
RACHEL Seriously? Tom, do you know Becky at all? It's much better to buy something that's her style. Something that you think she'll like. She doesn't need to show off.
T I'm getting this all wrong!
R That's why I'm here. Come on.
R How about that ring?
T Oh, that's a nice one.
R It's £1500.
T I don't believe it! That's ridiculous.
R Tom! It's Becky! Over there.
T You're kidding! What should we do?
R Quick! Let's go in.

167

▶ 2.37

JEFF I like eating out, but I don't really like expensive restaurants. It's not the money so much as the atmosphere. The waiters are often quite unfriendly and you feel you have to talk quietly, or I do anyway. No one seems to be very relaxed. And the food can be good, but you don't often get much on your plate. I'd much rather go somewhere where the food's good and you don't have to pay so much.

FABIO I love going to cafés, either with friends or on my own. I sometimes take a book or a newspaper to read, or I just order a coffee and sit there. I sometimes start talking to someone, in fact I've got quite a good friend who I met in a café. We started talking and then found out we both liked the same kind of music. I like pavement cafés best. You don't have to think about anything, you can just sit and watch the world go by. It's a great way to pass time I think, very relaxing.

CARLA I really love dancing, so I often go out with a group of friends to a club in the evening. It's such a good way to spend the evening. We usually order some food, maybe just some starters and some grilled meat, and something to drink, and then we start dancing. There's a favourite place of mine where they have live music and we all dance Latin American dances like *salsa* or *merengue*. It's quite cheap. You have to pay something to get in, but it's not much and it's always full of people, maybe 200 people all dancing. It's got an amazing atmosphere.

Unit 7

▶ 2.38

1 Well, it's very small so it can't belong to a big family, maybe a small family or an older couple who live on their own. Where is it? It's somewhere dry and sunny, so it could be Mexico, maybe, or Spain.
2 There can't be much space in there, so I think it must belong to a single person or a couple. And where is it? It could be in any big city, but on the outskirts of the city, I think. It might be somewhere like Tokyo, where land's expensive so you can't build big houses. It might not be a house, it might be two separate flats. No, they can't be flats, the ground floor one is too small, so it must be a house.
3 You can see tall buildings outside the window, so this flat must be somewhere like Dubai or some modern city. Whoever lives there can't have children, it's much too tidy. It might be someone who works a lot, or someone who doesn't spend much time there.
4 It's a huge house, so a very big family must live there, or maybe two or three different families. Or it might be a holiday home because it's in the mountains somewhere. It could be Switzerland or Austria, or perhaps Slovenia. Somewhere in Europe.

▶ 2.44

TIM What are you reading?
KATE Fran just sent me the link to this list of five reasons why small towns are better than cities.
T Ha-ha!
K What are you laughing at? Small towns are better than cities.
T Yes, if you want to have nothing to do and never meet anyone new!
K Well, I loved growing up in a small town. There's a real sense of community. People care about you. It's like you belong to one big family.
T Yes, I know you liked it. But I've always been a city boy. I love being in the centre of things – there's so much going on here. Cinemas, restaurants, museums. And there are lots more work opportunities in big cities than in a small town.
K But there's also more crime. Life's more dangerous here.
T Actually, research has shown that it's actually safer to live in the city.
K Really? I find that hard to believe.
T Yes, they did a study in the US that compared the number of accidents in country and city areas. And in the country there was a much higher number of accidents than in the city. Car crashes mainly, because people drive more in the countryside.
K That makes sense if you think about it. And hospitals are nearer, I suppose, so you get help quicker.
T Exactly. So it's actually safer to live in the city. And it's better for the environment.
K Really? How do you work that out?
T Well, you can't rely on public transport in the countryside like you can in the city, so you have to drive more. It's been proved that if you live in the city, you actually have a smaller carbon footprint, especially if you live somewhere with good public transport.
K I've definitely noticed that I walk more now I live in the city. Everything's closer, I guess. And it is nice not to have to get into the car just to go to a supermarket.
T You see! There are a lot of advantages to living in a city. You can't argue with that.
K No, I can't – there are definitely advantages. But I still miss my little home town.

▶ 2.50 **PART 1**

BECKY Do I look OK, Tom?
TOM You look great! You've got nothing to worry about.
B Oh, I really hope your parents like me.
T Of course they will. You'll be fine! After you, go on. … Dad, this is Becky.
MICHAEL Hello, Becky. I'm Michael. It's very nice to meet you.
B Nice to meet you.
T And this is my mum, Charlotte.
CHARLOTTE Hello! It's lovely to meet you at last!
B Oh, you too!
C Thank you. They're lovely.
M Take a seat, Becky.
B Oh, thank you.
C Would you excuse me for a moment? I just need to check on the food.
B Of course. Is there anything we can do to help?
C Oh no, it's all under control!
B So, Martin …
T Michael!
B Er, Michael. I expect you're excited about the match this afternoon.
M I'm not really a football fan, to be honest. I prefer golf.
B Oh, I see.
C Tom, do you think you could give me a hand in here?
T Sure.
M So, do you play golf?
B No.
B So Caroline, Tom tells me you're an architect. That must be very interesting.
C Oh, er, yes, I really enjoy it. In fact, at the moment, I'm working on –
M Here we go.
B Oh, this looks delicious.
M It's my own recipe.
B What's in it?
M It's chicken and mushroom.
B Oh. Um …
M Is something wrong?
T She's a vegetarian!
B And I'm allergic to mushrooms.
C What? Tom, why didn't you tell us?
T I sent you an email yesterday. Didn't you see it?
M Oh no, we didn't!

168

Audioscripts

C I'm really sorry, Becky. Let me get you something else.
B Oh no, Caroline, it's fine, really. Is it OK if I just have some bread and butter?
C No, we can do better than that. I'll get you a green salad.
B Oh OK, that would be lovely. Thanks.
T Becky, my mum's name is Charlotte, not Caroline!
B Oh no! How embarrassing!

▶ 2.51 PART 2

TOM Listen, I know today hasn't gone very well.
MICHAEL What do you mean?
T Well, Becky kept getting your names wrong. And she didn't eat the food you made.
M Oh, don't worry about that. It wasn't her fault. Becky seems really great.
T You really think so?
M Yes, of course.
T Well, I'm really happy to hear that, because, well, I'm thinking of asking her to marry me.
M Really? But that's great!

▶ 2.55

JON So you're going to Florida, Sue. Lucky you! It must be nice and warm – not like here.
SUE Yes, it's about 30°, I think.
J I'm so jealous! Where are you staying? In a hotel?
S No, we've got an apartment near Miami Beach, with a swimming pool. It actually belongs to my cousin, but she's going to New York so she said we can use it while she's away. And her car.
J And her car? Wow, she must like you a lot!
S Well, yes, it's really generous of her. It means we're just paying for the flight. We couldn't afford it otherwise, not with the four of us.
J So, what are you going to do? Are you going to travel around?
S Well, it depends on the weather. It's hurricane season so it might be quite windy. But we'll probably go to the beach for a start – we all like swimming. Then Mia, my daughter, she's really into wildlife, so she wants to go to the Everglades and see the alligators, so we'll definitely do that. And of course we're going to have to go to Disney World for a day. I don't really want to, but Mark – that's my son – he wants to go there, and he wants to go on all the rides.
J Oh, come on, it might be fun. You'll enjoy it.

S Yes, I might.
J Sounds like you're going to be busy, anyway.
S Yeah. Oh, and my husband says we've got to go to Cape Canaveral – he wants to see the Apollo space rockets, so I guess we'll spend a couple of days doing that. I don't really want to go there. It's so far away, I'm not sure I can cope with so much driving. But there's no point in arguing with him about it. Once he gets an idea in his head …
J So, you're doing everything your family wants. What about you? What do you want to do?
S Me? Oh, I'd just like to relax and do nothing – sit by the pool and read a few books.
J Well, it sounds like you're going to be too busy. You won't have time for that.
S No …

Unit 8

▶ 3.7

ERICA How do you like the sound of this restaurant, Harry? Have a look at the reviews.
HARRY Hmm. *Oscar's* restaurant, mostly five stars, 'One of the best places to eat in Britain', 'Magical place' …
E Sounds pretty good, doesn't it?
H Yeah? Why?
E There's only one problem. It doesn't exist! Lots of people read those reviews and wanted to go there. But when they tried to book a table, there was no response.
H Uh?
E People even went there to see if they could find it. But all they found was an empty street full of rubbish bins. Because the whole thing is a joke, a hoax, and there is actually no restaurant at all.
H So someone made it up, made the whole restaurant up, and then wrote reviews about it?
E Yeah, exactly.
H But why would someone do that, go to all that trouble?
E Well, apparently it was this businessman. He had a friend who owned a hotel. Another hotel owner wrote lots of bad reviews about the friend's hotel, and the hotel lost a lot of business and had financial problems because of the fake reviews. So this businessman wanted to make a point about online reviews.
H About how they can damage people's businesses?

E Exactly. He wanted to show that, really, anyone can write their opinion about anything online and a lot of people will believe it.
H Wow! I never knew these review sites had so much power.
E Yeah, they do. And I think this guy made a really good point. There should be much more control over which reviews are posted. People shouldn't just be able to write anything they like.
H Actually now I read these reviews again, they're not very realistic, are they? And all these fake reviewers have only written one review on the website. So yes, of course, they're all fake reviewers. Yes, it's obvious. I would have spotted that if I'd had more time to look at them.
E Ahem. Yes, of course.

▶ 3.9

1 HAIRDRESSER So I was thinking, maybe we could go for a much shorter style this time? What do you think? Something very different, really short.
WOMAN Yes, yes, really short! Do it!
H If you like, I can use this new product on your hair this time. It's very good. It'll make the cut a bit more expensive, though.
W Oh, no. No thanks.

2 WOMAN Here are the keys. It's been fantastic. Thank you.
RECEPTIONIST That's good to hear. Don't forget to write a review on our website when you get home!
W Yes, we will. We'll give you excellent feedback, don't worry!

3 WAITER Here's your bill.
WOMAN I'm sorry, but I'm not going to pay for the dessert. It was terrible.
WA But you ate it, madam.
WO Well yes, but …
WA Then you have to pay for it, madam.
WO But it wasn't …
WA Would you like me to get the manager?

▶ 3.11 PART 1

MARK Hi!
RACHEL Hi! What are you doing here?
M I left work a bit early, so I brought you some cakes.
R Really? Thank you! I was just getting hungry, actually. I haven't even had lunch yet. We've been really busy today.
M Well, that's good.
R Yes, yes it is.
M Are you still worried about that new florist's opening up down the road?
R Yes, kind of. I just don't know whether there's enough business around here for two places.

169

M Hmm. And have you heard anything from Becky? She's got her interview today, right?

R Yes, she should be there right now. I hope it goes well – she really wants a place on that course.

BEN And finally, what kind of photos do you enjoy taking the most? You have a couple of portraits in your portfolio.

BECKY Well, taking portraits can be really rewarding, especially if the person likes the final photo. But I think, on the whole, I prefer taking action shots – sport and that sort of thing. It's so satisfying when you manage to take the photo at just the right moment.

BEN OK, well that's all the questions I have. Do you have any questions for me?

B Actually, yes, I do. The course description mentions a work placement. Could you tell me a little more about that?

BEN Of course. It tends to either be working at a local gallery on a photography exhibition or working with a professional photographer as an assistant. The placement generally lasts two weeks and normally happens during the holidays.

B OK, and there are trips abroad too, aren't there?

BEN Yes, typically each class has two opportunities to go on study visits per year. Last year they went to Paris and Berlin to see exhibitions. In Berlin, they even had a private question and answer session with the photographer.

B That sounds fantastic.

TOM So, how did it go?

B Yeah. Pretty well I think, on the whole. But it was much more difficult than I thought it was going to be. I was there around two hours.

T Wow.

B Yeah. There was one question I didn't know how to answer, but otherwise, yeah, pretty well.

T What was the question?

B Oh, it was something about my opinion of a famous photographer. I'm not very good with that sort of thing.

T Don't worry. Surely that's what the course is for. Did you find out much about the course?

B Yeah, he told me quite a lot about it. It looks great. There's a job placement where we get to work with professional photographers. And the university itself seems really nice.

T When will you find out if you have a place?

B Well, normally they don't tell you during the interview, but the tutor said they'd be in touch this week.

▶ 3.13 **PART 2**

MARK Hi Tina, how are you?

TINA Hi Mark, I'm good, thanks. Listen, I just saw Sam from the newsagent's. Apparently that new shop's not going to be a florist's. It's going to be a clothes shop.

RACHEL Really?

TINA Really!

M That's brilliant.

R Yes, that's fantastic news. Though of course we'd have had no problem with a bit of competition!

BECKY Thank you. I've got an email from the university. Tom, I've got a place. They've accepted me on the course.

TOM Wow, that's fantastic. I knew they would!

B Oh, I'm so excited, I can't wait to start.

T We should celebrate!

B We should, but first I have to phone Rachel. After all, it was all her idea in the first place.

B Hi, Rachel. I've got some fantastic news!

R So have I! You first!

▶ 3.17

People were commenting online recently about an 11-year-old boy from Manchester in England, who flew to Rome on his own. He was out shopping with his mother at a shopping centre near Manchester Airport, and while she was busy looking at something, he slipped away and walked into the airport. Of course he had no money or anything, he was only 11 years old, but he followed a family who were going on holiday and no one noticed him – everyone thought he was part of that family.
Incredibly, he managed to get through security. It seems that no one noticed he didn't have a boarding pass, and they even let him get on the plane. Normally, of course, they check your boarding pass when you get on, but I guess they just thought he was with the family. Anyway, they let him on and he found an empty seat somewhere. They normally count the passengers to make sure they've got the right number, but it seems either they didn't do it this time or they didn't do it properly, so the plane took off and he flew to Rome. Then luckily, when he got to Rome they found out he was on his own without a passport and they put him on the next flight back to Manchester. Naturally, his mother was extremely worried about him and she complained about it. Both the airline and the airport admitted it was their fault straight away and they promised to look at their security. And they even offered her a free flight.

It's incredible that he managed to get through all the airport security controls without them noticing. But apparently, it happens quite often, and it's nearly always boys of about that age, between 11 and 14, who want to go on a plane.

Unit 9

▶ 3.21

ELLIE Nick, it's time to talk about cinema.

NICK OK.

E Yeah, the thing is I have a bit of a problem with films these days.

N What's that?

E Well, I'm getting a bit sick and tired of all the CGI. You know, I go to watch a drama, or an action film – and it just doesn't look real. It's the directors! They just seem to focus so much on cool special effects – they forget about the story. Think about classic films like *Casablanca*. They had absolutely no special effects. Just good story-telling, good characters, good acting.

N But Ellie, even *Casablanca* has special effects. You know those scenes where they're driving through the streets of Paris – well, that wasn't Paris – it was all filmed in a studio in California! I think CGI is a fantastic tool for directors. Nowadays we can tell stories that wouldn't have been possible 50 years ago. *The Hobbit*, *The Life of Pi,* even *Star Wars*. You couldn't make any of them without special effects.

E But still … I really think special effects are used so much more than necessary. Take Christopher Nolan …

N Christopher Nolan who made the Batman films? And *Inception*? He uses loads of special effects!

E Yes, but he only uses them when he really has to. When he was making *Inception*, he filmed in six different countries to get the different scenes he needed. And remember that fight scene in the room that was moving and turning?

N Oh yes, I do.

E Well, that wasn't done with special effects. They made a room that actually moved around. Leonardo DiCaprio and Joseph Gordon-Levitt had to fight in it.

N Wow, I didn't know that.

E Impressive, right?

N OK, yes, that's clever. But I think that just shows that good directors can have good actors and a good story and they can also use modern technology. And when the technology is used with imagination and creativity, the results can be amazing. Really spectacular.

Audioscripts

▶ **3.25**

ANNIE Well, my music experience sort of started when I was seven. It was my grandmother who started it. She gave me a CD of samba music. I loved the rhythms. I played it constantly. My mum says I was always dancing to it. Samba music is Brazilian music with African rhythms and it's very loud, very energetic. Eventually, I decided I wanted to play the music, not just listen to it, so I saved up and bought a drum. It was an *atabaque* … it's a drum you play with your hands. I taught myself to play it. And this year, I played in my first street carnival. We were playing in the street, and people around us were dancing, and it was like my whole body was part of the rhythm. It was incredible, the best thing I've ever done! So now I've decided that I want to be a music teacher.

JEFF Yeah, well, my music experience was going to the opera. I was travelling through Italy with a group from university. We got to Verona and there was this opera festival on. I wasn't really interested in opera, but my friends persuaded me to go. To be honest, it was a bit boring at first. But then it started to get dark. It was a clear night and you could see the stars. I was sitting next to one of the people who was in my group, Laura, and it was, you know, romantic, sitting under the stars, listening to this amazing music. And, well, we've been together ever since! We even went back to Verona for our honeymoon. Although we didn't go to the opera!

ERICA My friend Mark was living in Budapest, in Hungary, and I went to visit him. Mark knew a lot of places in the city and he took me to an old boat on the river, where you can hear bands practising. The atmosphere was great. It's the kind of place where you could sit and chat all night. Anyway, this band was amazing. They were playing folk music from Transylvania. I particularly remember the violinist. I'll never forget the way he played – so fast, but so relaxed. So there I was, in the middle of a freezing, icy river, listening to this amazing music. And I realised this is where I want to be. So a few months later, I quit my job, and Mark helped me find a job in Budapest. And I stayed there for nearly 10 years.

▶ **3.29** PART 1

RACHEL Hi, Becky.
BECKY Hi, Rachel!
R How are you?
B I'm good, thanks. Listen, Tom and I were thinking about going to see a band tomorrow night. Would you guys like to come?
R Oh, that's a great idea. Who were you planning to see?
B Well, we thought about going to that jazz club in town. They have live music every Friday and it's meant to be excellent.
R Wait a sec, I'll just ask Mark. … Mark, it's Becky. She wants to know if we'd like to go to a jazz club tomorrow evening. … Ah, sorry, Becky. Mark says he's not that keen on jazz. How about going to the classical music festival at the university? It's supposed to be really good.
B Hmm, I'm not a big fan of classical music. I'm sure Tom would like it, but not me. Hang on. Tom wants to say something.
TOM Why don't we go and see that local band, The Snowmen? They're playing at the Empire tomorrow and they've had great reviews.
B Did you hear what Tom said?
R Yes, but I'm not sure Mark would be interested. What kind of music do they play?
B What kind of music is it, Tom?
T It's rock, but it's a bit retro. They sound quite 1980s, so Mark should like it!
B Tom says it's rock, but a bit retro. 80s' music.
R I doubt Mark would be interested. He hasn't seen a rock band for about 10 years. Wait a moment, I'll ask him. Tom's suggesting an 80s' rock band.
MARK Um, yeah! Sounds good. Let's do it!
R Really?
M Yeah, why not? Something a bit different.
R Um, Becky, are you still there?
B Yeah.
R Mark says yes! So what time does it start?
B Hang on a moment. I'll pass you over to Tom. What time does it start?
T Hi, Rach. It starts at 8, so shall we meet outside at half past seven?
R Great. See you there.
T Oh, and tell Mark to wear something cool.

▶ **3.33** PART 2

BECKY Oh, there they are.
TOM What's he wearing?
B I don't know.
RACHEL Hi, guys.
B Hi.
T Mark, what are you wearing?
MARK It's my 'going out' jacket! Don't you like it?
T Er, not really!

▶ **3.34**

ANNA I got two free tickets to the Kanye West concert. I mean, I couldn't believe it! Kanye West, one of the biggest hip-hop stars, for free! So I invited my friend Camila and she said 'no thanks'. And I said 'What? Are you crazy? The ticket costs nothing'. But then she tells me she doesn't like live music. She'd prefer to stay at home and listen to music on her computer. I find that very strange because, for me, music is something full of … full of the singer's feelings, and if you can watch a singer perform, you can see what they're feeling and experience the music much more. But Camila thinks recorded music is better because you can hear everything more clearly. The quality's better, and you don't have crowds around you, and it's just easier to enjoy it. For me, it's more important to see the song come to life when the singer or band connects with the audience. And the other thing I love at the concert is the music is really loud. Anyway, Camila won't be coming with me, but lots of other people will want to.

CAMILA My friend Anna invited me to go to the Kanye West concert next month. She managed to get hold of two free tickets – she's very lucky. She asked me to go with her, but I said no. She thinks I must be mad, saying no to free tickets! I mean, I really like Kanye West and I've got all his albums, but I just don't like going to live concerts. I really prefer listening to music at home or through headphones. In a concert, singers and musicians always make mistakes. They get the rhythm a bit wrong or play notes that are wrong or something. And you see, mistakes can be fixed in recording. Well, that's part of it. The other thing is, but I didn't tell Anna this, I hate the crowds and there are usually so many people that you can only see the singer on the big screen. So what's the point? I know lots of friends who will want the ticket. It was very kind of Anna, but no.

171

Unit 10
▶ 3.36

LIBBY So, how are you, Gina? How was your holiday?
GINA Oh, it was great. Really good. Thailand was beautiful. And the food was amazing. But the best bit was when we went scuba diving.
L Scuba diving? I didn't realise you were going to do that!
G Neither did we! But we went to this gorgeous island called Koh Tao, and it turned out it's famous for its diving. Everyone there told us how amazing it is to dive there, so we decided to have a go.
L Wow. So did you have do some training before you went in the sea?
G Yes, we did a three-day course – PADI, it's called. We had to do a few sessions in a classroom and in a pool, but by the second day we were already diving in the open water.
L Was it scary? I think if I went, I'd be terrified!
G I was a bit worried about it before we went into the water for the first time. You start imagining sharks, and running out of oxygen, and all kinds of things! But once we got in, I relaxed really quickly. There were so many amazing fish to see – the colours were fantastic. In fact, I got so excited that I was moving around too much and using up all my oxygen. The instructor told me off. Apparently, diving is a sport for lazy people. You're not supposed to move around too much!
L Oh really? It sounds perfect for me!
G And on the third day we went to Shark Island. Luckily, it turns out that the name comes from the shape of the island – it looks like a fin – not the local wildlife! The coral there was just so beautiful – all these gorgeous colours.
L It all sounds so amazing.
G It really was. If you get the chance, you should definitely go scuba diving. If you went, you would absolutely love it.
L OK, well, if I ever go to somewhere like Thailand, I might try it.
G So, how are you? What's been happening here?
L Not much, really. Oh, I've just signed up for my first ever public run!
G Oh, great! I was wondering if you were still going running. A marathon?!
L No, not quite! I wouldn't do a full marathon – I'm not fit enough! It's only five kilometres, and it's not a timed race, or anything. It's just for fun, really. It's called the Colour Run, because every kilometre they cover you in coloured powder paint. So, by the end, you're all covered in different colours.
G Ha-ha, that sounds like fun.
L Yes, I think it'll be a bit more relaxed than a proper race – not quite so competitive. And at the end of the race, there's a big party, with music – and loads more powder paint. And it's popular with all kinds of people.
G Excellent!
L You should do it too! It would be great if there was a big group of us going. Would you like to try?
G Hmm, yes, I would, but I don't know. If I was a bit fitter, I would definitely do it. When is it?
L It's not for a couple of months. You've got time to prepare. And five kilometres is not very far.
G Hmm, OK then. I'll give it a try!

▶ 3.40

1 **A** How did the match go?
B Oh, I lost 5–1.
A Oh dear.
B Well, I wasn't playing my best. Of course I would have won easily if I hadn't hurt my arm.
A Oh, of course.
2 **C** It's no good. I can't start the engine.
D Oh great. This car's nothing but trouble.
C I know. I wouldn't have bought it if I'd known it was in such bad condition.
D Well, what did you expect for such a cheap price?
3 **E** Careful! Are you OK?
F Yes, thank you, I'm fine. Thank you. If you hadn't pushed me, that car would have hit me!
E Yes, I know. Some people just don't look.
F Yes. Thank you so much anyway.
E That's all right. You be careful, though.
4 **G** We found out that he was lying all the time. He had a daughter living in Hong Kong and he was sending her all the money.
H Ah, that explains why his bank account was empty.
G Yes, exactly. I wouldn't have discovered the truth if I hadn't read her letters. I found them in a box in his attic.
H Well done. Good work.

▶ 3.43 PART 1

MARK Thanks Tom. So have you …?
TOM Not yet.
M Right.
T I'm going to ask her tonight.
M Oh! How do you feel?
T A bit nervous! How did you feel when you did it?

▶ 3.44 PART 2

TOM How did you feel when you did it?
MARK When I asked Rachel to marry me? Um, fine, I think. You've got nothing to worry about. I'm sure it'll be ok.
T I wish I had your confidence.
M So, where are you taking her?
T I've booked a table at *Bella Vita*. It's the place where we went on our first date.
M That's a good idea.
T Do you think so? You don't think it's a bit boring?
M No, not at all.
T Hmm. I'm still worried that something will go wrong. What if she says no?
M She's definitely not going to say no. You two are perfect for each other.
T Hmm, but what if?
M All right, enough!

▶ 3.47 PART 3

BECKY Thank you!
TOM Thanks!
B So what are you going to get? I'm starving!
T I don't know. Maybe a pizza.
B Yeah, the pizzas do look really good.
T So, um, Becky, ever since I've known you …
B It's been a long time since we were here last.
T Yeah, we came here on our first date, didn't we?
B Really? I thought we went somewhere else. That reminds me, I need to book the restaurant for the office party. Let me just make a note of that before I forget. Were you trying to give me a ring earlier?
T A ring? What?! No!
B I've got a missed call from you on my phone.
T Oh! Oh, yeah, I just wanted to check that you knew which restaurant it was.
B Oh, OK.
T So, anyway, as I was saying, you've really changed my life.
WAITER Are you ready to order?
B Oh, we haven't even looked at the menus yet! Could you give us a couple more minutes?
W Of course.

172

Audioscripts

T Becky, there's something I want to ask you.
B Oh yes, me too. Are you free this weekend? My parents are coming to stay and –
T Listen, I'm trying to ask you to marry me!
B What? Tom! Oh I had no idea. How long have you been planning this? … This ring is gorgeous. When did you buy that? Oh, I know! That's what you were doing with Rachel in the shopping centre. I was sure something was going on!
T Becky, will you marry me?
B Of course I will!

▶ 3.49

GREG I finished training as a nurse in Auckland and I was expecting to get a job in a small hospital somewhere. But then a friend told me about *NowVolunteer* and I decided to apply. I'd always wanted to go to an African country and use my nursing skills to help people and here was a chance to do that, so I decided to take the opportunity while I could. I had to raise $500 before I went, but that was quite easy – I got two hospitals to sponsor me and then I borrowed some money from the bank.

So I went to Madagascar and joined a team of people working with a local supervisor. We set up a program where we went round villages and taught basic ways to improve hygiene and to avoid catching diseases. For example, we gave instruction about how to avoid catching malaria and distributed mosquito nets to some of the homes. I think we did some good, I hope so anyway, but I also learned a huge amount from it. I was suddenly in a completely different culture, teaching people who had such a different lifestyle from my own, so I think it made a big difference to the way I see the world. And I also made some very good friends out there, both local people and the other volunteers. We had such good times together and we've kept in touch since then.

After I came back, I got accepted straight away for a job at the university hospital, which is one of the best hospitals in Auckland. I'm sure I wouldn't have managed to do that if I hadn't worked in Madagascar and got this practical experience.

So I'd recommend *NowVolunteer* to anyone. I think their programs are great.

Phonemic Symbols

Vowel sounds

Short

/ə/	/æ/	/ʊ/	/ɒ/
teach**er**	m**a**n	p**u**t	g**o**t
/ɪ/	/i/	/e/	/ʌ/
ch**i**p	happ**y**	m**e**n	b**u**t

Long

/ɜː/	/ɑː/	/uː/	/ɔː/	/iː/
sh**ir**t	p**a**rt	wh**o**	w**a**lk	ch**ea**p

Diphthongs (two vowel sounds)

/eə/	/ɪə/	/ʊə/	/ɔɪ/	/aɪ/	/eɪ/	/əʊ/	/aʊ/
h**ai**r	n**ear**	t**our**	b**oy**	f**i**ne	l**a**te	wind**ow**	n**ow**

Consonants

/p/	/b/	/f/	/v/	/t/	/d/	/k/	/g/	/θ/	/ð/	/tʃ/	/dʒ/
picnic	**b**ook	**f**ace	**v**ery	**t**ime	**d**og	**c**old	**g**o	**th**ink	**th**e	**ch**air	**j**ob
/s/	/z/	/ʃ/	/ʒ/	/m/	/n/	/ŋ/	/h/	/l/	/r/	/w/	/j/
sea	**z**oo	**sh**oe	televi**si**on	**m**e	**n**ow	si**ng**	**h**ot	**l**ate	**r**ed	**w**ent	**y**es

Irregular verbs

Infinitive	Past simple	Past Participle
be	was /wɒz/ / were /wɜː/	been
become	became	become
begin	began	begun
blow	blew /bluː/	blown /bləʊn/
break /breɪk/	broke /brəʊk/	broken /ˈbrəʊkən/
bring /brɪŋ/	brought /brɔːt/	brought /brɔːt/
build /bɪld/	built /bɪlt/	built /bɪlt/
buy /baɪ/	bought /bɔːt/	bought /bɔːt/
catch /kætʃ/	caught /kɔːt/	caught /kɔːt/
choose /tʃuːz/	chose /tʃəʊz/	chosen /ˈtʃəʊzən/
come	came	come
cost	cost	cost
cut	cut	cut
deal /dɪəl/	dealt /delt/	dealt /delt/
do	did	done /dʌn/
draw /drɔː/	drew /druː/	drawn /drɔːn/
drink	drank	drunk
drive /draɪv/	drove /drəʊv/	driven /ˈdrɪvən/
eat /iːt/	ate /et/	eaten /ˈiːtən/
fall	fell	fallen
feel	felt	felt
find /faɪnd/	found /faʊnd/	found /faʊnd/
fly /flaɪ/	flew /fluː/	flown /fləʊn/
forget	forgot	forgotten
get	got	got
give /gɪv/	gave /geɪv/	given /ˈgɪvən/
go	went	gone /gɒn/
grow	grew /gruː/	grown /grəʊn/
have /hæv/	had /hæd/	had /hæd/
hear /hɪə/	heard /hɜːd/	heard /hɜːd/
hit	hit	hit
hold /həʊld/	held	held
keep	kept	kept
know /nəʊ/	knew /njuː/	known /nəʊn/

Infinitive	Past simple	Past Participle
leave /liːv/	left	left
lend	lent	lent
let	let	let
lose /luːz/	lost	lost
make	made	made
meet	met	met
pay /peɪ/	paid /peɪd/	paid /peɪd/
put	put	put
read /riːd/	read /red/	read /red/
ride /raɪd/	rode /rəʊd/	ridden /ˈrɪdən/
ring	rang	rung
run	ran	run
sit	sat	sat
say /seɪ/	said /sed/	said /sed/
see	saw /sɔː/	seen
sell	sold /səʊld/	sold /səʊld/
send	sent	sent
set	set	set
sing	sang	sung
sleep	slept	slept
speak /spiːk/	spoke /spəʊk/	spoken /ˈspəʊkən/
spend	spent	spent
stand	stood /stʊd/	stood /stʊd/
steal /stiːl/	stole /stəʊl/	stolen /ˈstəʊlən/
swim /swɪm/	swam /swæm/	swum /swʌm/
take /teɪk/	took /tʊk/	taken /ˈteɪkən/
teach /tiːtʃ/	taught /tɔːt/	taught /tɔːt/
tell	told /təʊld/	told /təʊld/
think	thought /θɔːt/	thought /θɔːt/
throw /θrəʊ/	threw /θruː/	thrown /θrəʊn/
understand	understood /ˌʌndəˈstʊd/	understood /ˌʌndəˈstʊd/
wake /weɪk/	woke /wəʊk/	woken /ˈwəʊkən/
wear /weə/	wore /wɔː/	worn /wɔːn/
win	won	won
write /raɪt/	wrote /rəʊt/	written /ˈrɪtən/

Acknowledgements

The publishers would like to thank the following teachers and ELT professionals for the invaluable feedback they have provided during the development of the B1+ Student's Book:

Andre Alipio, Brazil; Peggy Altpekin, Turkey and the Gulf; Natalia Bayrak, Russia; Kate Chomacki, UK; Leonor Corradi, Argentina; Ludmila Gorodetskaya, Russia; Ludmila Kozhevnikova, Russia; Steve Laslett, UK; Rabab Marouf, Syria; Christina Maurer Smolder, Australia; Mariusz Mirecki, Poland; Catherine Morley, Spain; Antonio Mota Cosano, Spain; Julian Oakley, UK; Litany Pires Ribeiro, Brazil; Elena Pro, Spain; Wayne Rimmer, Russia; Ruth Sánchez, Spain; Hilda Zubiria, Peru.

The publishers are grateful to the following contributors:
Gareth Boden: commissioned photography
Leon Chambers: audio recordings
Hilary Luckcock: picture research
Rob Maidment and Sharp Focus Productions: video recordings, video stills
Ann Thomson: commissioned photography

The authors and publishers acknowledge the following sources of copyright material and are grateful for the permissions granted. While every effort has been made, it has not always been possible to identify the sources of all the material used, or to trace all copyright holders. If any omissions are brought to our notice, we will be happy to include the appropriate acknowledgements on reprinting.

The publisher has used its best endeavours to ensure that the URLs for external websites referred to in this book are correct and active at the time of going to press. However, the publisher has no responsibility for the websites and can make no guarantee that a site will remain live or that the content is or will remain appropriate.

The publishers are grateful to the following for permission to reproduce copyright photographs and material:
Key: L = left, C = centre, R = right, T = top, B = bottom
p67: Corbis/Hugh Sitton; pp68/69(B): Superstock/Franck Binewald/Imagebroker.net; p69(L)(firefighters): PA/Eraldo Peres/AP; p69(L)(jeep): Alamy/patrick nairne; p69(L)(hospital): Rex/Sipa Press; p69(TR): BBC Photo Sales; p70: Alamy/imageBroker; p71(a): Alamy/Julie Woodhouse; p71(b): Alamy/Martin Turzak; p71(c): Alamy/Food and Drink Photos; p71(d): Alamy/amana images inc.; p71(e): Shutterstock/Sean Wandzilak; p71(B): Alamy/Robert Harding Picture Library Ltd; p72(TL): Shutterstock/racorn; p72(TR): Alamy/MBI; p72(B): Alamy/JLImages; p73(L): Corbis/Inspirestock; p73(C): Alamy/ Simon Reddy; p73(R): Alamy/ Bon Appetit; p76(1): Shutterstock/Radu Bercan; p76(2): Alamy/Robert Harding Picture Library Ltd; p76(3): Shutterstock/jan kranendonk; p77: Shutterstock/posztos; p79: Corbis/Michael Freeman; p80(a): Shutterstock/Natali Glado; p80(b): Superstock/View Pictures Ltd; p80(c): Alamy/Peter Donaldson; p80(d): Alamy/ CulturalEyes-N; p81(T): Shutterstock/Breadmaker; p81(BL): Alamy/Greg Balfour Evans; p81(BR): Superstock/View Pictures Ltd; p82(L): Alamy/les polders; p82(a): Alamy/Jon Arnold Images Ltd; p82(b): Alamy/Images&Stories; p82(c): Alamy/David J. Green; p82(d): Alamy/Adam Burton; p82(e): Alamy/Clive Sawyer; p82(f): Alamy/Doug Houghton; p83(T): Getty/Folio Images; p83(B): Alamy/David Lyon; pp84/85: Corbis/Atlantide Phototravel; p85(Pablo): Masterfile; p85(Jen): Masterfile/Beth Dixson; p85(Kira): Masterfile; p88(TR): Shutterstock/Richard Goldberg; p88(CR): Alamy/North Wind Picture Archives; p88(main): Science Photo Library/National Reconnaissance Office; p89: Shutterstock/Richard Cavalleri; p91: Real Madrid via Getty Images; p93(T): Corbis/Gary Hershorn/Reuters; p93(B): Science Photo Library/Ria Novosti; p94: Getty/Nicolas McComber; p95(TR): Shutterstock/Goodluz; p95(CL): Corbis/Rick Friedman; p95(BL): Masterfile/Al Accardo; p100(a): Shutterstock/pio3; p100(b): Rex/Isopix; p100(c): Getty/Daniel Reiter/Stock4B; p103: Corbis/Lucas Jackson/Reuters; p104(TR): Rex/Moviestore; p104(CL): Rex/Moviestore; p104(CC): Rex/c.W. Disney/Everett; p104(CR): Kobal/Lucasfilm/20th Century Fox; p104(BL): Ronald Grant Archive/New Line Cinema/Wingnut Films/Lord Dritte Productions Deutschland Filmproduktion GmbH/Saul Zaentz Co.; p105(TR): Rex/Courtesy Everett Collection; p105(CL): Capital Pictures/NFS; p105(CR): Alamy/AF Archive; p105(BL): Capital Pictures/NFS; p105(BR): Photofest/Walt Disney Studios; p106: Corbis/enewsimage.com/Splash News; p107(L)(1): Alamy/Rob Ball; p107(L)(2): Alamy/Juice Images; p107(L)(3): Alamy/Ted Foxx; p107(R)(a): Shutterstock/ Igor Bulgarin; p107(R)(b): Lebrecht Music & Arts/Leemage; p107(R)(c): Alamy/Jose Elias/StockPhotosArt – Events; p108/109: Splash UK; p108(L): Rex/Gonzales Photo/Christian Hjorth/PYMCA; p109: Getty Images Entertainment; p112(T): Alamy/John Warburton-Lee Photography; p112(B): Alamy/Juice Images; p113(L): Alamy/Geraint Lewis; p113(C): Shutterstock/ Martin Lehmann; p113(TR): Rex/ Benjamin Lozovsky/BFAnyc.com; p113(BR): Lebrecht Music & Arts/Chris Christodoulou;

p115: Corbis/Andrew Fox; p116(TL): Getty Images Sport; p116(BL): Alamy/Zuma Press Inc.; p116(BR): Getty/Shannon Stent; p117(T): Shutterstock/Richard Whitcombe; p117(B): Corbis/Remko de Waal/epa; p118(CL): Alamy/Mikhail Kondrashov "fotomik"; p118(BL): Alamy/imageBroker; p118(BR): Rex/Terry Harris; p119(a)(T): Shutterstock/Monkey Business Images; p119(b)(C): Shutterstock/Jacek Fulawka; p119(c)(L): Alamy/Robert Stainforth; p119(c)(R): Alamy/PYMCA; p119(c)(B): Shutterstock/Brian Eichhorn; p119(background): Shutterstock/ Songquan Deng; p120(TR): Shutterstock/Monkey Business Images; p120(BR): Shutterstock/ Image Point Fr; p124(T): Masterfile; p124(B): Masterfile/R. Ian Lloyd; p125(T): Corbis/Oliver Rossi; p125(B): Alamy/Yvette Cardozo; p130: Kobal/RKO; p160(1): Kobal/ Paramount Pictures; p160(2): Corbis/Radius Images; p160(3): Rex/Ken McKay; p160(4): Kobal/New Line Productions/Michael Ginsberg; p160(5): Disney-ABC via Getty Images; p160(6): Kobal/Universal; p160(7): Ronald Grant Archive/Walt Disney Pictures/Pixar Animation Studios; p160(8): Rex/ITV; p160(9): Kobal/Dream Works Animation; p160(10): Rex/FremantleMedia Ltd; p160(11): Ronald Grant Archive/Ariescope Pictures; p160(12): Kobal/Samson Films/Summit Entertainment.

Commissioned photography by Gareth Boden: pp95(BR), 119(a)(C), p119(b)(T,B) and 120(L).

We are grateful to Barratt Developments plc and Neide's Deli Cafe for their help with the commissioned photography.

Front cover photograph by Alamy/imageBROKER.

The publishers would like to thank the following illustrators: Beatrice Bencivenni, Mark Bird, Mark Duffin, Jo Goodberry, Mark (KJA Artists), Jerome Mireault, Gavin Reece, Gregory Roberts, Sean (KJA Artists), David Semple, Sean Sims, Marie-Eve-Tremblay.

Corpus Development of this publication has made use of the Cambridge English Corpus (CEC). The CEC is a computer database of contemporary spoken and written English, which currently stands at over one billion words. It includes British English, American English and other varieties of English. It also includes the Cambridge Learner Corpus, developed in collaboration with the University of Cambridge ESOL Examinations. Cambridge University Press has built up the CEC to provide evidence about language use that helps to produce better language teaching materials.

English Profile This product is informed by the English Vocabulary Profile, built as part of English Profile, a collaborative programme designed to enhance the learning, teaching and assessment of English worldwide. Its main funding partners are Cambridge University Press and Cambridge ESOL and its aim is to create a 'profile' for English linked to the Common European Framework of Reference for Languages (CEFR). English Profile outcomes, such as the English Vocabulary Profile, will provide detailed information about the language that learners can be expected to demonstrate at each CEFR level, offering a clear benchmark for learners' proficiency. For more information, please visit www.englishprofile.org

CALD The Cambridge Advanced Learner's Dictionary is the world's most widely used dictionary for learners of English. Including all the words and phrases that learners are likely to come across, it also has easy-to-understand definitions and example sentences to show how the word is used in context. The Cambridge Advanced Learner's Dictionary is available online at dictionary.cambridge.org. © Cambridge University Press, Third Edition, 2008 reproduced with permission.

This page is intentionally left blank

Cambridge English

EMPOWER

Combo B
WORKBOOK
WITH ANSWERS

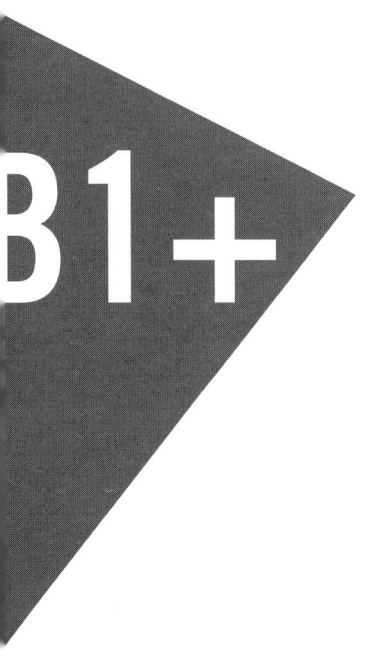

B1+

Peter Anderson

Contents

Unit 6 Different cultures			Page
6A	You have to use pedestrian crossings	**Grammar** Modals of obligation **Vocabulary** Compound nouns; Multi-word verbs	**Pronunciation** Word stress	34
6B	It's tastier than I expected	**Grammar** Comparatives and superlatives **Vocabulary** Describing food		35
6C	Do you think I should take her somewhere special?	**Everyday English** Asking for and giving recommendations	**Pronunciation** Sounding interested	36
6D	It's definitely worth a visit	**Reading** Restaurant reviews	**Writing skills** Positive and negative language; Adverbs **Writing** Positive and negative restaurant reviews	37
Reading and listening extension		**Reading** An article about disabled access in a city	**Listening** A conversation about restaurants	38
Review and extension		**WORDPOWER** go		39
Unit 7 House and home			
7A	It might be a holiday home	**Grammar** Modals of deduction **Vocabulary** Buildings	**Pronunciation** Final sounds in modal verbs	40
7B	There are plenty of things to do	**Grammar** Quantifiers **Vocabulary** Verbs and prepositions		41
7C	Is there anything we can do to help?	**Everyday English** Offers, requests and asking for permission	**Pronunciation** Sounding polite	42
7D	Make yourselves at home	**Reading** A note for a visitor	**Writing skills** Offering choices **Writing** A note for a babysitter	43
Reading and listening extension		**Reading** An article about Detroit	**Listening** A conversation between a group of friends	44
Review and extension		**WORDPOWER** over		45
Unit 8 Information			
8A	He said he'd read the news online	**Grammar** Reported speech: statements and questions **Vocabulary** The news		46
8B	I recommended visiting a local restaurant	**Grammar** Verb patterns **Vocabulary** Shopping; Reporting verbs		47
8C	On the whole, I prefer taking action shots	**Everyday English** Generalising; Being vague	**Pronunciation** Sound and spelling: /h/ and /w/	48
8D	Fortunately, everything was all right	**Reading** A news story	**Writing skills** Summarising information **Writing** A news story	49
Reading and listening extension		**Reading** An article about careers	**Listening** A conversation about shopping	50
Review and extension		**WORDPOWER** in/on + noun		51

Unit 9 Entertainment			
9A The film is still loved today	**Grammar** The passive **Vocabulary** Cinema and TV		52
9B I went to a concert which changed my life	**Grammar** Defining and non-defining relative clauses **Vocabulary** Music; Word-building: nouns	**Pronunciation** Defining and non-defining relative clauses	53
9C It's meant to be excellent	**Everyday English** Recommending and responding	**Pronunciation** Showing contrast	54
9D I like going out, but …	**Reading** An opinion article	**Writing skills** Contrasting ideas **Writing** An opinion article	55
Reading and listening extension	**Reading** A blog article	**Listening** A conversation about choosing a film	56
Review and extension	WORDPOWER *see, look at, watch, hear, listen to*		57
Unit 10 Opportunities			
10A If I was fitter, I'd do it!	**Grammar** Second conditional **Vocabulary** Sport; Adjectives and prepositions	**Pronunciation** Strong and weak forms: *would*	58
10B Making the most of opportunities	**Grammar** Third conditional **Vocabulary** Expressions with *do, make* and *take*	**Pronunciation** Strong and weak forms: *have, had* and *hadn't*	59
10C You've got nothing to worry about	**Everyday English** Talking about possible problems and reassuring someone	**Pronunciation** Sounding sure and unsure	60
10D I think you should go for it	**Reading** Emails asking for and giving advice	**Writing skills** Advising a course of action **Writing** An email giving advice	61
Reading and listening extension	**Reading** An email about a football team	**Listening** A conversation about a medical school interview	62
Review and extension	WORDPOWER Easily confused words		63
Vox pop video			68
Audioscripts			74
Answer key			82

6A You have to use pedestrian crossings

1 GRAMMAR Modals of obligation

a Underline the correct words to complete the conversation.

PAUL I've got my English exam tomorrow morning.
MUM Oh, really? So what time do you ¹*should / have to / must* be at school?
PAUL Well, the exam starts at 9 o'clock, so I ²*mustn't / don't have to / can* be late.
MUM I think you ³*shouldn't / mustn't / ought to* leave earlier than normal, in case there's a lot of traffic.
PAUL Yes, that's a good idea.
MUM And what are you going to do after the exam?
PAUL Well, I ⁴*mustn't / shouldn't / don't have to* stay at school in the afternoon, so I ⁵*can / should / must* come home for lunch.
MUM Fine, just two more things. It says on this information sheet that students ⁶*can / must / shouldn't* show their identity cards to the examiner before the exam.
PAUL Don't worry. I always take my ID card with me to school.
MUM It also says you ⁷*don't have to / must / can't* use a dictionary during the exam, so don't take one with you.
PAUL Yes, I know. I'll leave it at home.
MUM OK, good. By the way, it's 10 o'clock. You ⁸*shouldn't / have to / must* go to bed late tonight.
PAUL No, you're right. I'll go up now.
MUM OK, good night. And good luck for tomorrow!

b ▶ 6.1 Listen and check.

c Match 1–6 with a–f to make sentences.
1 [f] The service was terrible, so you shouldn't
2 [ ] Go slower! We're near a school so you mustn't
3 [ ] In my experience you don't usually have to
4 [ ] I'm worried about hiring a car in the USA. I think we should
5 [ ] It's all right here. The sign says you can
6 [ ] It's Mum's birthday tomorrow. You've got to

a take off your shoes when you go into a British person's house.
b drive more than 50 kilometres per hour.
c buy her a present this afternoon.
d park your car here after 6.30 pm.
e read about the rules for driving in the guidebook before we decide.
f give the waiter a tip.

2 VOCABULARY Compound nouns

a Match 1–6 with a–f to make sentences.
1 [c] When I go into the town centre I normally use public
2 [ ] I haven't got any money on me, so I'll go to the cash
3 [ ] The car didn't stop when the traffic
4 [ ] I think they should put a pedestrian
5 [ ] It's safe to cycle to work because there are cycle
6 [ ] I hate driving into London in the rush

a lanes so you're not on the road with all the cars.
b crossing outside the school, as it's a dangerous road to cross.
c transport, as the car parks are very expensive.
d machine outside the bank opposite the station.
e hour, so I leave home at 6.30 most days.
f lights turned red and crashed into a bus.

3 VOCABULARY Multi-word verbs

a Underline the correct words to complete the sentences.
1 The easiest way to get *out / around / away* London is to take the underground.
2 Restaurants are quite expensive in Paris so my wife and I only eat *around / away / out* once or twice a month.
3 If Sarah doesn't turn *away / out / up* soon, I think we should buy our tickets for the film and go in without her.
4 I've got a cousin that lives in New York, so I'm sure he'll be able to show us *around / up / out* the city.
5 Although I lived in Stockholm for a year, I didn't pick *out / up / back* much Swedish because everyone speaks English.
6 We've got three hours before we need to go, so why don't we look *back / around / up* the town for a couple of hours?
7 I'm tired after all this sightseeing, so I'd like to go *out / up / back* to the hotel now, if that's OK with you.
8 We normally go *away / out / back* for two or three weeks every summer but we can't afford a holiday this year.

4 PRONUNCIATION Word stress

a ▶ 6.2 Listen to the compound nouns and underline the stressed syllables.

1 swimming pool
2 rush hour
3 washing machine
4 cycle lane
5 lunchtime
6 cash machine

6B It's tastier than I expected

1 GRAMMAR
Comparatives and superlatives

a Put the words in the correct order to make sentences.
1. wasn't / as / my / nearly / I / nice / as / meal / expected .
   My meal wasn't nearly as nice as I expected.
2. by far / is / luxurious / the / most / I've / hotel / stayed in / this / ever .
   _____
3. than / tennis / much / I do / plays / she / better .
   _____
4. nearly / today / hot / as / was / as / isn't / yesterday / it .
   _____
5. most / these / are / ever / shoes / expensive / I've / the / bought .
   _____
6. cheaper / go to / the restaurant / we / far / normally / this restaurant / is / than .
   _____
7. hardest / that was / the / I've / my / in / exam / taken / life .
   _____
8. got / yesterday / than / usual / earlier / home / she / evening .
   _____

b ▶ 6.3 Listen and check.

c Correct *two* mistakes in each sentence.
1. He speaks quicklier that I do.
   He speaks more quickly than I do.
2. London is many expensive than Edinburgh.
   _____
3. They make the better pizzas of Rome.
   _____
4. Colin is more clever that his brother.
   _____
5. That was the most sad film I ever seen.
   _____
6. The exam wasn't near as hard that I expected.
   _____
7. I think this is most simple recipe in the book.
   _____
8. At the moment the weather in France is a little more warm that in the UK.
   _____

d ▶ 6.4 Listen and check.

2 VOCABULARY Describing food

a <u>Underline</u> the correct words to complete the sentences.
1. This coffee is too *sour / bitter / <u>sweet</u>*. You know I don't take sugar!
2. To make a Spanish omelette add the *creamy / heavy / cooked* onions and potatoes to the eggs and then fry the mixture for about five minutes.
3. When you make a salad, it's better to use *cooked / raw / sour* carrots so they don't lose their vitamins.
4. Sorry, I can't eat these cornflakes quietly. They're really *crunchy / sour / raw*.
5. It's the butter and the milk in this sauce that makes it taste so *crunchy / creamy / sour*.
6. This cream's horrible. It tastes really *dried / heavy / sour*. When did you buy it?
7. It's always better to use *fresh / sweet / heavy* herbs when you're cooking. They taste much nicer.
8. I had a really *light / raw / heavy* dinner last night so I didn't sleep very well.

b Complete the sentences with the words in the box.

| add | stir | mix | mash | chop |
| fry | <s>squeeze</s> | serve | heat up | |

1. You need to __*squeeze*__ the juice from four large oranges to make a glass of orange juice.
2. When the potatoes are cooked, take them out of the water and then _____ them with a little butter and milk until they are smooth and creamy.
3. Using a sharp knife, _____ the onions and peppers finely and then _____ them in a little olive oil for about five minutes.
4. _____ a little salt and pepper to the tomato sauce and cook it slowly for about twenty minutes.
5. To make the salad, _____ the lettuce, tomatoes, onions and cucumber together, put a little olive oil and balsamic vinegar on top and _____ with some fresh bread and butter.
6. _____ the mixture of milk, butter and flour in a saucepan and _____ continuously with a wooden spoon to ensure a smooth, creamy sauce.

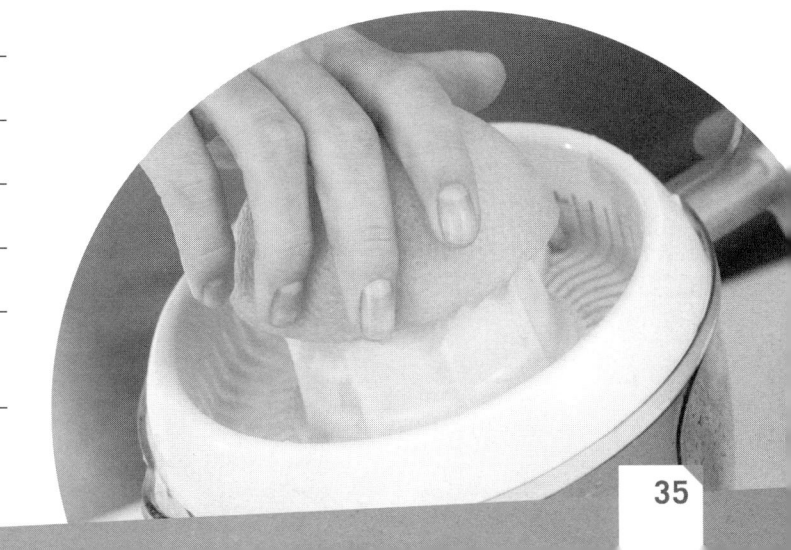

35

6C Everyday English
Do you think I should take her somewhere special?

1 USEFUL LANGUAGE Asking for and giving recommendations

a Complete the conversation with the words in the box.

| worth | should | ~~think~~ | idea | kidding | were |
| better | recommend | would | definitely | | |

A So, where do you ¹___think___ I should take my mother on holiday?
B If I ²_____ you, I'd take her somewhere warm, like Italy.
A You've been to Italy lots of times, haven't you? Where would you ³_____ taking her?
B Well, you should ⁴_____ go to Rome – it's such a beautiful city.
A That's a good idea. And when ⁵_____ you go?
B Er, let me see. Well, it's not a good ⁶_____ to go in July or August, as it's much too hot for sightseeing then. It's much ⁷_____ to go in May or June, when it isn't quite as hot.
A And where do you think we ⁸_____ stay in Rome?
B Well, there are some lovely hotels in the centre, but they're at least €200 a night.
A You're ⁹_____! I had no idea it would be that expensive. I can't afford to pay that much!
B Oh, well, in that case it's probably ¹⁰_____ finding a hotel outside the centre, then.
A Yes, that makes sense. Thanks for your advice.

b ▶6.5 Listen and check.

c Underline the correct words to complete the sentences.
1 You should definitely *to visit / visiting / visit* the British Museum when you're in London.
2 What dress would you *wearing / wear / to wear* to the party?
3 It's much better *take / to take / taking* the train from London to Paris.
4 Would you recommend *going / to go / go* to Athens in August?
5 It's probably worth *book / booking / to book* a hotel before you go.
6 If I were you, *I'll / I did / I'd* take the job in San Francisco.
7 Do you think I *would / should / shall* buy this watch?
8 It's not a good idea *to change / changing / change* your money at the airport.

d ▶6.6 Listen and check.

2 PRONUNCIATION Sounding interested

a ▶6.7 Listen to the exchanges. Does Speaker B sound excited or bored? Tick (✓) the correct box.

1 **A** My boyfriend's taking me to Paris this weekend!
  B Wow! That's amazing. excited ✓ bored ☐
2 **A** I've been offered a place at Harvard University!
  B Oh, really? That's good. excited ☐ bored ☐
3 **A** I got the best exam grades in my class!
  B That's amazing! Well done! excited ☐ bored ☐
4 **A** My dad's going to buy me a rabbit!
  B Wow! That's brilliant. excited ☐ bored ☐
5 **A** John's asked me to marry him!
  B Great! I'm so happy for you. excited ☐ bored ☐
6 **A** We're going on holiday on Saturday!
  B I know. I can't wait! excited ☐ bored ☐

6D Skills for Writing
It's definitely worth a visit

'The tastiest Italian food in London?' — Review A

I took my Italian friend here for his birthday and he absolutely loved it. The atmosphere was really relaxing and the waiters were friendly and extremely helpful. All the food was really fresh and the portions were generous. The tiramisu that we had for our dessert was absolutely delicious. Paolo says it's the best he's ever had – apart from his mum's, of course! Although our meal was rather expensive, we didn't mind paying a bit more than usual because the food was so good. I'd definitely recommend this restaurant if you want to eat lovely food in a relaxing atmosphere. **EMMA T**

'Not the most relaxing evening …' — Review B

A colleague at work recommended this place but we thought it was rather disappointing. First of all, the atmosphere wasn't very relaxing. It was a bit noisy, perhaps because it was a Friday night and the restaurant was rather busy. Also, the music was too loud so it was hard to talk. Secondly, although the waiters were very friendly, there weren't enough of them when we were there and so the service was slow. Unfortunately, when our food eventually arrived it wasn't very good. Our steaks were a bit overcooked and the salad wasn't very fresh. Finally, the portions weren't very big and we thought the meal was rather overpriced. All in all, I'm afraid I wouldn't recommend it. **DAVID M**

1 READING

a Read the reviews and tick (✓) the correct column.

	Review A	Review B
1 The reviewer really enjoyed the meal.		
2 The service wasn't very good.		
3 The quality of the food was good.		
4 The review of the restaurant is positive.		

b Read the reviews again. Are the sentences true or false?
1 In Emma's opinion, the service was good.
2 Emma didn't enjoy her dessert.
3 Emma thought the price of her meal was too high.
4 There weren't many people there when David went to this restaurant.
5 David had to wait a long time for his food to arrive.
6 David was rather disappointed by the quality of his food.

2 WRITING SKILLS Positive and negative language; Adverbs

a Underline the correct words to complete the sentences with a 'strong' or a 'weak' adverb, following the instruction in brackets.
1 The chocolate cake was *fairly / absolutely* delicious. (strong)
2 Unfortunately, all the vegetables were *rather / completely* overcooked. (weak)
3 The food in that new restaurant was *extremely / a bit* boring. (weak)
4 I thought the portions were *absolutely tiny / rather small*. (weak)
5 That new café is *extremely / fairly* expensive. (strong)
6 I thought the tomato soup was *rather / completely* tasteless. (strong)
7 The staff in the hotel were *reasonably / really* friendly. (weak)
8 When we were there the service was *quite / terribly* slow. (strong)

3 WRITING

a Write two reviews, one for each of the restaurants in the fact files below. One review should be mostly positive, the other mostly negative.

RESTAURANT FACT FILE
NAME: Chez Pierre
LOCATION: city centre
TYPE OF FOOD: French e.g. meat (steak, lamb, etc.), fish / seafood, salads
QUALITY OF FOOD:
ATMOSPHERE:
MUSIC:
TYPE OF CUSTOMER: businessmen and women, romantic couples
SERVICE/ATTITUDE OF WAITERS:
PRICE: ££££
VALUE FOR MONEY:
WHEN BUSY: Weekday lunchtimes, weekends

RESTAURANT FACT FILE
NAME: Villa Borghese
LOCATION: at the beach
TYPE OF FOOD: Italian e.g. pizzas, pasta risotto, fish, meat, ice cream
QUALITY OF FOOD:
ATMOSPHERE:
MUSIC:
TYPE OF CUSTOMER: families and groups of young people
SERVICE/ATTITUDE OF WAITERS:
PRICE: £
VALUE FOR MONEY:
WHEN BUSY: every evening

UNIT 6
Reading and listening extension

1 READING

a Read the text. Are the sentences true or false?
1. This text is a newspaper article.
2. The writer's name is Alex Walker.
3. The writer says that she enjoyed her first visit to the city despite one or two problems.
4. The writer says that the city has improved.

b Read the text again and tick (✓) the correct answers.
1. How long has Alex Walker been mayor of the city?
   - a ☐ at least one year
   - b ☐ exactly one year
   - c ☐ less than one year
2. What does Ayesha say about taxis during her first visit?
   - a ☐ It was impossible for her to find one.
   - b ☐ She was not able to use them.
   - c ☐ They were better than public transport.
3. Why is Ayesha writing another report about the city?
   - a ☐ She had been invited to an anniversary party in the city.
   - b ☐ She has become a professional journalist.
   - c ☐ She heard that a lot of money had been spent on the city.
4. How has the train station improved since Ayesha's last visit?
   - a ☐ Men are employed to help her get from the platform to the exit.
   - b ☐ She can get from the platform to the exit by herself.
   - c ☐ They have repaired the old lifts on the platform.
5. How many of the cash machines at the station can Ayesha use easily?
   - a ☐ one
   - b ☐ two
   - c ☐ three
6. How many different forms of transport did Ayesha use to get around the city?
   - a ☐ one
   - b ☐ two
   - c ☐ three

c Think about the place where you live. How easy or difficult do you think it might be for wheelchair users to get around your hometown? Make notes about:
- public transport (do buses/trains/trams have disabled access?)
- things to do and places to visit (is it easy to visit a museum or go shopping?)

Use your notes to write a short review of disabled access for wheelchair users where you live.

CITY MAKES PROGRESS FOR DISABLED

This week is the first anniversary of mayor Alex Walker's promise to make life in our city easier for disabled people. One year on, we asked disabled athlete Ayesha Omar to tell us about her experiences in the city.

Just over a year ago, City News invited me here for the day to do an interview; it turned out to be a visit I will never forget – unfortunately, for all the wrong reasons. As someone in a wheelchair, it was almost impossible for me to get around the city. There was not nearly enough access to public transport and I discovered that taxis were no better: none of them had the special doors I need to carry my wheelchair. The day was such a nightmare that I decided to write a story about my experience in the paper. After I wrote my story, mayor Alex Walker promised to make things better in the city and gave £6 million to the project. Last week, I returned to see if the city had improved.

I arrived at the train station early in the morning. One year ago, the station had only had stairs up to the exit. That meant that three men had to carry me off the platform which was by far the most embarrassing thing that happened to me during my last visit. This year, I saw immediately that they had built a new lift. 'Wonderful!' I thought – but then I remembered something – the buttons. On 'normal' lifts, the buttons are sometimes too high for a person in a wheelchair. That means that I have to ask someone to push the buttons for me. However, the lift in the station had buttons that were much lower so I was able to push them myself. I was really pleased with this.

I decided to take a taxi into the city centre, so first of all I needed to get some money from the bank. Again, I am very pleased to say that when I found the line of three cash machines outside the station, one of them was lower than the other two and so it was the right height for wheelchair users. Later that day, I took a bus and a tram and visited all the main museums, galleries and shopping centres. There was access for wheelchair users everywhere I went. Things are still not perfect and there is a long way to go but I can honestly say that Alex Walker has kept his promise to disabled people in the city!

2 LISTENING

a ▶6.8 Listen to a conversation between three students, Peeraya, Sylvie and Matt, and tick (✓) the correct answers.

1 Which two students are meeting for the first time?
 a ☐ Peeraya and Matt
 b ☐ Peeraya and Sylvie
 c ☐ Sylvie and Matt

2 How do Peeraya and Sylvie know each other?
 a ☐ They are going to Liverpool together.
 b ☐ They study English together.
 c ☐ They met on holiday in Thailand.

3 Peeraya and Sylvie ask Matt to …
 a ☐ recommend a good, local restaurant.
 b ☐ explain how to make fish and chips.
 c ☐ tell them the best place to get a burger.

4 At the end of the conversation, Peeraya and Sylvie …
 a ☐ agree with Matt's recommendation.
 b ☐ ask Matt to recommend something else.
 c ☐ decide to ask someone else.

b Listen again. Underline the correct words to complete the sentences.

1 Peeraya and Sylvie are planning a celebration for *the end of their English course* / *their friend's birthday* / *passing their English exams*.
2 Matt says that he has lived in Liverpool *for quite a long time* / *for quite a short time* / *all his life*.
3 Peeraya and Sylvie will be inviting *18* / *20* / *21* people to the celebration.
4 Sylvie does not want to go to a *big* / *chain* / *family* restaurant.
5 Both Peeraya and Sylvie would like to try *British fish and chips* / *hot and spicy Thai seafood* / *traditional English dishes*.
6 'Scouse' is a traditional *dessert* / *meat dish* / *vegetarian dish* from Liverpool.
7 To get to 'Sarah's Bistro' Peeraya and Sylvie should *turn right* / *turn left* / *go straight on* at the cash machine on Double Street.

c Write a conversation between two people discussing how to celebrate the end of their English course. Use the questions below to help you.
- How many people will go?
- Where will they go to eat? Will the place be big enough?
- Is anyone in the class a vegetarian?
- Is there any type of food that someone in the class cannot eat (for example, fish)?

Review and extension

1 GRAMMAR

Correct the sentences.

1 You must to arrive 30 minutes before the exam starts.
 You must arrive 30 minutes before the exam starts.
2 I think this is the better Greek restaurant in London.
3 Last night we must take a taxi because we'd missed the bus.
4 His house is more near the university than yours.
5 You mustn't parking outside that school.
6 He's more taller than his older brother.
7 You don't have to feed the animals in the zoo – it's forbidden.
8 I think French is easyer to learn than English.

2 VOCABULARY

Correct the sentences and questions.

1 When he realised he'd forgotten his passport, he came back to his house to get it.
 When he realised he'd forgotten his passport, he went back to his house to get it.
2 Can I borrow your spoon so I can mix my coffee?
3 We had three hours to wait so we saw round the old town.
4 The best way to move around New York is to take the subway.
5 Mash the lemon and pour the juice over the fish.
6 If you put in too much sugar, it will be too sour to drink.

3 WORDPOWER *go*

Match 1–6 with a–f to make sentences.
1 [d] I don't think anything can go
2 ☐ My English exam went
3 ☐ Unfortunately, all the tickets had gone
4 ☐ The stairs next to the lift go
5 ☐ The tie you bought yesterday goes
6 ☐ My father's hair has all gone

a really well with your blue shirt.
b down to the car park.
c by the time we got there.
d wrong because it's a brilliant plan.
e grey now but it was fair when he was young.
f really well. I think I passed.

REVIEW YOUR PROGRESS

Look again at Review your progress on p.78 of the Student's Book. How well can you do these things now?
3 = very well   2 = well   1 = not so well

I CAN …	
talk about advice and rules	☐
describe food	☐
ask for and give recommendations	☐
write a review of a restaurant or café.	☐

7A It might be a holiday home

1 GRAMMAR Modals of deduction

a Match 1–8 with a–h to make pairs of sentences.

1. [g] They may have some relatives in Miami.
2. [ ] She can't live in that tiny flat.
3. [ ] Their car's outside the house, but I haven't seen them for a few days.
4. [ ] There are a lot of people in our neighbour's garden.
5. [ ] Why's Sam wearing a suit and tie?
6. [ ] She can't still be living with her parents.
7. [ ] He might not have a well-paid job at the moment.

a They could be away on holiday.
b That's why he isn't taking his family on holiday this year.
c They might be having a party.
d She's nearly 40 years old.
e She told me she had four bedrooms and two bathrooms.
f He must be going to London today for his job interview.
g Perhaps that's why they always go there every January?

b Underline the correct words to complete the conversation.

A Some new people have just moved into the house opposite.
B Yes, I know. I saw them yesterday when they arrived. I think they're French.
A No, they ¹*mustn't / can't / must* be French. Their car has a 'P' sticker on the back.
B Oh, really? They ²*can't / couldn't / might* come from Poland, then.
A Or they ³*mustn't / could / can't* be Portuguese?
B That's true – both countries begin with a 'P'.
A Is it a family or a couple?
B It ⁴*must / can't / couldn't* be a family. They ⁵*couldn't / must / mustn't* have two or three children.
A How do you know that?
B Because I saw some children's bikes in their garden. Also, there was another woman in the car when they arrived yesterday – she was older than the mother.
A She ⁶*might / can / couldn't* be the children's grandmother.
B No, she ⁷*can / mustn't / can't* be their grandmother. She only looked about 45.
A Or she ⁸*must / can't / could* be their aunt? Or she ⁹*can't / might not / can* be a relative at all. She ¹⁰*may / can't / can* be just a friend. She ¹¹*can't / might / can* be helping them to unpack their things.
B Why don't we go and say 'hello'?
A But they ¹²*might not / can't / couldn't* speak English – it ¹³*can't / could / mustn't* be really embarrassing.
B They ¹⁴*can't / couldn't / must* speak English. I just saw them speaking to one of their neighbours and they seemed to understand each other.

c ▶7.1 Listen and check.

2 VOCABULARY Buildings

a Complete the crossword puzzle.

→ **Across**
2 I used to live in a very noisy ___block___ of flats.
6 I'd like to live in a friendly _____ that has a good primary school for my children.
7 I had a good _____ of the sea from my hotel window.
8 My office is on the 22nd _____ so I take the lift.

↓ **Down**
1 His new house is in a very convenient _____. He can walk to the city centre in five minutes.
3 We had a lovely hotel room with a large _____ outside, where I could read my book and sunbathe.
4 A lot of American houses have a large _____ under the house where the children can watch TV and play.
5 When you get to my building, ring the _____ and I'll come down to meet you.

b Underline the correct words to complete the sentences.

1 At the top of my house there's *a balcony / an attic / a basement* where we keep all the things we don't use any more.
2 When I lived in Rome I *located / hired / rented* a tiny *house / flat / landing* which only had two rooms.
3 Go up the stairs to the *landing / hall / basement* on the first *level / step / floor*. My bedroom is the first on the right.
4 The *principal / front / in front of* door has two *locks / views / steps* so take both keys when you leave the house.
5 I'm moving *off / out of / away* this flat next Saturday and moving *in / on / into* my new flat on Sunday.
6 On the *ground / earth / land* floor there's a huge *pavement / terrace / balcony* where you can sit and relax.

3 PRONUNCIATION Final sounds in modal verbs

a ▶7.2 Listen. Tick (✓) the sentences where you hear the final /t/ or /d/ of the modal verbs.

1 [✓] He mus**t** have rich parents.
2 [ ] She can'**t** be revising for her exams tonight.
3 [ ] They migh**t** enjoy going to the zoo.
4 [ ] You coul**d** invite Jenny to your party.
5 [ ] We mus**t** be quite near the centre now.
6 [ ] John mus**t** earn a lot more money than her.

7B There are plenty of things to do

1 GRAMMAR Quantifiers

a Complete the sentences with the words in the box.

| too many   plenty   many   no |
| some   a few   little   enough (x2) |

1 She doesn't have ___many___ clothes so she needs to buy _____.
2 There isn't _____ time to have a meal before the film.
3 There are _____ cars on the roads these days.
4 We've got _____ of time before the film starts, so let's go for a coffee.
5 He knows quite _____ people in London, so he won't be lonely.
6 I'm sorry but there are _____ tickets left for tonight's show.
7 She isn't fit _____ yet to run a marathon.
8 I have very _____ money left so I'm not going out tonight.

b Correct the sentences.

1 I'm late because there was much traffic in the city centre.
   I'm late because there was a lot of traffic in the city
   centre.
2 Unfortunately, there aren't no good restaurants near here.
   _____
3 He won't pass his exams because he hasn't worked enough hard this year.
   _____
4 **A** Is there many milk left?
   _____
   B Yes, we've got plenty of.
   _____
5 There were too much people at the bus stop to get on the bus.
   _____
6 There are too little eggs in the fridge to make a Spanish omelette.
   _____
7 My father's too much old to play tennis these days.
   _____
8 She made lot of mistakes in her translation.
   _____

2 VOCABULARY Verbs and prepositions

a Underline the correct words to complete the sentences.

1 He paid *about / around / for* the shopping with his credit card.
2 I complained to the receptionist *about / for / from* the dirty towels in my room.
3 They apologised to their teacher *about / for / with* not doing all their homework.
4 We try to recycle all of our rubbish because we care *for / about / with* the environment.
5 If you get into trouble, you can always depend *about / for / on* your family to help you.
6 She's thinking *about / in / at* her boyfriend.
7 It was very hard for the children to cope *about / with / for* their parents' divorce.
8 After five years in Tokyo he succeeded *for / on / in* learning Japanese.

b Complete the sentences with one word from each of the boxes.

| rely   complained   believe   apologised |
| belongs   argued   cope   worried |

| to (x2)   with (x2)   about (x2)   in   on |

1 When I was little I used to ___believe___ ___in___ ghosts.
2 She's finding it hard to _____ _____ the stress of her new job.
3 I _____ _____ Jane for forgetting her birthday.
4 You can always _____ _____ the metro as the trains run very regularly.
5 Dan's getting _____ _____ his job because his company wants to save money.
6 I think that cat _____ _____ one of my neighbours.
7 He went over the road and _____ _____ the noise his neighbour was making.
8 At the end of the meal they _____ _____ the waiter about the bill.

41

7C Everyday English
Is there anything we can do to help?

1 USEFUL LANGUAGE Offers, requests and asking for permission

a Match the questions 1–6 with the responses a–f.

1. [d] Do you think you could help me with the shopping bags?
2. [ ] Is there anything I can do to help?
3. [ ] Do you think I could have a quick shower?
4. [ ] May I use your phone?
5. [ ] Is it OK if I watch the news on TV?
6. [ ] Would you mind taking your shoes off?

a Sure, no problem. Let me turn it on for you.
b No, not at all. Where shall I leave them?
c Yes, of course. It's in the hall.
d Sure, I'll take them into the kitchen for you.
e Yes, of course. Let me get you a towel.
f Yes, there is, actually. Could you lay the table for me?

b ▶ 7.3 Listen and check.

c Complete the responses with the words in the box. There is one extra word you do not need.

~~course~~ lovely mind sure better control really

1. **A** Do you think I could borrow your camera tomorrow?
   B Yes, of _course_. It's in the living room. Here.
2. **A** I'm sorry about the problem with your computer. Is there anything I can do to help?
   B No, it's fine, _____. I think I can fix it.
3. **A** Do you think you could give me a hand with this maths homework?
   B _____. Let me have a look at it.
4. **A** Are you OK in the kitchen? Let me help you.
   B Don't worry! It's all under _____.
5. **A** Is there anything I can do for the party? I could organise some games for the kids.
   B That would be _____, thanks.
6. **A** Is it OK if I have a cheese sandwich?
   B We can do _____ than that. Come in the kitchen and I'll make you something special for lunch.

d <u>Underline</u> the correct words to complete the sentences.

1. Would you mind *open* / <u>*opening*</u> / *to open* that door for me?
2. Is it OK if I *leave* / *left* / *could leave* my coat here?
3. **A** Do you think *I'd* / *I would* / *I could* have a cup of tea?
   B Yes, of course. *I shall* / *I'll* / *I would* make one for you.
4. **A** Would you mind if *I used* / *I use* / *I'll use* your toilet?
   B Not at all. *Leave* / *Let* / *Allow* me show you where it is.
5. Is there *anything* / *nothing* / *a thing* I can do to help?
6. Excuse me. Do you think you *will* / *could* / *would* turn the music down a little, please? It's really hard to talk in here.

e ▶ 7.4 Listen and check.

2 PRONUNCIATION Sounding polite

a ▶ 7.5 Listen to the pairs of questions. Tick (✓) the question which sounds more polite: a or b.

1. a Would you mind getting me some more water? [✓]
   b Would you mind getting me some more water? [ ]
2. a Do you think you could lend me some money? [ ]
   b Do you think you could lend me some money? [ ]
3. a Is it OK if I make myself a coffee? [ ]
   b Is it OK if I make myself a coffee? [ ]
4. a Do you think I could borrow your car? [ ]
   b Do you think I could borrow your car? [ ]
5. a Do you mind if I make a quick phone call? [ ]
   b Do you mind if I make a quick phone call? [ ]

42

7D Skills for Writing
Make yourselves at home

1 READING

a Read the note and tick (✓) the correct answer.
- a ☐ Sarah hasn't left any food in her fridge for Paul.
- b ☐ You can't walk to the city centre from Sarah's house.
- c ☐ Paul's children won't get bored in York.
- d ☐ You can go swimming in Rowntree Park.

b Read the note again. Are the sentences true or false?
1. Paul needs to go to the supermarket to buy some bread for breakfast.
2. There aren't any big supermarkets in York.
3. It's easy to take the bus from Sarah's house to the city centre.
4. Paul's children would enjoy a visit to the railway museum.
5. Paul can't go swimming with his children in York.

Hi Paul!

Welcome to York! Hope you had a good journey from London and that it wasn't difficult to find my house and get the keys from my next-door neighbour.

Help yourself to anything you find in the fridge and the kitchen cupboards. For breakfast tomorrow morning you can have cereal with milk. Otherwise, there's plenty of bread to make toast and you'll find butter and strawberry jam in the fridge.

If you need to go shopping for lunch or dinner, the nearest supermarket is the little SPAR in Clifton, the main road from the city centre. You probably passed it on your way to my house. Alternatively, you can drive to the big Tesco on the A1237 at Clifton Moor, which has everything you need.

By the way, you can take the number 2 bus to the centre from the end of my road. The buses run every five minutes or so. Another option is to walk. It takes about 25 minutes to walk to the centre from here but it's good exercise.

There are plenty of things to do and see in York. You can take the kids to the Jorvik Viking Centre where they can learn all about the Vikings. Another possibility is to visit the National Railway Museum near the station. I think they'll enjoy going to both places. Apart from that, there are lots of good shops in the city centre and also plenty of nice cafés and restaurants if you prefer to eat out.

Finally, if you need some exercise there's an excellent swimming pool in Haxby Road. Alternatively, if the weather's nice you and the kids can play tennis in Rowntree Park in Terry Avenue.

Anyway, enjoy your stay and speak soon.

Love,

Sarah

2 WRITING SKILLS Offering choices

a Use one of the words or phrases in the box to connect the sentences. Make any necessary changes. There is more than one possible answer.

> Another option is   Otherwise   Alternatively
> Apart from that   Another possibility is

1. You can take the train from here to Granada. Or there is a coach which runs every two hours.
   <u>You can take the train from here to Granada. Apart from that, there is a coach which runs every two hours.</u>
2. There's a good shop at the end of my road. You could also go to the huge supermarket which is just before you get to the motorway.
3. You can get a good view of London from the London Eye. Or you can go to the top of The Shard building.
4. I suggest you go to the beach early in the morning, before it gets too hot. You could also go late in the afternoon.
5. Why don't you go to that Italian restaurant opposite Covent Garden Underground Station? Or you could try that new Japanese restaurant near Leicester Square.

3 WRITING

a Read the notes. Write a note for Pascale, the babysitter who is going to look after your two young children this evening.

Note for Pascale
1) Drinks & snacks
   - Tea & coffee by kettle. Hot chocolate in cupboard.
   - Chocolate biscuits on table. Cheesecake in fridge.
2) Dinner for children
   - Chicken soup & fish pie in fridge. Sandwiches.
3) Entertainment
   - OK to watch TV (both like X Factor).
   - Favourite DVDs are Toy Story & Pirates of the Caribbean.
4) Bedtime
   - Read bedtime story e.g. Harry Potter / The Lion, the Witch and the Wardrobe.
5) If any problems, phone:
   - 07700 900221 (Me)
   - 07700 900834 (Other person's mobile. Whose?)

43

UNIT 7
Reading and listening extension

1 READING

a Read the article. Match the paragraphs A–D with functions 1–6. There are two extra functions you do not need.

☐ Paragraph A   ☐ Paragraph C
☐ Paragraph B   ☐ Paragraph D

1 To describe how Detroit changed
2 To explain that education in Detroit has become worse
3 To make a prediction about the future of Detroit
4 To show that Detroit helped a singer become famous
5 To show that Detroit might be improving
6 To show the reader why Detroit is an important place

b Read the text again and put the information in the correct order of the article.

☐ a possible benefit of recent changes to Detroit
☐ businessmen whose relatives are from Detroit
☐ how old parts of Detroit have changed recently
☐ other names for Detroit
☐ popular songs that came from Detroit
☐ 1 a businessman who made Detroit famous
☐ the number of people who live in Detroit
☐ a famous singer who made records in Detroit
☐ the way people might think about Detroit in the future
☐ where many people in the city used to work

c Think about your hometown or another place that you know well. Make notes about:

- where it is
- how old it is
- some famous people who have lived there
- some things it is famous for / things that you can only find in that place
- some important changes that have happened there in the last 50 years.

Write a short essay about this place.

DETROIT A TALE OF TWO CITIES

A **DETROIT** was at one time one of the most famous cities in the United States, and perhaps even the world. This was the city where Henry Ford built the Ford Motor Company in 1903, and it didn't take long for Detroit to become known as 'Motor City'. Later, 'Motor City' became simply 'Motown', which was, of course, the name given to the popular American music of the 1960s and '70s that came out of the city, including The Jackson 5 – the band where Michael Jackson sang such hits as 'I Want You Back' and 'ABC'. Today, however, Detroit is a very different place.

B In 1950, the city had a population of 1.8 million and there were nearly 300,000 men and women working in its car factories. Nowadays, that population is just 700,000 and only 27,000 have jobs connected with the car industry. So many people moved out of Detroit after 2001 that by 2010, more than a third of Detroit's houses, factories and schools were empty. In lots of neighbourhoods, not only was there no more noise from the traffic but there was also no more music. The city was so cold and dark that many people thought the city had died. Then businessmen John Hantz and Michael Score moved in.

C Hantz and Score, who both have family connections in Detroit, cared about what was happening there. They also both believed in the same very simple idea – urban farms. Together, they bought lots of empty land in the city and then pulled down 50 old houses. Instead of broken buildings, there are now fields of trees. Once Hantz and Score had succeeded in showing what could be done with all that empty land, lots of other people started to create their own gardens. Men and women who used to build cars and lorries are now planting fruit and vegetables. And now something even better has happened.

D In the first ten years of the 21st century, crime increased and many residents became worried about safety on the streets at night. But now, incredibly, crime has fallen and many residents believe this must be due to the new urban farms and gardens. Although it has not been proven whether the new green spaces are the reason that crime has gone down, you can be sure that no one in the city is complaining about it! Perhaps this could be a change other cities around the world could learn from, and it might not be long before 'Motor City' becomes known as 'Green City'.

2 LISTENING

a ▶7.6 Listen to a group of friends talking. Match 1–6 with a–f to make sentences.

1. [b] They must
2. [ ] They can't
3. [ ] One of them has to
4. [ ] Some of them have to
5. [ ] Katia is the person who is
6. [ ] Ben is the person who is

a describe a place to the others.
b be playing some kind of game.
c talking about a house.
d explaining how to play the game.
e draw something.
f be in the university library.

b Listen to the conversation again. Tick (✓) the correct answer.

1. On her turn, Katia gets …
   a [ ] three. b [ ] twelve. c [ ] sixteen.
2. Luis and Daniela have to draw what she describes …
   a [ ] on the same piece of paper.
   b [ ] using a special kind of pencil.
   c [ ] without looking at their picture.
3. Where would Katia's dream home be?
   a [ ] in a village
   b [ ] in a small town
   c [ ] in a big city
4. What would Katia be able to see from her dream home?
   a [ ] a beautiful mountain lake
   b [ ] her favourite shopping centre
   c [ ] some famous places
5. What would Katia's dream home be?
   a [ ] an apartment
   b [ ] a cottage
   c [ ] a palace
6. What size would Katia's dream home be?
   a [ ] small and cosy
   b [ ] medium-sized
   c [ ] very large
7. Where would Katia like to have picnics and parties?
   a [ ] in Pushkin Square
   b [ ] on her balcony
   c [ ] in her kitchen
8. What kind of kitchen would she like to have?
   a [ ] a kitchen with gold tables and chairs
   b [ ] a modern kitchen with lots of technology
   c [ ] an old-fashioned kitchen

c Write about your dream home. Remember to include:
- the location
- the views
- the size / number of rooms
- the type of home
- what the building looks like.

Review and extension

1 GRAMMAR

Correct the sentences.

1. He isn't answering the phone so he must to be away on holiday.
   He isn't answering the phone so he must be away on holiday.
2. George isn't enough good at football to play for the school team.
3. She mustn't be the manager – she looks too young!
4. There's much traffic in the town centre during the rush hour.
5. They mustn't be doing their homework at this moment – it's nearly midnight!
6. The maths exam was too much difficult for most of the people in my class.

2 VOCABULARY

Correct the sentences.

1. His new flat is in an excellent place. There's a beautiful park opposite and the metro station's only 200 metres away.
   His new flat is in an excellent location. There's a beautiful park opposite and the metro station's only 200 metres away.
2. She complained to the waiter about the dirty glass.
3. I can't afford to buy a flat at the moment so I'm going to hire a flat in the city centre.
4. Don't worry about the bill. I'll pay the meal.
5. I live in a really nice neighbour – everyone's very friendly.
6. When he told me about the accident, I didn't believe in him at first.

3 WORDPOWER *over*

Match 1–6 with a–f to make sentences.

1. [b] I've only seen her three or four times over
2. [ ] After about three minutes, turn the steak over
3. [ ] It usually takes about seven hours to fly over
4. [ ] If the match starts at 3 o'clock, it should be over
5. [ ] By 2050 there will be over
6. [ ] There's glass all over

a the Atlantic from New York to London.
b the past 20 years.
c and cook the other side.
d the floor because I dropped a vase.
e 10 billion people living on the planet.
f by a quarter to five.

REVIEW YOUR PROGRESS

Look again at Review your progress on p.90 of the Student's Book. How well can you do these things now?
3 = very well   2 = well   1 = not so well

I CAN …

describe a building	☐
describe a town or city	☐
make offers and ask for permission	☐
write a note with useful information.	☐

45

8A He said he'd read the news online

1 GRAMMAR Reported speech: statements and questions

a Correct the mistakes in the sentences with reported speech. There may be more than one mistake in each sentence.

1 Yesterday John said, 'I'm going to phone my mother this evening.'
Yesterday John said me that he's going to phone my mother this evening.
<u>Yesterday John told me that he was going to phone his mother that evening.</u>

2 'You should wait behind this line until it is your turn.'
She said I should wait behind this line until it is your turn.
_____

3 'Are you going to Harry's party tomorrow?'
When I met her last Friday she asked to me if I'm going to Harry's party tomorrow.
_____

4 'He might be about fifty years old.'
She said me he might be about fifty years old.
_____

5 He said, 'I'm sorry but I can't come to your party this evening.'
He told he's sorry but he can't come to my party this evening.
_____

6 'Did you see your uncle when you were in New York last year?'
She asked me did I see your uncle when I were in New York last year.
_____

7 'Goodbye, Anna. I'll see you next week.'
He told Anna he will see me next week.
_____

b Complete the reported speech with the correct verb form. Change the tense where possible.

1 'Mandy's coming to stay with me next week.'
She said that <u>Mandy was coming to stay with her the following week.</u>

2 'Martin has just sent me a text message.'
He said that _____.

3 'I'll phone you when I get home from work.'
He told me _____.

4 'Are you going to buy your brother a present this afternoon?'
He asked me _____.

5 'Why can't you lend me some money?'
She asked me _____.

6 'You must stop writing immediately and give me your papers.'
The examiner said that we _____.

7 'I want you to take these flowers for your grandmother.'
She told me _____.

2 VOCABULARY The news

a Underline the correct words to complete the sentences.

1 The *reporter* / <u>*editor*</u> / *presenter* is the most important journalist at a newspaper.
2 Let's listen to the *notices* / *journals* / *news* on the radio to see if they say anything about tomorrow's underground drivers' strike.
3 If you want to know what's happening in Hollywood, you should watch the *business* / *entertainment* / *political* news.
4 News of the explosion in Washington *posted* / *communicated* / *spread* very quickly on Facebook.
5 My newspaper has four pages of *current affairs* / *celebrity gossip* / *feeds* about the lives of Hollywood actors and sports stars.
6 He's a billionaire who owns the biggest news *company* / *feed* / *organisation* in Europe.
7 There's a *current* / *news* / *politics* affairs programme on TV tonight about the presidential elections in the USA.
8 I want to watch the *entertainment* / *political* / *business* news because I'm interested in next week's local elections.

b Complete the crossword puzzle.

→ **Across**
4 Most companies advertise their products on social ___<u>media</u>___ like Facebook and Twitter.
6 She's going to be the new _____ of *The X Factor* on Channel 6.
7 Have you heard the _____ news about the accident on the motorway?
8 He _____ a comment about the concert on Facebook five minutes after it finished.

↓ **Down**
1 When she saw the _____ TRAIN CRASH DISASTER, she immediately called her husband to make sure he was all right.
2 He wrote a fascinating _____ in *The Times* about the problems of air pollution in London.
3 The local TV station sent their sports _____ to interview the new manager of the town's football team.
5 In the _____ news section of the newspaper there was an interesting article about the economic crisis.

46

8B I recommended visiting a local restaurant

1 GRAMMAR Verb patterns

a Complete the sentences with the *-ing* form or the *to* + infinitive form of the verb in brackets.

1. _Reading_ (read) a good book is an excellent way to relax before _____ (go) to bed.
2. She remembered _____ (see) the film in the cinema when she was a little girl.
3. It will be extremely difficult _____ (get) a ticket for the World Cup Final.
4. We promised _____ (come) back at the same time the following day.
5. He didn't enjoy _____ (visit) his grandparents.
6. Would you mind _____ (wait) here for me while I get changed?
7. Instead of _____ (go) to the bookshop they went to the library _____ (see) if they could borrow a copy of *Oliver Twist*.
8. In my view it isn't worth _____ (pay) to see the new Spielberg film.

b Correct the sentences.

1. I phoned Philip ask him if he wanted playing tennis at the weekend.
   I phoned Philip to ask him if he wanted to play tennis at the weekend.
2. Don't forget giving me back my book when you've finished read it.
   _____
3. He admitted to steal the old lady's handbag.
   _____
4. We hoped finding a good place to eat in one of the streets near the station.
   _____
5. He threatened telling my parents what I had done.
   _____
6. It's really important teach your children how crossing the road safely.
   _____
7. She didn't know which book buying her brother for his birthday.
   _____
8. You promised helping me with my homework!
   _____

2 VOCABULARY Shopping

a Complete the conversation with the words in the box.

sale	bargain	refund	priced
~~browsing~~	come	back	afford	value

SHOP ASSISTANT Good morning. Can I help you?
CUSTOMER 1 No, thank you. I'm just [1] _browsing_.
CUSTOMER 2 So what kind of present do you want to buy for your nephew?
CUSTOMER 1 I'm not really sure.
CUSTOMER 2 It's difficult, isn't it? Let's have a look in the computer games section. I think they said on the radio that 'Mayhem 5' was going to [2] _____ out this week.
CUSTOMER 1 Yes, I think I heard that, too. Let's see if it's on [3] _____.
CUSTOMER 2 Look, there it is. €49.90.
CUSTOMER 1 49.90! I can't [4] _____ that!
CUSTOMER 2 You're right. That's a lot of money for a computer game. Let's have a look at the special offers over there. Here's one that's reasonably [5] _____. It's from last year and it's only €19.99. That's a [6] _____, isn't it?
CUSTOMER 1 Yes, that's good [7] _____ for money. I'll buy him that one. I hope he doesn't already have it.
SHOP ASSISTANT Don't worry. He can always take it [8] _____ to his local store and change it for another one or get a [9] _____.
CUSTOMER 1 OK, that's great. I'll take it, then.

b ▶ 8.1 Listen and check.

3 VOCABULARY Reporting verbs

a Complete the sentences with the correct form of the verbs in the box.

warn	~~advise~~	refuse	offer	agree	suggest

1. 'You should apply for the Head of Marketing job.'
   He _advised_ her to apply for the Head of Marketing job.
2. 'Yes, that's fine. I'm happy to sell you my car for £5,000.'
   She _____ to sell me her car for £5,000.
3. 'Why don't we go to the beach tomorrow?'
   He _____ going to the beach the following day.
4. 'Be careful! Don't touch that plate – it's hot!'
   He _____ her not to touch the plate as it was hot.
5. 'I'm not going to lend you any more money.'
   I _____ to lend her any more money.
6. 'If you like, I can give you a lift to the station.'
   He _____ to give us a lift to the station.

47

8C Everyday English
On the whole, I prefer taking action shots

1 USEFUL LANGUAGE
Generalising

a Put the words in the right order to make sentences.
1 be / film / of / honest, / the / was / boring / kind / to .
   <u>To be honest, the film was kind of boring.</u>
2 my / tend / Americans / be / experience, / friendly / to / very / in .
   _____
3 normally / that / thing / of / I / like / kind / don't .
   _____
4 whole, / I / his / liked / film / the / new / on .
   _____
5 songs / of / his / can / depressing / some / rather / be .
   _____
6 a / coffee / Italian / is / rule, / excellent / as .
   _____

b ▶8.2 Listen and check.

2 CONVERSATION SKILLS Being vague

a Complete the sentences with the words in the box.

| whole   stuff   ~~that~~   couple   sort |

1 He likes hip hop and rap music – you know, stuff like ___that___.
2 We had a _____ of days when it was cloudy and rainy, but on the _____ we had pretty good weather.
3 Don't touch all that _____ in his office, please.
4 She likes watching documentaries about animals and nature and that _____ of thing.

b ▶8.3 Listen and check.

3 PRONUNCIATION
Sound and spelling: /h/ and /w/

a ▶8.4 Listen to the sentences. Put the words in **bold** in the correct columns.
1 **When** did you last see her?
2 They **went** the **wrong way** and got lost.
3 **Whose** suitcase was the **heaviest**?
4 I **wrote** a long letter to my uncle in Scotland.
5 I didn't know **which** book to get my **husband**.
6 She **had** to wait two **hours** for the next train to London.

Sound 1 /h/ (e.g. *h*ot)	Sound 2 /w/ (e.g. *w*ith)	First letter silent (e.g. *h*onest)

b ▶8.5 Listen and check.

48

8D Skills for Writing
Fortunately, everything was all right

1 READING

a Read the email and tick (✓) the correct answer.

a ☐ The alligator attacked Blackie and broke his leg.
b ☐ The alligator bit Pam and broke her leg.
c ☐ Blackie was afraid of the alligator and didn't stay with Pam.
d ☐ Pam broke her leg while she was walking with Blackie.

✉ I read an amazing story in the newspaper this morning about a dog called Blackie who saved his owner's life in Florida. It seems that his owner, Pam Evans, who is 79 years old, was walking near a lake when she fell over and broke her leg. Unfortunately, she couldn't move and didn't have a mobile phone so she couldn't call for help. At that moment, a huge alligator came out of the lake and started walking towards Pam, threatening to attack her. Incredibly, Blackie wasn't frightened by the alligator and, apparently, he started fighting it to try and protect Pam. Amazingly, after a few minutes, the alligator gave up trying to attack Pam and went back into the lake. Fortunately, a man who was near the lake with his dog heard Blackie barking and came to rescue Pam. It seems that he then phoned for an ambulance, which immediately took Pam to hospital. Luckily, neither Pam nor Blackie were hurt in the attack and Pam has now made a full recovery.

b Read the news story again. Are the sentences true or false?

1 Pam Evans has a dog called Blackie.
2 Pam couldn't call for help because her mobile phone was broken.
3 When Blackie saw the alligator he was very frightened and ran away.
4 The man near the lake called for an ambulance.
5 Blackie was seriously injured by the alligator.

2 WRITING SKILLS
Summarising information

a Use one of the words in the box to connect the sentences. Make any necessary changes. Sometimes there is more than one possible answer.

before   who   but   with   and   which

1 The man spent several hours looking for his son. Unfortunately, he couldn't find him anywhere.
   <u>The man spent several hours looking for his son but,</u>
   <u>unfortunately, he couldn't find him anywhere.</u>

2 I heard a story on the radio about an elephant. Apparently, it sat on a car in a safari park.

3 The 12-year-old girl stole her father's motorbike. She rode it for 40 km along the motorway. The police stopped her near Oxford.

4 The woman hit the teenager hard on his head with her umbrella. Then she used his mobile phone to call the police.

5 Amanda escaped from the burning building by breaking a window. She used her shoe to break the window.

6 There was an incredible story on the news about a baby in China. She fell from a fourth-floor window. She wasn't hurt because a man in the street caught her.

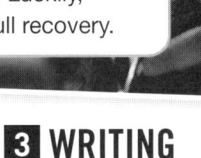

3 WRITING

a Read the notes. Write the story.

FAMILY'S LUCKY ESCAPE WHEN CAR CRASHES INTO HOUSE

Car crashed into house. Manchester.
Family watching TV in living room at time of accident. Heard loud noise.
Driver lost control of car. Drove straight through front door. Stopped 2 metres from kitchen.
No-one seriously hurt. Driver & 3 passengers only minor injuries.
Police were called. Arrived 5 minutes later.
Front of house badly damaged.
Car removed. Took fire service 6 hours.

UNIT 8
Reading and listening extension

1 READING

a Read the article and tick (✓) the correct answers.
1. Why has the article been written?
   - a ☐ to encourage more students to take courses in journalism
   - b ☐ to explain why careers in journalism have become popular with students
   - c ☐ to show the advantages and disadvantages of a career in journalism
2. Who has the article been written for?
   - a ☐ owners of news organisations
   - b ☐ professional journalists
   - c ☐ students who study journalism
3. Which of these things do Mercedes and Frankie have in common?
   - a ☐ They both earn good money at their job.
   - b ☐ They both love their work.
   - c ☐ They both studied journalism at university.
4. Mercedes and Frankie both agree that people who want to become journalists …
   - a ☐ need to travel all over the world.
   - b ☐ should be really interested in journalism.
   - c ☐ will have to work at weekends.

b Read the text again and tick (✓) the correct answers.

Who …	Mercedes	Frankie	Neither Mercedes nor Frankie
1 works when they are travelling?	✓		
2 enjoys thinking about the readers of their stories?			
3 has a parent that was also a journalist?			
4 does not sleep very much?			
5 won a prize for journalism while at university?			
6 often writes more than one story in a day?			
7 always knew they wanted to be a journalist?			
8 became a journalist by accident?			
9 takes their own photos for their stories?			
10 has no free time in the mornings?			
11 works from home?			
12 writes stories of 1,000 words?			

c Read the notice from a student magazine. Write a short article.

We are looking for people to tell us about their experiences of work or study. We would like you to write a short article explaining:
- what your job is or what you are studying
- why you have chosen the job or course you are doing
- a typical day at work or at university.

CAREERS FOR LIFE

*A report this week announced that **journalism courses** are now more popular than ever with students. But what is it like to work as a journalist? Here, two young journalists tell Careers for Life about their experience.*

THE NEWSPAPER JOURNALIST
Mercedes Alvarado, 24

A typical day for me starts at 7 am. The morning is always the hardest part of the day because I have to work all the time without any breaks. I only have about 7 or 8 hours to finish a story and there is a lot to do in that time.

First, I have to interview people for the story and sometimes that means travelling quite a long way. I usually go by train so that I can carry on working on my laptop. I also need to think about photos for the story. These days I usually buy pictures from a photo agency but sometimes a photographer goes with me on a story. I usually have to write a story of about 1,000 words and it can be very difficult to do that in only a few hours. By 4 pm I'm usually exhausted, but I don't normally leave work until 5 pm.

I have wanted to be a journalist since I was five years old and I studied journalism at university, so working for a newspaper has been a dream come true. Journalism is a great career but can be a very stressful one that does not pay very well. Anyone who is thinking of becoming a journalist needs to know that.

THE BUSINESS BLOGGER
Frankie Kaufman, 20

I had never had any plans to become a journalist but then I started my business blog when I was still at university. I wasn't enjoying life as a student so when a news organisation offered to pay me for my reports I immediately accepted. I eventually quit university to blog full time, even though I've never actually had any training as a reporter.

My day starts at 4 am when I check Twitter in bed to find out what has happened around the world during the night. I start preparing my first report at around 4.30 am and it is usually finished and on my website by 5.30 am. In a normal day I can expect to write maybe five or six reports and I usually manage to sell at least two or three of them to news agencies. It's really exciting when an agency from another country buys one of my reports. I love the idea that something that I wrote in my kitchen is being read by someone in Dubai or Dallas.

I make good money but I work hard for it. I often don't go to bed until 11 pm and I usually work 7 days a week. I would say that unless you are really in love with journalism this is not a career for you.

50

2 LISTENING

a ▶8.6 Listen to a conversation between two friends, Cathy and Cindy. Are the sentences true or false?

1. One of the women bought a painting.
2. One of the women bought something that she is not happy with.
3. One of the women has been in an argument in a shop.
4. One of the women has bought a pair of boots.
5. One of the women has some good news.
6. One of the women is an artist.
7. One of the women is complaining about something.
8. One of the women is the manager of a shop.

b Listen to the conversation again and tick (✓) the correct answers.

1. When did Cathy buy the boots?
   a ☐ in the morning
   b ☐ yesterday
   c ☐ last week
2. Why did Cathy think the boots were 'good value'?
   a ☐ They were half price.
   b ☐ They were designer boots.
   c ☐ They only cost £50.
3. The problem was that Cathy was given …
   a ☐ boots that had been damaged.
   b ☐ boots of the wrong size.
   c ☐ boots in white instead of brown.
4. Cathy didn't notice the problem until later because the shop assistant …
   a ☐ didn't open the box for her.
   b ☐ hid the problem from her.
   c ☐ gave her the wrong box.
5. The manager of the shop …
   a ☐ offered to give Cathy another pair of boots.
   b ☐ promised to give Cathy a refund.
   c ☐ refused to give Cathy her money back.
6. What is Cathy going to do next?
   a ☐ She is going to call the police.
   b ☐ She is not sure what to do next.
   c ☐ She is going to sell the boots.

c Write a conversation between two people who are Cathy's friends. Person A tells Person B what happened to Cathy; Person B asks questions. Listen to the conversation again and make notes to help you retell the story.

Review and extension

1 GRAMMAR

Correct the sentences.

1. She said me she didn't like horror films.
   She told me she didn't like horror films.
2. They asked me was I going to the football match.
3. He has agreed taking us to the airport.
4. When I phoned him last night, he said he has just finished his exams.
5. She advised me not tell anyone about our meeting.
6. Yesterday he told he would help me with my homework.
7. I'm really looking forward to see you on Sunday.

2 VOCABULARY

Correct the sentences.

1. I was shocked when I heard the notices on the radio about the explosion.
   I was shocked when I heard the news on the radio about the explosion.
2. The new song by Rihanna is going to come across next week.
3. My sister likes reading the celebrity gossips pages in the Sunday paper.
4. He adviced me to buy a new laptop because mine is over five years old.
5. I don't usually watch programmes about politic on TV.
6. She remembered me to book a table at the restaurant.
7. The main title on the front page of my newspaper today is BARACK WINS U.S. ELECTION.

3 WORDPOWER in/on + noun

Underline the correct words to complete the sentences.

1. There are some beautiful photos of Venice *in* / *on* this magazine.
2. I sent him a message *in* / *on* Facebook but he hasn't replied yet.
3. It's better to watch this film *in* / *on* a big screen at the cinema.
4. You always look so pretty *in* / *on* photos!
5. There's always an easy crossword *in* / *on* my newspaper.
6. Is there anything good *in* / *on* TV tonight?
7. Can you pay me *in* / *on* US dollars, please?
8. Do you have this T-shirt *in* / *on* a large size, please?

REVIEW YOUR PROGRESS

Look again at Review your progress on p.102 of the Student's Book. How well can you do these things now?
3 = very well   2 = well   1 = not so well

I CAN …

talk about the news	☐
talk about what other people say	☐
generalise and be vague	☐
write an email summary of a news story.	☐

9A The film is still loved today

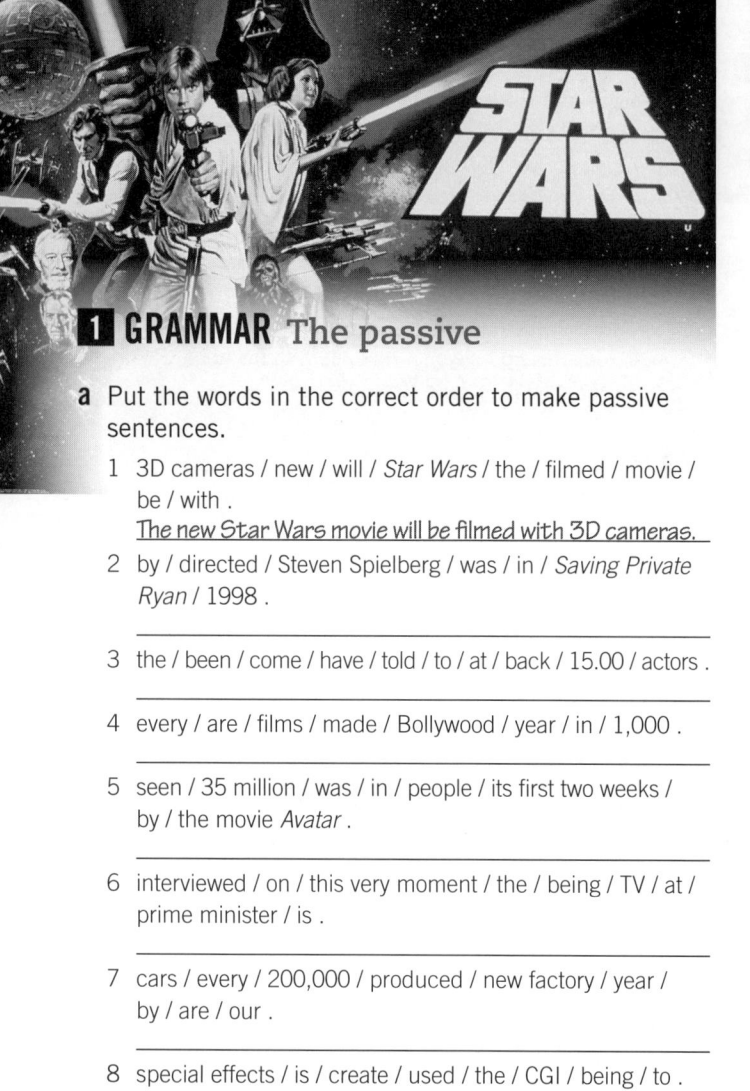

1 GRAMMAR The passive

a Put the words in the correct order to make passive sentences.

1. 3D cameras / new / will / *Star Wars* / the / filmed / movie / be / with .
   The new Star Wars movie will be filmed with 3D cameras.
2. by / directed / Steven Spielberg / was / in / *Saving Private Ryan* / 1998 .
3. the / been / come / have / told / to / at / back / 15.00 / actors .
4. every / are / films / made / Bollywood / year / in / 1,000 .
5. seen / 35 million / was / in / people / its first two weeks / by / the movie *Avatar* .
6. interviewed / on / this very moment / the / being / TV / at / prime minister / is .
7. cars / every / 200,000 / produced / new factory / year / by / are / our .
8. special effects / is / create / used / the / CGI / being / to .

b Rewrite the sentences. Use the passive.

1. They built 250,000 new houses each year in the 1990s.
   250,000 new houses were built each year in the 1990s.
2. They grow five different varieties of orange in this region.
   Five _____
3. The government will give students a loan to pay for their university fees.
   Students _____
4. They are creating the special effects with the latest animation software.
   The special effects _____
5. They've asked the actors to give some of their fees to charity.
   The actors _____
6. He was driving the car really fast when the accident happened.
   The car _____
7. The journalist asked the pop star about his new album.
   The pop star _____
8. A little girl in a pink dress gave the president a big bunch of flowers.
   The president _____

2 VOCABULARY Cinema and TV

a Complete the sentences with the words in the box.

drama   chat show   horror   action   thriller   game show
documentary   science fiction   soap opera   animated

1. *Captain Phillips* is a ___drama___ starring Tom Hanks about an American boat that is hijacked by Somali pirates.
2. *Dracula* is one of the most famous _____ films of all time.
3. I saw a really exciting _____ at the cinema on Saturday. It was about a detective who was trying to prevent a gang from stealing a famous painting from the National Gallery.
4. I'm not very keen on _____ _____ films like *Star Wars* or *The Matrix*.
5. My friend was on the _____ _____ *Who Wants to Be a Millionaire?* and won £5,000!
6. There was a fascinating wildlife _____ on TV last night about African elephants.
7. I think *Shrek* is one of the best _____ films for children I've ever seen.
8. They had some brilliant guests on that _____ _____ on Channel 4: Brad Pitt and Lady Gaga!
9. I love _____ films like *Mission: Impossible* and the James Bond series.
10. *EastEnders* is a very popular _____ _____ on British TV about the everyday lives of a group of people who live in the East End of London.

b Complete the crossword puzzle.

→ Across
2. It took six months to ___film___ *Titanic* and it cost over $200 million to make.
4. In *The Curious Case of Benjamin Button*, Brad Pitt plays a _____ who gets younger and younger as the film progresses.
5. The film *Romeo and Juliet* stars Leonardo DiCaprio and Claire Danes, and is _____ _____ the famous play by William Shakespeare.

↓ Down
1. The _____ is the person who gives instructions to the actors and takes all the important decisions when a film is being made.
3. In my opinion, the best _____ in the film is when Paul and Sarah meet again after 25 years.

9B I went to a concert which changed my life

1 GRAMMAR Defining and non-defining relative clauses

a Rewrite the sentences. Use the information in brackets as a non-defining relative clause.

1 The opera singer gave us some free tickets for her concert. (Her husband is a famous author.)
   The opera singer, whose husband is a famous author, gave us some free tickets for her concert.

2 While you're in Italy you should visit the town of Verona. (There is a lovely Roman amphitheatre in Verona.)
   _____

3 John Lennon was murdered in 1980. (He was a member of the pop group The Beatles.)
   _____

4 Pelé was a famous Brazilian footballer. (His real name is Edson Arantes do Nascimento.)
   _____

5 Steven Spielberg was the director of the film *Saving Private Ryan*. (It was about a group of American soldiers in the Second World War.)
   _____

6 First we went to Paris and then we took the train to Lyon. (In Paris we visited the Eiffel Tower.)
   _____

7 In my view, Bruce Springsteen's best album is *The River*. (He recorded it in 1980.)
   _____

8 Bill Clinton is giving a talk at our university next month. (He was President of the USA from 1993 to 2001.)
   _____

2 VOCABULARY Music

a Complete the words in the text.

① When I was in London last summer I went to a superb concert during the BBC Proms, which is a ¹f_estival_ of classical music at the Royal Albert Hall. It's great to hear a symphony or a concerto when it's ²p_____ by an ³o_____ of professional ⁴m_____ who are playing ⁵l_____. They played symphonies by Mahler and Beethoven and there was also a huge ⁶c_____ of 80 people that sang Mozart's Requiem. At the end of the concert everyone in the ⁷a_____ stood up and gave the performers a standing ovation which lasted for over five minutes.

② I've just heard on the radio that the band have been in the ⁸r_____ studio for the last month. They're making a new ⁹a_____ of jazz, soul and blues songs, which they're bringing out in September. I've just listened to an amazing ¹⁰p_____ of their old songs on the Internet. It's got about 30 ¹¹t_____ on it and most of them are old songs of theirs from the 80s and 90s.

b ▶9.1 Listen and check.

3 VOCABULARY Word-building: nouns

a Complete the sentences with the noun forms of the words in brackets.

1 Lots of writers have tried to describe the __beauty__ (beautiful) of the Taj Mahal in India.
2 My football team gave its best _____ (perform) of the season and won the match 4 – 0.
3 He has donated £100 to a _____ (charitable) that is providing schools for poor villages in Africa.
4 We believe that staff _____ (develop) is very important so we provide regular training courses for all of our employees.
5 In my view, money can't buy you _____ (happy).
6 You need plenty of _____ (creative) to write good children's stories.
7 There will be a huge _____ (celebrate) in Edinburgh this New Year's Eve, with live performances by bands and a big fireworks display.
8 There is a fascinating exhibition of Aztec art and _____ (cultural) at the British Museum at the moment.

4 PRONUNCIATION Defining and non-defining relative clauses

a ▶9.2 Listen to the sentences. Is the relative clause defining or non-defining? Tick (✓) the correct box.

	Defining	Non-defining
1 … which have a lot of adverts …	✓	
2 … which they recorded in 2010 …		
3 … whose brother is also a musician …		
4 … who eat healthily…		
5 … which my sister went to …		
6 … which last more than three hours …		

53

9C Everyday English
It's meant to be excellent

1 USEFUL LANGUAGE
Recommending and responding

a Underline the correct words to complete the conversation.

PAM Hi, Mel. Listen. Ian and I were thinking of ¹*go / going* out for a meal this weekend. ²*Do / Would* you guys like to ³*come / coming* with us?
MEL Yes, ⁴*it's / that's* a great idea. Where were you planning ⁵*going / to go*?
PAM We ⁶*think / thought* about going to that new Chinese restaurant in town. It's ⁷*meaning / meant* to be really good.
MEL ⁸*Hang / Wait* on a second. I'll just ask Tony … Sorry, Pam, but Tony isn't a big fan ⁹*from / of* Chinese food.
PAM OK, never mind. We could go somewhere ¹⁰*other / else*.
MEL Oh, I know. How about ¹¹*go / going* to that new Italian restaurant near the station?
PAM Mmm, that ¹²*seems / sounds* interesting.
MEL Yes, it's ¹³*supposed / suggested* to be excellent, and very good value for money.
PAM Yes, I'm sure Ian ¹⁴*likes / would like* it. He loves pizzas and pasta.
MEL Good. ¹⁵*Shall / Will* I book a table for Saturday evening?
PAM Yes, that would be perfect for us. Why ¹⁶*won't / don't* we get a table for 8 o'clock?
MEL Yes, OK. I'll book one.

b ▶9.3 Listen and check.

c Complete the words.
1 Sorry, but Sean isn't a big f*an*____ of science fiction films. What other films are on?
2 The new novel by JK Rowling, who wrote the Harry Potter books, is s_____ to be really good.
3 The new animated film from Pixar has had great r_____ in the papers.
4 **A** There's a documentary about the Roman occupation of Britain on TV tonight.
  B Really? That s_____ interesting.
5 I'm not s_____ my father would be i_____ in going to an exhibition of surrealist paintings.
6 This hotel was r_____ by a friend of mine, who stayed here last year.
7 That's a great i_____. I'm sure Andy would l_____ it.
8 The new Greek restaurant near my house is m_____ to be very good.

d ▶9.4 Listen and check.

2 PRONUNCIATION
Showing contrast

a ▶9.5 Listen to the exchanges. Underline the word or words which are stressed in the responses.

1 **A** Did you go to the concert with Luke?
  B No, I went with Will.
2 **A** Did James go to Edinburgh by bus?
  B No, he went on the train.
3 **A** So, your friend's a famous actor?
  B No, she's a famous dancer.
4 **A** So, you're from Lecce, in the south of Italy?
  B No, I'm from Lecco, in the north of Italy.
5 **A** Are you meeting your friend Pam on Thursday?
  B No, I'm meeting my friend Sam, on Tuesday.

9D Skills for Writing
I like going out, but …

1 READING

a Read the text and tick (✓) the correct answer.

Mike likes watching sport on TV because …
a ☐ he can't see the players when he is in the stadium.
b ☐ it's less expensive than going to the stadium.
c ☐ it's dangerous to go to the stadium.
d ☐ it's more exciting to watch the match at home.

b Read the text again. Are the sentences true or false?
1 Everyone in Mike's family likes watching their local team.
2 The sports channels that show live football matches are free.
3 It is easier to see what is happening when you are in the stadium.
4 The TV commentator tells you lots of interesting things about the players.
5 Mike doesn't like being in a huge stadium with thousands of other people.

Why I prefer watching sport on TV
by Mike Adams

I love all kinds of sport, especially football, rugby and tennis. However, I prefer watching it live on TV instead of going to the stadium.

The first reason for staying at home to watch sport is the cost. Although my whole family are big fans of our local football team, I can't afford to pay for four tickets to watch a match at the stadium every two weeks. While I have to pay extra to get the sports channels which show live football matches every week, it is much cheaper than going to the stadium.

Another reason I prefer watching sport live on TV is that you get a better view of the action. In a stadium the spectators are not usually very close to the players so it is sometimes difficult to see everything that happens clearly. Furthermore, on TV they show you the action from lots of different angles and they replay the most important parts of the match again and again. And when you watch a match on TV the commentator explains what is happening and gives you lots of interesting information about the players and the teams, which you don't get when you're watching in the stadium.

Finally, I don't enjoy being in a place where there are 50,000 other people. It's true that these days football stadiums are very safe places to watch matches. However, I sometimes get claustrophobic when I'm in a big crowd of people so it's much better to be at home, where I can watch a match with my family or just a few friends.

So, although watching a match on TV probably isn't as exciting as being in the stadium, I generally prefer watching sport live on TV. It's cheaper, I can see the action more easily and I can share the experience with my family and friends.

2 WRITING SKILLS Contrasting ideas

a Underline the correct words to complete the sentences.
1 I enjoyed seeing the new film *Julius Caesar* at the cinema, *although / in spite of / while* the noisy family who were sitting behind me.
2 *However / Despite / Although* I generally enjoy science fiction films, I wouldn't recommend the film *Black Hole*.
3 Steven Spielberg is a great director. *However / While / Although*, I thought his last film was actually rather boring.
4 *However / Although / Despite* the loud rock music that accompanied most of the action scenes, I really enjoyed the film.
5 *Despite / While / However* I agree with you that George Clooney is a good actor, I think he's mainly famous because of his looks.
6 *Although / Despite / However* it's more convenient to download movies from the Internet, more and more people are watching films at their local cinemas.
7 *Despite / While / Although* the superb acting and the exciting action scenes, I thought the film was too long and rather boring.
8 *While / However / In spite of* the amazing special effects, I wouldn't recommend seeing that film because the story wasn't very interesting.

3 WRITING

a Read the notes. Write an article explaining why you prefer reading the original book rather than a film which has been adapted from a book.

Why I prefer reading a book
Paragraph 1
• Introduction: State your position.
Paragraph 2
• Longer to read a book than watch a film. More enjoyment from books.
• Interesting details often cut from films.
Paragraph 3
• Need to use your imagination when reading a story.
• In films, director decides appearance of people and places, not you.
Paragraph 4
• Books a great way to relax. Can enter a world that author created.
• Can read a book anywhere. Very convenient.
Paragraph 5
• Conclusion: Repeat the main points.

55

UNIT 9
Reading and listening extension

1 READING

a Read the text. Are the sentences true or false?
1. The main topic of the text is Marc Boulanger.
2. Marc Boulanger knows a lot about popular African music.
3. Marc Boulanger is from France.
4. Konono Nº1 is the name of a music festival.
5. 'Tommo23' is interested in what Marc Boulanger wrote.
6. 'ShSh41' agrees with Marc Boulanger.

b Read the text again and tick (✓) the correct answer.
1. Why was Konono Nº1's concert so interesting for Marc?
   a ☐ because Fela Kuti had recommended the band to him
   b ☐ because he had never visited Paris before
   c ☐ because it was the first time he had ever heard popular African music
   d ☐ because their music was not similar to anything else he knew
2. Who used to make traditional instruments out of elephant tusks?
   a ☐ Fela Kuti
   b ☐ Kanda Bongo Man
   c ☐ People from Angola
   d ☐ The Bazombo people
3. What is a *likembé*?
   a ☐ a kind of elephant
   b ☐ a kind of instrument
   c ☐ a kind of musician
   d ☐ a kind of sound
4. All the instruments used by Konono Nº1 have been made by hand …
   a ☐ apart from the instruments they found in the street.
   b ☐ except the electric instruments, which they bought.
   c ☐ including all the electric instruments which they use.
   d ☐ except for the piano and drums.
5. According to 'ShSh41', who combined music with politics?
   a ☐ Fela Kuti
   b ☐ Kanda Bongo Man
   c ☐ Konono Nº1
   d ☐ Mawangu Mingiedi

c You are going to write a blog for *Heroes of Music*. First, make notes about a singer, musician or band whose music you like very much. Use the Internet to help you make notes about:
- the name of the singer/musician/band
- the history of the singer/musician/band
- any interesting details about the singer/musician/band

HEROES OF MUSIC

Marc Boulanger, on the sweet sounds of Congolese band, Konono Nº1:

I was just 15 when I saw Konono Nº1 perform live. They were playing a concert in Paris, my hometown, and although I had been serious about playing music since the age of 10, I had never seen or heard anything like this band before. I don't mean that I had never heard any popular African music before. Even at 15, I had already heard of musicians such as Fela Kuti and Kanda Bongo Man. So what was different about this folk orchestra?

First of all, I think it is the way that they mix modern culture with the cultural traditions of the Bazombo people, who live near the border with Angola. In that ancient tradition, musical instruments were made out of elephant tusks*. But Mawangu Mingiedi, the musician who started Konono Nº1, introduced electric *likembé* (a traditional *likembé* is part piano, part drum). They have a really special sound – they have a beauty which you just won't hear anywhere else.

Secondly, the instruments they use are really interesting. Every one of them has been made out of old bits of wood and metal and other rubbish that they have found just lying around. Even the electric instruments that they use have been made using batteries from old cars and broken lamps as well as small magnets. Again, this all helps to create a sound that is unlike anything else you might hear.

Finally, there is the amazing rhythm they use. Every time I listen to it I get a really strong feeling of excitement. Everyone who hears that beat is filled with so much happiness that they just have to start dancing.

💬 COMMENTS

Posted by: Tommo23 09:13

Thanks for this. I've just read Marc's full article. Really great story. They're going to do a performance at this year's Edinburgh festival in August. I can't wait to go.

Posted by: ShSh41 10:23

Yeah, I don't know. In spite of my love of African music I think there are other bands who are more important than these guys. Fela Kuti is just the best. Now there was a guy who managed to put music and politics together. Definitely a hero for me.

56

Review and extension

1 GRAMMAR

Correct the sentences.

1 *Romeo and Juliet* is written from Shakespeare.
   Romeo and Juliet was written by Shakespeare.
2 A new bridge is built at the moment with a Chinese construction company.
3 I interviewed the actor which had just won an Oscar.
4 *Sunflowers* was painted from Vincent Van Gogh.
5 Where the new James Bond film being made?
6 He's the player used to be in our team.

2 VOCABULARY

Correct the sentences.

1 There was a brilliant documentation about the Antarctic on TV last night.
   There was a brilliant documentary about the Antarctic on TV last night.
2 The actor was annoyed because someone in the crowd had forgotten to switch off his mobile phone.
3 My father's a professional music who plays the clarinet in the London Philharmonic Orchestra.
4 In *Titanic*, Leonardo DiCaprio plays a personality who falls in love with the daughter of an American millionaire.
5 When I was about sixteen I saw The Rolling Stones play life at a festival in Germany.
6 I'm not very keen on terror films like *Dracula*.

3 WORDPOWER
see, look at, watch, hear, listen to

Correct the sentences. Use the correct form of the verbs *see*, *look (at)*, *watch*, *hear*, or *listen (to)*.

1 Why don't we see the match on TV at your house?
   Why don't we watch the match on TV at your house?
2 Have you watched my brother? He said he'd meet me here.
3 I don't hear why you're so angry with us.
4 She always hears pop music in her bedroom.
5 I'm looking at my grandparents next Sunday.
6 Sorry, this phone's terrible. I can't listen to you very well.
7 I've finished this exercise. Please see it for me.

REVIEW YOUR PROGRESS

Look again at Review your progress on p.114 of the Student's Book. How well can you do these things now?
3 = very well   2 = well   1 = not so well

I CAN ...

talk about films and TV	☐
give extra information	☐
recommend and respond to recommendations	☐
write an article.	☐

2 LISTENING

a ▶9.6 Listen to three people talking and tick (✓) the correct answers.

1 The speakers must be ...
   a ☐ at a local cinema.
   b ☐ at someone's house.
   c ☐ in a classroom.
2 The speakers are trying to decide ...
   a ☐ what to buy.
   b ☐ what to eat.
   c ☐ what to watch.
3 Which type of film do the women not want to watch?
   a ☐ comedy
   b ☐ documentary
   c ☐ science fiction
4 Which type of film do they all agree to watch?
   a ☐ comedy
   b ☐ documentary
   c ☐ science fiction

b Listen again. Complete the sentences with the words you hear in the conversation.

1 The man says he remembered to order a __vegetarian__ pizza.
2 They are going to watch the films on the _____.
3 *Blackfish* is the name of a _____ film.
4 The man thinks the film *Blackfish* will probably be quite _____.
5 According to one of the women, the film *Man on the Moon* has amazing _____, beautiful photography and a great story.
6 The man does not think that *Man on the Moon* is a _____.
7 The film they all agree to watch is an _____ film.

c Write about the kind of films you like. Think about these questions:

- Do you think animated films are only for children? Why / Why not?
- If you could direct a film, what type of film would you most like to direct? Why?
- Which book would you most like to be made into a film? Why?

57

10A If I was fitter, I'd do it!

1 GRAMMAR Second conditional

a Complete the sentences with the correct forms of the verbs in brackets. Use contractions where possible.

1 If you __weren't__ (not be) so busy, you _____ (can) train to run a marathon.
2 I _____ (take) my daughter to the match if she _____ (be) interested in football.
3 I _____ (go) to the theatre at least once a month if I _____ (live) in London.
4 If I _____ (speak) Spanish, I _____ (apply) for a job in Madrid.
5 I'm sure you _____ (like) her if you _____ (know) her better.
6 I _____ (learn) another foreign language if I _____ (not have) so much work at the moment.
7 My sister _____ (buy) a new car if she _____ (can) afford it.
8 Germany don't have a very strong team at the moment, so I _____ (not be) surprised if England _____ (beat) them tomorrow.

b Decide if the first or second conditional is more suitable for each situation. Complete the sentences using the correct form of the verbs in the box. Use contractions where possible.

| be (x3)   have   not live   visit   come |
| pass   train   pay   not lose   finish |

1 You've studied really hard this year. If you __pass__ your exams, I _____ for your holiday to the USA.
2 He never goes to football training. If he _____ every day, he _____ a much better player.
3 Our team has won its last 10 matches. If we _____ our next match, we _____ champions again.
4 My current salary isn't very high. I _____ able to afford to buy a house if I _____ a job with a better salary.
5 Unfortunately, I live over 250 kilometres from my parents' house. If I _____ so far away, I _____ them more often.
6 I've nearly done all my homework. I _____ and watch the match at your house if I _____ it before nine o'clock.

2 VOCABULARY Sport

a Underline the correct words to complete the sentences.

1 If your *competitor* / <u>opponent</u> / *referee* doesn't return the ball, you *miss* / *beat* / *score* a point.
2 No, I didn't enjoy the cup final. My team *lost* / *beat* / *missed* the match 2 – 0.
3 We *didn't win* / *didn't beat* / *didn't score* the match because you *lost* / *missed* / *attacked* that penalty.
4 The last time we played tennis together, I *won* / *lost* / *beat* you easily.
5 If you love swimming in the sea, perhaps you should *have a go* / *compete* / *win* at scuba diving?
6 A standard athletics *court* / *pitch* / *track* has eight lanes and each lap is 400 metres.

3 VOCABULARY Adjectives and prepositions

a Complete the sentences with one word from each box.

| essential   ~~proud~~   scared   similar   worried   interested   good |
| of (x2)   for   to   in   about   at |

1 That was the day my son won his gold medal. I was so __proud__ __of__ him.
2 Plenty of exercise and a good diet are _____ _____ a healthy lifestyle.
3 I'm not very _____ _____ current affairs.
4 I'm not very _____ _____ skiing. I love it but I always fall over and I have to go on the easiest slopes!
5 I think Portuguese is very _____ _____ Spanish.
6 My son hasn't done enough work so he's really _____ _____ his exams.
7 She didn't want to go to the top of the Eiffel Tower because she was _____ _____ heights.

4 PRONUNCIATION Strong and weak forms: *would*

a ▶10.1 Listen to the pronunciation of *would* in these sentences. Is it strong (stressed) or weak (not stressed)? Write S (strong) or W (weak).

1 [W] I **would** go to the gym more often.
2 [ ] **A Would** he apply for a job in London?
  [ ] **B** No, he **wouldn't**.
3 [ ] She **wouldn't** lend you any money.
4 [ ] You **wouldn't** enjoy that film – it's too scary.
5 [ ] **A Would** you like to go for a pizza?
  [ ] **B** Yes, I **would**.

10B Making the most of opportunities

1 GRAMMAR Third conditional

a Underline the correct words to complete the sentences.
1 She *had won / might have won / would win* the gold medal if she *hadn't fallen / didn't fall / wouldn't have fallen* over at the start.
2 I *wouldn't have been able to / couldn't / hadn't been able to* get back into my house if *I would've lost / I've lost / I'd lost* my keys.
3 She *hadn't married / wouldn't have married / didn't marry* him if *she would've known / she knew / she'd known* that he'd been in prison.
4 If she *hadn't / wouldn't have / hasn't* helped him so much, he *mightn't have / hadn't / won't have* passed his exams.
5 We *hadn't / wouldn't have / won't have* got lost if you *hadn't / wouldn't have / had* forgotten to bring the map.
6 If she *wouldn't read / didn't read / hadn't read* that letter, she *didn't find / wouldn't have found / hadn't found* out about her family in Russia.
7 They *would have won / had won / would win* the match if their captain *didn't miss / hadn't missed / wouldn't miss* that penalty!
8 If it *didn't start / hadn't started / wouldn't have started* raining, we *had finished / would finish / could have finished* our game of tennis.

b Complete the text with the third conditional form of the verbs in brackets. Use contractions where possible.

This is the story of how I met my wife Jane. It all started when I was going to work by taxi and it suddenly broke down. If my taxi ¹ **hadn't broken** (not/break) down, I ² _____ (get) to the station on time. If I ³ _____ (arrive) at the station on time, I ⁴ _____ (not/miss) my train. If I ⁵ _____ (not/miss) the train, I ⁶ _____ (not/have to) wait an hour for the next one. If I ⁷ _____ (not/have to) wait for an hour, I ⁸ _____ (not/go) to the café for a coffee. If I ⁹ _____ (not/have) a coffee, I ¹⁰ _____ (not/meet) my friend Sarah – and if I ¹¹ _____ (not/meet) Sarah, she ¹² _____ (not/introduce) me to her friend Jane. So Jane and I met because my taxi broke down that morning!

c ▶10.2 Listen and check.

2 VOCABULARY Expressions with *do*, *make* and *take*

a Match 1–6 with a–f to make sentences.
1 [c] They've offered me a job in Paris but I'm not sure if I want to take it or stay here. I have to make
2 [ ] If I had trained seriously over the past six months, I would have taken
3 [ ] I realise he isn't a very sociable person but please do
4 [ ] It's such a lovely day, so why don't we take
5 [ ] If we can rent the film on DVD, it doesn't make
6 [ ] His final exams are next month. If he did

a your best to persuade him to come to the party.
b advantage of the nice weather and go for a picnic by the river?
c a decision by the end of this week.
d sense for all five of us to go to the cinema to see it.
e badly he would have to repeat the whole year.
f part in last Sunday's marathon.

b Underline the correct words to complete the sentences.
1 Joe's a very outgoing and sociable boy so I'm sure he'll *do / make / take* new friends easily when he starts his new school.
2 You've *made / done / taken* a lot of progress with your English over the past six months. Well done!
3 We've been driving for over two hours now. Let's stop at the next service station and *make / do / take* a rest.
4 We're *doing / making / taking* some research into our family history. It's amazing what we've discovered.
5 I *did / made / took* a big mistake and called my father-in-law 'Tim' instead of 'Tom'. It was so embarrassing.
6 Who would *take / do / make* care of your grandmother if she were ill?
7 I've been *making / taking / doing* this maths homework all night and I still don't understand it.

3 PRONUNCIATION Strong and weak forms: *have*, *had* and *hadn't*

a ▶10.3 Listen to the pronunciation of *have* in these sentences. Is it strong (stressed) or weak (not stressed)? Write S (strong) or W (weak).
1 If I **hadn't** fallen over, [S]
   I wouldn't **have** hurt my knee. [ ]
2 We wouldn't **have** missed the bus [ ]
   if you **had** got up on time. [ ]
3 Julia would **have** passed her exams [ ]
   if she **had** worked harder. [ ]
4 If they **had** saved some money each week, [ ]
   they might **have** had enough to buy a car. [ ]
5 She would never **have** married him [ ]
   if she **had** known what a strange person he is. [ ]

59

10C Everyday English
You've got nothing to worry about

1 USEFUL LANGUAGE
Talking about possible problems and reassuring someone

a Complete the conversation with the words in the box.

| about | feeling | think | worried | nothing |
| happen | it'll | ~~feel~~ | definitely | what if |

A How do you ¹___feel___ about the party tonight, then?
B Er, I'm ²_____ OK …
A Good. Is everything ready?
B Yes, but I'm ³_____ that not many people will come.
A You've got ⁴_____ to worry ⁵_____. You've invited lots of people.
B Yes, but ⁶_____ only a few people come?
A That's ⁷_____ not going to ⁸_____. Everyone I've spoken to says they're coming.
B Oh, good. You don't ⁹_____ we'll run out of food?
A No, I'm sure ¹⁰_____ be fine. You've made a lot of food and most people will probably bring something.
B Oh, OK, that's good.

b ▶10.4 Listen and check.

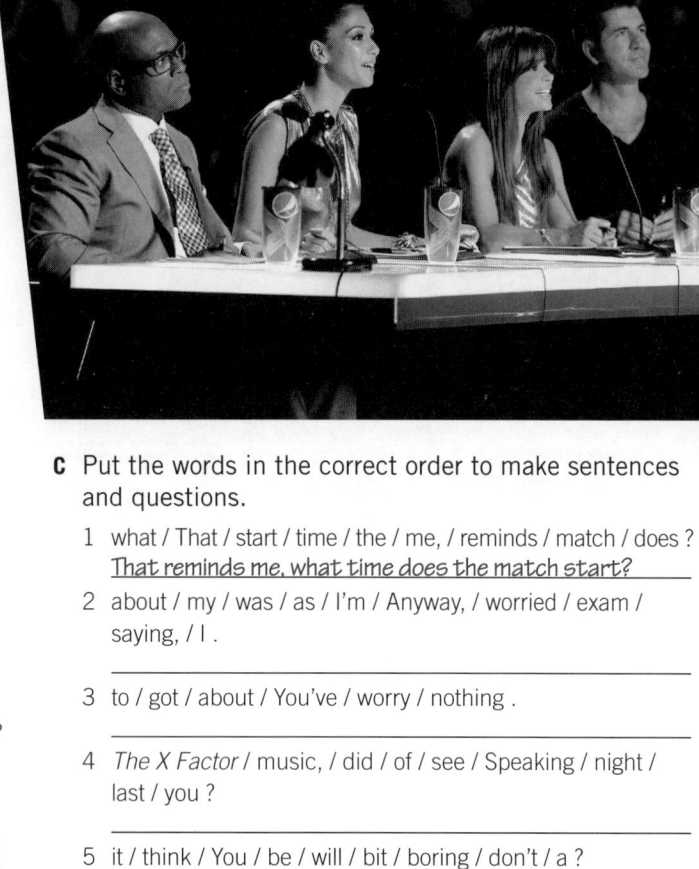

c Put the words in the correct order to make sentences and questions.

1 what / That / start / time / the / me, / reminds / match / does ?
   That reminds me, what time does the match start?
2 about / my / was / as / I'm / Anyway, / worried / exam / saying, / I .
   _____
3 to / got / about / You've / worry / nothing .
   _____
4 *The X Factor* / music, / did / of / see / Speaking / night / last / you ?
   _____
5 it / think / You / be / will / bit / boring / don't / a ?
   _____
6 the / definitely / She's / like / going / ring / to .
   _____
7 go / afraid / something / will / that / wrong / I'm .
   _____
8 girlfriend / new / way, / have / By / you / the / his / met ?
   _____

d ▶10.5 Listen and check.

2 PRONUNCIATION
Sounding sure and unsure

a ▶10.6 Listen to the exchanges. Does speaker B sound sure (falling intonation) or unsure (rising intonation)? Write S (sure) or U (unsure).

1 **A** How much will an engagement ring cost?
  B About £500. [S]
2 **A** How long has your sister known her boyfriend?
  B About four years. ☐
3 **A** What time does the film start?
  B At half past eight. ☐
4 **A** How often is there a train to York?
  B Every 45 minutes. ☐
5 **A** How fast was the car going when the accident happened?
  B About 100 kilometres an hour. ☐
6 **A** How much does it cost to fly to New York?
  B Around £600. ☐

10D Skills for Writing
I think you should go for it

✉ Hi Joe and Tom

My bank have offered me the chance to go to Brazil! Apparently, we're going to open a new branch in Rio de Janeiro and my manager has asked me if I'd like to go and work there. They would want me to stay for at least two years. I think it would be an amazing opportunity to live abroad and to get some experience of working in a foreign country. It seems that they would provide me with free accommodation and pay for me to have Portuguese lessons. What do you guys think? Would it be good for my career if I worked in Brazil for two years?

Please let me know what you think.

Speak soon

Brian

✉ Hi Brian

No wonder you sound so excited! Everyone says Rio is a fantastic place to live and that the Brazilians are such friendly people. I think you should definitely accept the offer. I'm pretty sure you'd enjoy living and working in Brazil and that you'd make lots of new friends. Also, it would look good on your CV if you worked abroad for a couple of years. And I'm sure it would be useful if you learned another foreign language. So, if I were you, I'd go for it.

Let me know what you decide to do.

Joe

P.S. I'd definitely come to visit you for a holiday!

✉ Hi Brian

I'm not sure what I think about the opportunity you've been given to spend two years in Brazil. I can see that it would be exciting to live in Rio, but, if I were you, I'd think about it very carefully before making a decision.

I expect you'd have a great time in Rio but you also need to think about your career with the bank. You've worked for your bank for over five years now so maybe it would be better to apply for a management job either with them or with another bank in the UK? I'm not sure experience of working in a bank in Brazil would help when you come back to look for a better job in London. I think you should discuss with your manager what kind of job your bank would give you if you came back after two years.

Let me know if you want to meet up to talk about it in more detail.

Best

Tom

1 READING

a Read the emails and tick (✓) the correct answer.
   a ☐ Brian isn't sure if he should accept the job in Rio.
   b ☐ Brian has already accepted the offer of a job in Brazil.
   c ☐ Brian wants to leave his bank and get a new job.
   d ☐ Brian has decided not to accept the job in Rio.

b Read the emails again. Are the sentences true or false?
   1 Brian's bank want him to be the manager of their branch in Rio de Janeiro.
   2 Brian wouldn't have to pay to rent a flat or a house in Rio.
   3 Joe thinks that if Brian moves to Brazil he'll probably feel lonely.
   4 Joe thinks it would be good for Brian's career to work in Brazil.
   5 Tom doesn't think Brian would enjoy living in Rio.
   6 Tom thinks working in Brazil for two years would definitely help Brian to get a better job in London.

2 WRITING SKILLS
Advising a course of action

a Complete the sentences with the words in the box.

should	better	definitely	would
I'd	pretty	expect	suggesting

   1 If I were you, ___I'd___ apply for that new job in Marketing.
   2 I'm not sure you _____ enjoy working for that company.
   3 It would _____ be good for your career.
   4 I'm _____ sure you'd be a good manager.
   5 Maybe it would be _____ to try and get another job in London?
   6 I _____ you'd find that training course extremely interesting.
   7 I think you _____ definitely discuss it with your manager.
   8 I'm just _____ that you should think about it very carefully before you decide.

3 WRITING

a Read the email from Jane and write a reply. It can be positive and enthusiastic (in favour of her accepting the job) or more careful (advising her to consider going to university instead).

✉ Hi

I've got some good news but I also need some advice.

I've just received my exam results and, fortunately, I passed all my subjects and even got a distinction in maths and IT. As a result, I've been offered a place at university to do a three-year degree in Business Studies. However, the problem is that my parents don't think I should go to university. Although my dad didn't go to university he's become a very successful businessman with a chain of small hotels around the country. Anyway, he wants me to start working as a trainee manager in one of these hotels. I worked there during the summer holidays last year as a receptionist and I really enjoyed it. So, I'm thinking of accepting his offer of a permanent job now instead of going to university. Apparently, I could become a hotel manager within five years.

Please let me know what you think.

Speak soon

Jane

61

UNIT 10
Reading and listening extension

1 READING

a Read the email. Complete the sentences with the names in the box. You need to use some names more than once.

| Alex | Dean | Luis | Micky | Pilar | Robin | Stevo |

1 ___Dean___ wrote the email.
2 _____ received the email.
3 _____ and _____ are managers of local football teams.
4 _____ and _____ are football trainers.
5 _____ is the wife of one of the people in the email.

b Read the email again. Are the sentences true or false?
1 Dean respects Luis's knowledge of football.
2 Dean was mostly disappointed in the results of his team.
3 Dean thinks his team was most successful when they were attacking.
4 Dean has told his players that they are not allowed to have a rest.
5 Dean wants to reorganise his team.
6 Dean believes that most of his players try to avoid the ball during a game.
7 Dean agrees with Luis that the referee missed an important part of a recent game.
8 In general, Dean's email has been written in a formal style of English.

c Read the end of an email from your English friend, Emily. Write a positive and enthusiastic reply to Emily's email. Think about the following:
- how to begin your email
- how to advise her on the best course of action
- ways of encouraging Emily to become the manager.

Hi Luis!

How are things in Madrid these days? How are Pilar and the kids?

Thanks for your last email and for your excellent advice about goalkeepers. Your knowledge of football is just fantastic. Speaking of which, I need to ask your advice about something. So now that the team is taking a break from football for a couple of months, I thought that this would be a good time to think about next year.

Generally, I was quite proud of the players but I think we were beaten too many times. I'm convinced that we would have won more games if we had attacked better. The defence is strong but our attacking is just not so good. Although it's the summer holidays, I've already told the team that they cannot take it easy.

First of all, they're just not fit enough so they're all going to be doing more training. As I explained to them, 'If you're going to take part in this beautiful game, then you are going to have to work much harder. I don't want you to do your best – I want you to win, win, and then win again.' So from now on, they are going to do a good workout three times a week. Micky and Stevo (do you remember those guys?) are helping me do the training so I know that they'll have to work really hard.

I also want to have a go at changing the team. I don't think Alex or Robin should be in defence any more. I think both of them will be right for playing up front. I think they'd be good because they are the only two who aren't scared of the ball (you should see the rest of them!).

Anyway, that's what I thought after watching the videos of this year's games. For instance, that game we played against the All Stars in March. I think if we'd had those two at the front, then we would have won easily. Can I ask you to take a look at the video (the link's below)? Tell me what you think. That reminds me – I saw the video of your team's last game and I think you were right. If the referee had seen what number 7 had done to your goalkeeper, there would have been a penalty for sure.

Well, I won't write any more. As you know, there's no time to relax when you're the manager of the local primary school's seven-year-old girls' football team!

Best,
Dean

… so the local primary school is looking for a new manager for their girls' football team. The kids are seven years old, so they're quite little. I've been thinking about doing it.

I'm quite fit and I love football. Plus, I still haven't decided what to do after I finish university next year. Maybe if I do this, it will be good experience if I want to become a teacher later. It's voluntary, of course, and it's about 10 or 12 hours of my time every week.

What do you think? Does it sound worth doing?

Emily

2 LISTENING

a ▶10.7 Listen to a conversation between two students, Wendy and Phil, and tick (✓) the correct answers.

	Wendy	Phil
1 Who seems to be unhappy?	☐	☐
2 Who has had an interview recently?	☐	☐
3 Who wishes that they had got better marks at school?	☐	☐
4 Who describes a time when they felt very worried?	☐	☐
5 Who encourages the other?	☐	☐
6 Who needs some advice for a future interview?	☐	☐

b Listen to the conversation again. Tick (✓) the correct answers.

1 According to Wendy, how many people apply for each place at medical school?
   a ☐ 2
   b ☐ 10
   c ☐ 12
2 Phil reminds Wendy that she had excellent results in …
   a ☐ all her subjects.
   b ☐ more subjects than Phil.
   c ☐ most of her subjects.
3 When she describes her interview to Phil, what does Wendy compare herself to?
   a ☐ an animal
   b ☐ her mother
   c ☐ the Sahara desert
4 Phil is sure that the people who interviewed Wendy …
   a ☐ have all had a similar experience to Wendy.
   b ☐ must have understood how intelligent Wendy is.
   c ☐ were all experienced and professional people.
5 Wendy says that all doctors should be …
   a ☐ confident.
   b ☐ friendly.
   c ☐ patient.
6 Which of these things does Phil suggest might help Wendy improve?
   a ☐ taking up a sport
   b ☐ finding a job in a theatre
   c ☐ having a go at acting

c Choose a job from the box below. Write a conversation between two people. Person A has an interview for this job next week. Person B gives advice for the interview to Person A.

   doctor   engineer   astronaut   politician   salesperson

Review and extension

1 GRAMMAR

Correct the sentences.

1 If I would speak French, I would apply for that job in Paris.
   If I spoke French, I would apply for that job in Paris.
2 If there wasn't an accident, we didn't miss our flight.
3 If I were you, I will wait until the shop has a sale to buy a jacket.
4 She didn't fail her exam if she studied harder.
5 If she would be nicer, she will make more friends.
6 We had caught the train on time if we left the house earlier.
7 I will buy a new car if I would have more money.
8 If it didn't rain yesterday, we would play tennis.

2 VOCABULARY

Correct the sentences.

1 The match finished 4 – 1 and Messi took three goals, including one penalty.
   The match finished 4 – 1 and Messi scored three goals, including one penalty.
2 I'm making some research into how children spend their pocket money.
3 In the final set Roger Federer won Rafael Nadal 6 – 2.
4 I'm terribly sorry, Madam, for doing a mistake with your bill.
5 My cousin's really good in languages – she speaks German, French and Russian.
6 Samantha's very worry about her exams.
7 He did a lot of money when he worked in the City of London, but now he's a teacher.
8 We've been working for two hours now, so let's do a short break and have a coffee.

3 WORDPOWER Easily confused words

Underline the correct words to complete the sentences.
1 Can you *bring* / *take* these flowers to your grandmother's house, please?
2 That man *stole* / *robbed* my mobile phone!
3 If we don't get to the station soon, we'll *lose* / *miss* our train.
4 In summer the sun *raises* / *rises* at 4.30 in the morning.
5 Can you *lend* / *borrow* me ten dollars, please?
6 He's *currently* / *actually* writing his third novel.

◉ REVIEW YOUR PROGRESS

Look again at Review your progress on p.126 of the Student's Book. How well can you do these things now?
3 = very well   2 = well   1 = not so well

I CAN …

talk about new things I would like to do	☐
talk about imagined past events	☐
talk about possible problems and reassure someone	☐
write an email with advice.	☐

63

Vox pop video

Unit 6: Different cultures

6a ◀ **Do you like visiting foreign countries?**

a Watch video 6a. Underline the correct words to complete the sentences.

1. Martina likes going to foreign countries because the *weather / culture / coffee* is different.
2. Maibritt thinks it's *boring / interesting / exciting* to visit other countries.
3. Matt thinks it's *exciting / interesting / expensive* to travel to different parts of the world.
4. Anna thinks it's interesting to see what the *houses look like / public transport looks like / shops look like*.

b Watch video 6a again. Match 1–4 with a–d to make sentences.

1. [b] Martina talks about
2. [ ] Maibritt talks about
3. [ ] Matt talks about
4. [ ] Anna talks about

a. the architecture in other countries.
b. the fruit in other countries.
c. the trains in other countries.
d. the weather in other countries.

6b ◀ **Have you ever experienced culture shock?**

c Watch video 6b. Match 1–8 with a–h to make sentences.

1. [c] Martina worked as a volunteer in
2. [ ] Martina was surprised
3. [ ] Maibritt spent two years in
4. [ ] Maibritt was surprised
5. [ ] Matt taught English in
6. [ ] Matt was surprised
7. [ ] Anna had a job as a teaching assistant in
8. [ ] Anna was surprised

a. Japan.
b. by how different it was from Great Britain.
c. Russia.
d. by the role of women.
e. that people didn't use 'small talk'.
f. Germany.
g. by how people spoke to each other.
h. Italy.

d Watch video 6b again and tick (✓) the correct answers.

1. Martina spent _____ in Russia.
   a. [ ] a month
   b. [✓] half a year
   c. [ ] six years
2. Maibritt mentions that she had problems with _____ abroad.
   a. [ ] eating new things
   b. [ ] finding her way around
   c. [ ] working
3. Matt felt _____ during his first weeks in Japan.
   a. [ ] angry
   b. [ ] excited
   c. [ ] scared
4. Anna had problems getting to know her colleagues in Germany because _____.
   a. [ ] she didn't speak the language
   b. [ ] she was extremely shy around new people
   c. [ ] there was an age difference between her and them

6c ◀ **What advice would you give someone visiting this country for the first time?**

e Watch video 6c. Match 1–4 with a–d to make sentences.

1. [c] Martina says that
2. [ ] Maibritt says that
3. [ ] Matt says that
4. [ ] Anna says that

a. tourists should try English food and go to a football match.
b. it can rain at any time in the UK.
c. tourists should explore the British countryside.
d. the weather in the UK changes all the time.

Vox pop video

Unit 7: House and home

7a◀ Did you grow up in a big city or a small town?

a Watch video 7a. Underline the correct words to complete the sentences.
1 Deborah liked the *parks / people / weather* in Manchester.
2 Tony *lives / would like to live / doesn't live* in the village where he was born.
3 Andrew liked living in Cardiff because of the *culture / weather / people*.
4 Arian liked Cambridge because there were lots of *friendly people / parks for children / good schools*.

b Watch video 7a again and tick (✓) the correct answers.
1 Deborah complains about the _____ in Manchester.
   a ☐ prices
   b ☐ public transport
   c ✓ weather
2 Tony is _____ the place where he lives.
   a ☐ fed up with
   b ☐ frustrated with
   c ☐ happy with
3 Andrew describes Cardiff as good for _____.
   a ☐ shopping
   b ☐ outdoor activities
   c ☐ tourism
4 Arian thinks that Cambridge is _____.
   a ☐ enormous
   b ☐ not large
   c ☐ a typical city

7b◀ What are the advantages of living in a big city?

c Watch video 7b. Match 1–4 with a–d to make sentences.
1 [c] Deborah thinks that in a big city
2 ☐ Margaret thinks that in a big city
3 ☐ Andrew thinks that in a big city
4 ☐ Arian thinks that in a big city

a there are lots of people to meet.
b there are always plenty of interesting things to do.
c it's easy to see a film or an exhibition.
d everything you need is near to where you live.

7c◀ What are the disadvantages of living in a big city?

d Watch video 7c and tick (✓) the correct answers.
1 Deborah _____ living in a big city.
   a ☐ loves
   b ☐ doesn't enjoy
   c ✓ doesn't mind
2 Tony thinks that if you live in a big city, you might miss _____.
   a ☐ your friends
   b ☐ the countryside
   c ☐ your village
3 Andrew thinks that cities are _____ than villages.
   a ☐ cleaner
   b ☐ more polluted
   c ☐ friendlier
4 Arian says that people _____ in a big city.
   a ☐ don't know all their neighbours
   b ☐ don't have many friends
   c ☐ are always very busy

69

Unit 8: Information

8a ◀ When did you last read a newspaper?

a Watch video 8a and tick (✓) the correct answers.

1. Alyssia read the *i* newspaper because it _____.
   - a ☐ was the only one on sale
   - b ☐ was given to her free
   - c ✓ wasn't expensive
2. Tom _____ a copy of the *Metro* newspaper.
   - a ☐ bought
   - b ☐ was given
   - c ☐ couldn't find
3. Lottie _____ newspapers.
   - a ☐ doesn't usually buy
   - b ☐ doesn't like reading
   - c ☐ can't afford to buy
4. Tim read the *Independent* newspaper _____.
   - a ☐ last weekend
   - b ☐ yesterday
   - c ☐ today
5. Elizabeth read *The Times* because _____.
   - a ☐ it's her favourite newspaper
   - b ☐ her father left it
   - c ☐ it was cheap to buy

b Watch video 8a again. Underline the correct words to complete the sentences.

1. Alyssia says she last read a newspaper <u>the day before yesterday</u> / yesterday / that morning.
2. Tom read the newspaper at home / in a café / on the train.
3. Lottie looks at the papers when she's at home / shopping / waiting for the bus.
4. Tim read the *Guardian* / the *Independent* / the *Metro*.
5. Elizabeth always / occasionally / usually reads *The Times*.

8b ◀ Where do you get most of your news from?

c Watch video 8b. Match 1–5 with a–e to make sentences.

1. *c* Alyssia gets her news
2. ☐ Tom sometimes reads the news
3. ☐ Lottie gets her news
4. ☐ Tim normally gets his news
5. ☐ Elizabeth reads about the week's news

- a from BBC1.
- b on the Internet.
- c from television news channels.
- d in a magazine.
- e from newspapers.

8c ◀ What kinds of news are you most interested in?

d Watch video 8c. Underline the correct words to complete the sentences.

1. Alyssia is most interested in entertainment news / local news / <u>world affairs</u>.
2. Tom likes sports / entertainment / business news.
3. Lottie is most interested in celebrity / entertainment / international news.
4. Tim likes local / business / celebrity news.
5. Elizabeth is interested in news about fashion / world affairs / people.

e Watch video 8c again and tick (✓) the correct answers.

1. Alyssia says she is interested in _____ news.
   - a ☐ culture
   - b ✓ politics
   - c ☐ technology
2. Tom is studying _____.
   - a ☐ economics
   - b ☐ film studies
   - c ☐ history of art
3. Lottie thinks that reading gossip about stars is _____.
   - a ☐ boring
   - b ☐ fun
   - c ☐ terrific
4. Tim is originally from _____.
   - a ☐ Canada
   - b ☐ Ireland
   - c ☐ the USA
5. Elizabeth isn't interested in news about _____.
   - a ☐ entertainment
   - b ☐ finance
   - c ☐ other cultures

Unit 9: Entertainment

9a ◀ How much TV do you watch?

a Watch video 9a and tick (✓) the correct answers.

1. Colin watches _____ a day.
   - a ✓ 1 hour
   - b ☐ 2 hours
   - c ☐ 3 hours
2. Jessie watches _____ a day.
   - a ☐ half an hour
   - b ☐ 1 hour
   - c ☐ 2 hours
3. Caroline watches _____.
   - a ☐ 30 minutes a day
   - b ☐ 1 hour a day
   - c ☐ only at weekends
4. Dave _____ watches TV.
   - a ☐ often
   - b ☐ rarely
   - c ☐ never
5. Gary watches _____.
   - a ☐ 1 hour a day
   - b ☐ 1 hour a week
   - c ☐ 1 hour a month

Vox pop video

9b ◀ What kind of TV programmes do you like?

b Watch video 9b. Match 1–4 with a–d to make sentences.
1. [c] Colin likes watching
2. [ ] Jessie likes watching
3. [ ] Caroline likes watching
4. [ ] Dave likes watching

a sports programmes.
b reality TV programmes.
c documentaries.
d crime dramas.

9c ◀ Can you recommend a great film?

c Watch video 9c. Underline the correct words to complete the sentences.
1. The film Colin recommends is a *comedy* / *drama* / *horror film*.
2. Jessie saw a great film *last week* / *last month* / *several years ago*.
3. The film Caroline recommends is a good film for *children* / *adults* / *the whole family*.
4. When you watch Dave's film, you will feel *happy* / *excited* / *sad*.

d Watch video 9c again. Match 1–4 with a–d to make sentences.
1. [b] Colin recommends his film because
2. [ ] Jessie recommends her film because
3. [ ] Caroline recommends her film because
4. [ ] Dave recommends his film because

a it gives people hope.
b it stars great actors.
c it's very funny.
d it has an interesting central idea.

Unit 10: Opportunities

10a ◀ How often do you play sport?

a Watch video 10a and tick (✓) the correct answers.
1. Chloe plays sport _____.
   a [ ] once a week
   b [✓] several times a week
   c [ ] once a month
2. Alwyn plays golf _____.
   a [ ] once a week
   b [ ] every day
   c [ ] at least once a month
3. Steph goes skiing _____.
   a [ ] once a year
   b [ ] twice a year
   c [ ] several times a year
4. Trevis _____ plays sport.
   a [ ] often
   b [ ] sometimes
   c [ ] never
5. Claire goes to the gym _____.
   a [ ] every day
   b [ ] twice a week
   c [ ] once a week

10b ◀ Would you like to run a marathon?

b Watch video 10b. Match 1–5 with a–e to make sentences.
1. [c] Chloe wouldn't like to run a marathon because
2. [ ] Alwyn wouldn't like to run a marathon because
3. [ ] Steph wouldn't like to run a marathon because
4. [ ] Trevis wouldn't like to run a marathon because
5. [ ] Claire wouldn't like to run a marathon because

a it would be too tiring.
b she finds it uncomfortable to run.
c she's afraid of pain.
d it's not a good idea for an old person.
e she hasn't got enough energy.

c Watch video 10b again. Underline the correct words to complete the sentences.
1. Chloe would *never run a marathon* / *run a full marathon* / *run a half-marathon*.
2. Alwyn says his *best friend* / *daughter* / *wife* has run a marathon.
3. Steph *criticises* / *respects* / *wants to be like* people who run marathons.
4. Trevis *is not interested in* / *has stopped* / *got injured* running marathons.
5. Claire only runs *for the bus* / *when she's on holiday* / *in the gym*.

10c ◀ If you could try one new sport, what would it be?

d Watch video 10c. Match 1–5 with a–e to make sentences.
1. [e] If Chloe had a lot of money,
2. [ ] If Alwyn were fit enough,
3. [ ] Steph likes doing crazy things, so
4. [ ] If Trevis could try a new sport,
5. [ ] If Claire could try a new sport,

a she would choose beach volleyball.
b she would try base-jumping.
c she would choose paddle boarding.
d he would try snowboarding.
e she would try paraskiing.

Audioscripts

Unit 6

6.1
PAUL I've got my English exam tomorrow morning.
MUM Oh, really? So what time do you have to be at school?
P Well, the exam starts at 9 o'clock, so I mustn't be late.
M I think you ought to leave earlier than normal, in case there's a lot of traffic.
P Yes, that's a good idea.
M And what are you going to do after the exam?
P Well, I don't have to stay at school in the afternoon, so I can come home for lunch.
M Fine, just two more things. It says on this information sheet that students must show their identity cards to the examiner before the exam.
P Don't worry. I always take my ID card with me to school.
M It also says you can't use a dictionary during the exam, so don't take one with you.
P Yes, I know. I'll leave it at home.
M OK, good. By the way, it's 10 o'clock. You shouldn't go to bed late tonight.
P No, you're right. I'll go up now.
M OK, good night. And good luck for tomorrow!

6.2
1 swimming pool
2 rush hour
3 washing machine
4 cycle lane
5 lunchtime
6 cash machine

6.3
1 My meal wasn't nearly as nice as I expected.
2 This is by far the most luxurious hotel I've ever stayed in.
3 She plays tennis much better than I do.
4 Today isn't nearly as hot as it was yesterday.
5 These are the most expensive shoes I've ever bought.
6 This restaurant is far cheaper than the restaurant we normally go to.
7 That was the hardest exam I've taken in my life.
8 Yesterday evening she got home earlier than usual.

6.4
1 He speaks more quickly than I do.
2 London is much more expensive than Edinburgh.
3 They make the best pizzas in Rome.
4 Colin is cleverer than his brother.
5 That was the saddest film I've ever seen.
6 The exam wasn't nearly as hard as I expected.
7 I think this is the simplest recipe in the book.
8 At the moment the weather in France is a little warmer than in the UK.

6.5
A So, where do you think I should take my mother on holiday?
B If I were you, I'd take her somewhere warm, like Italy.
A You've been to Italy lots of times, haven't you? Where would you recommend taking her?
B Well, you should definitely go to Rome – it's such a beautiful city.
A That's a good idea. And when would you go?
B Er, let me see. Well, it's not a good idea to go in July or August, as it's much too hot for sightseeing then. It's much better to go in May or June, when it isn't quite as hot.
A And where do you think we should stay in Rome?
B Well, there are some lovely hotels in the centre, but they're at least 200 euros a night.
A You're kidding! I had no idea it would be that expensive. I can't afford to pay that much!
B Oh, well, in that case it's probably worth finding a hotel outside the centre, then.
A Yes, that makes sense. Thanks for your advice.

6.6
1 You should definitely visit the British Museum when you're in London.
2 What dress would you wear to the party?
3 It's much better to take the train from London to Paris.
4 Would you recommend going to Athens in August?
5 It's probably worth booking a hotel before you go.
6 If I were you, I'd take the job in San Francisco.
7 Do you think I should buy this watch?
8 It's not a good idea to change your money at the airport.

6.7
1 **A** My boyfriend's taking me to Paris this weekend!
   B Wow! That's amazing.
2 **A** I've been offered a place at Harvard University!
   B Oh, really? That's good.
3 **A** I got the best exam grades in my class!
   B That's amazing! Well done!
4 **A** My dad's going to buy me a rabbit!
   B Wow! That's brilliant.
5 **A** John's asked me to marry him!
   B Great! I'm so happy for you.
6 **A** We're going on holiday on Saturday!
   B I know. I can't wait!

6.8
PEERAYA Hi Matt!
SYLVIE Hi!
MATT Hi Peeraya, how are you doing?
P Very well, thank you! This is my friend Sylvie, who I'm always talking about.
S Hi, Matt. Nice to finally meet you.
M Hi, Sylvie. You too. So, what are you two up to?
P Well, you know I said in my text message that our English course is almost over.
M Yeah, right. It's gone really quickly, hasn't it?
P It really has. Anyway, we're planning to celebrate with a meal out …
S Yes, but, uh, we don't really know Liverpool very well.
P So … we were sort of hoping you might be able to recommend some places to eat out?
S That would be really great.
M Yeah, sure. No problem at all. I mean, I'm not from Liverpool either but I've lived here for quite a few years now and so I think I know it pretty well. Um, OK, so how many people is the dinner for?
S Oh, uh, 18 I think?
P Yes, well. There are 18 students in our class but we'd like to invite our teachers, Phillipa and Sarah, too.
S Oh, yes, we definitely want them to come too.
M OK, so that's dinner for 20 people?
S Yes. Oh, actually, no. I've just remembered – Hiromi, one of the students, she wants to bring her husband, Shigeru. So that would be 21.
M OK, so you'll need quite a big restaurant then. There's nothing worse than waiting all night for one poor chef to try to prepare hundreds of starters and main courses.
P Yes, that's true!
S But, also, we'd like to go to a place that's, uh, how do you say this in English? Um, we don't want to go to a big company place. You know, one of those places like 'Star Noodles' or 'Wonderful Burgers' or any of those kinds of places. We want to go to a, you know, something more like a family restaurant.
M Yes, I know what you mean. You don't want to go to any chain restaurants.
S That's right! No chain restaurants.
M Sure. OK, so places to eat out. Hmm. Well, you should definitely look at restaurants in East Village. In fact, if I were you I'd go to The Thai House. It's a really nice restaurant and their seafood dishes are especially delicious. They're not too spicy but the food is always really fresh there.
P That sounds nice. But we were thinking that this is an English course, so we'd like to go to an English restaurant.
S Yes. I mean, do you know any places that do British food, or even better, food from Liverpool?
M Ah! I see what you mean –
P But not …
P/S Fish and chips!
M Don't worry! I knew what you meant. Well, it's probably worth going to Sarah's Bistro. They do a really good 'scouse'.
S 'Scouse'? What's that?
M It's a dish that's local to Liverpool. It's a kind of lamb stew, really tasty. Although you can get vegetarian scouse there now too.
P That sounds perfect!
S Yes, where is it?
M Well, do you know the traffic lights on the corner of Danielle Street and Porch Road?
P Yes.
M Well, you turn left there and go up Double Street until you see a cash machine. Turn right there and – you're there!
P Oh, thanks so much, Matt!
S Yes, thank you. That's great.
M No problem.

Unit 7

7.1
A Some new people have just moved into the house opposite.
B Yes, I know. I saw them yesterday when they arrived. I think they're French.
A No, they can't be French. Their car has a 'P' sticker on the back.
B Oh, really? They might come from Poland, then.
A Or they could be Portuguese?
B That's true – both countries begin with a 'P'.
A Is it a family or a couple?
B It must be a family. They must have two or three children.
A How do you know that?
B Because I saw some children's bikes in their garden. Also, there was another woman in the car when they arrived yesterday – she was older than the mother.
A She might be the children's grandmother.
B No, she can't be their grandmother. She only looked about 45.
A Or she could be their aunt? Or she might not be a relative at all. She may be just a friend. She might be helping them to unpack their things.
B Why don't we go and say 'hello'?
A But they might not speak English – it could be really embarrassing.
B They must speak English. I just saw them speaking to one of their neighbours and they seemed to understand each other.

7.2
1 He must have rich parents.
2 She can't be revising for her exams tonight.
3 They might enjoy going to the zoo.
4 You could invite Jenny to your party.
5 We must be quite near the centre now.
6 John must earn a lot more money than her.

74

Audioscripts

▶ 7.3

1. **A** Do you think you could help me with the shopping bags?
   B Sure, I'll take them into the kitchen for you.
2. **A** Is there anything I can do to help?
   B Yes, there is, actually. Could you lay the table for me?
3. **A** Do you think I could have a quick shower?
   B Yes, of course. Let me get you a towel.
4. **A** May I use your phone?
   B Yes, of course. It's in the hall.
5. **A** Is it OK if I watch the news on TV?
   B Sure, no problem. Let me turn it on for you.
6. **A** Would you mind taking your shoes off?
   B No, not at all. Where shall I leave them?

▶ 7.4

1. Would you mind opening that door for me?
2. Is it OK if I leave my coat here?
3. **A** Do you think I could have a cup of tea?
   B Yes, of course. I'll make one for you.
4. **A** Would you mind if I used your toilet?
   B Not at all. Let me show you where it is.
5. Is there anything I can do to help?
6. Excuse me. Do you think you could turn the music down a little, please? It's really hard to talk in here.

▶ 7.5

1. a Would you mind getting me some more water?
   b Would you mind getting me some more water?
2. a Do you think you could lend me some money?
   b Do you think you could lend me some money?
3. a Is it OK if I make myself a coffee?
   b Is it OK if I make myself a coffee?
4. a Do you think I could borrow your car?
   b Do you think I could borrow your car?
5. a Do you mind if I make a quick phone call?
   b Do you mind if I make a quick phone call?

▶ 7.6

LUIS OK, is it my turn yet?
BEN Erm, not yet. You have to miss your turn this time because you only got three 'ones', remember?
L Oh, yes, I forgot. So whose turn is it now?
KATIA It's mine, yay!!! OK, come on, come on – be lucky! Give Katia the score she needs. OK, so I've got two 'sixes'. And what's that one? I can't see it from here.
B It's a 'four'.
K OK, so a 'four' and two 'sixes', sixteen. Is that good?
B Yes. You can move three places and you get – a 'Dream' question.
K Ooh! Excellent! Go on then.
B OK, 'You have one minute to describe your dream home to the other players – so just to Luis and Daniela – but not me. Every player has to draw what you describe – but with their eyes closed!'
L/DANIELA What? / No! / I can't draw to save my life!
B Yes, yes. Just take a pencil and be quiet. OK, Katia? Close your eyes, Luis! OK, so Katia, are you ready? Good! So, one minute from now!
K OK, so, my dream home! Let me see, oh OK, I know! I know! So, it would be in Moscow, right in the centre, in a fantastic location somewhere in a really nice neighbourhood near to Pushkin Square. OK, and it would have to be on the top floor of a really big building so that I could see the Kremlin and even Red Square from my window.
B What kind of building?
K A really big one.
B Yes, but what kind of building? Old? New?
K Oh, I see! OK, you're right, yes. OK, well, really new. Like from the 1990s or 2000s. In fact, from any time after 2010. So it would have lots of shiny metal and glass on the outside and lots of gold and marble on the inside. Because, actually, my dream home isn't a house but a luxury apartment. And it would be huge, I mean really, really big. And it would have a balcony along one side. The balcony would be really wide so that I'd have enough space for lots of flowers and a garden and a table where I could have picnics and parties. Oh, and actually, it would also have a big, a really, really big, square dance floor.
B What about inside the apartment? They have to draw that too!
L Oh man, you're kidding, right?
B No, no. And close your eyes!
L Uff!
K OK, inside the apartment would be completely different from the building. It would be decorated just like a room in an Irish country cottage. So, there would be lots of white walls and dark, brown wood. And really old things. The kitchen would have an old metal oven where I could make cakes and bread and things. And I'd also …
B Time's up! OK, Picasso, let's have a look at, oh …

Unit 8

▶ 8.1

SHOP ASSISTANT Good morning. Can I help you?
CUSTOMER 1 No, thank you. I'm just browsing.
CUSTOMER 2 So what kind of present do you want to buy for your nephew?
C1 I'm not really sure.
C2 It's difficult, isn't it? Let's have a look in the computer games section. I think they said on the radio that 'Mayhem 5' was going to come out this week.
C1 Yes, I think I heard that, too. Let's see if it's on sale.
C2 Look, there it is. €49.90.
C1 49.90! I can't afford that!
C2 You're right. That's a lot of money for a computer game. Let's have a look at the special offers over there. Here's one that's reasonably priced. It's from last year and it's only 19.99. That's a bargain, isn't it?
C1 Yes, that's good value for money. I'll buy him that one. I hope he doesn't already have it.
SA Don't worry. He can always take it back to his local store and change it for another one, or get a refund.
C1 OK, that's great. I'll take it, then.

▶ 8.2

1. To be honest, the film was kind of boring.
2. In my experience, Americans tend to be very friendly.
3. I don't normally like that kind of thing.
4. On the whole, I liked his new film.
5. Some of his songs can be rather depressing.
6. As a rule, Italian coffee is excellent.

▶ 8.3

1. He likes hip hop and rap music – you know, stuff like that.
2. We had a couple of days when it was cloudy and rainy, but on the whole we had pretty good weather.
3. Don't touch all that stuff in his office, please.
4. She likes watching documentaries about animals and nature and that sort of thing.

▶ 8.4

1. When did you last see her?
2. They went the wrong way and got lost.
3. Whose suitcase was the heaviest?
4. I wrote a long letter to my uncle in Scotland.
5. I didn't know which book to get my husband.
6. She had to wait two hours for the next train to London.

▶ 8.5

/h/: whose, heaviest, husband, had
/w/: when, went, way, which
First letter silent: wrong, wrote, hours

▶ 8.6

CATHY Hi, Cindy!
CINDY Hi, Cathy. How's it going?
CA Well, I've had better days.
CI Oh dear, what's happened?
CA Well, do you remember those boots I was looking at last week?
CI The brown leather ones?
CA Yes. Well anyway, yesterday I decided to go back and buy them.
CI Oh cool!
CA Ah, well …
CI Oh.
CA Yes, 'Oh'. I thought they were really good value when I bought them. I mean, fifty per cent off a pair of designer boots that had just come out only six months ago!
CI So what happened? Were they the wrong size or something?
CA That's what typically happens to me but no, not this time. When I got home and took them out of the box, realised why they had fifty per cent off.
CI What do you mean?
CA As soon as I took them out of the box and turned them over, I saw that one of them had a big black mark on the side.
CI That's absolutely awful. I hope you took them back to the shop.
CA Yes, of course I did, but …
CI They didn't refuse to give you a refund, did they?
CA Ha! Yes, you've got it! I couldn't believe it!
CI I'm not surprised. But how …? I mean, what did they say?
CI Well, I went back to the shop and I found the manager and told him what had happened, that I'd been into the shop last week and tried on the boots and then I'd gone back yesterday to buy them. I couldn't see them on the shelves so I asked the assistant and he brought them out already in the box.
CI But didn't he show you the boots before you paid for them?
CA Well, yes he did. He took the top off the box and asked me if everything was OK but by that time, you see, the boots were already lying flat inside the box. So I could only see the good side of them. I didn't think to ask him to take them out of the box again.
CI Of course not. Why would you? So what did the manager say to that?
CA He told me that as a rule they would always give someone a refund but that that wasn't possible this time because they were in the sale.
CI You're kidding? So, what happened?
CA Well, he asked me if the shop assistant had shown me the boots in the box before I'd paid for them and I admitted that he had. But I said that I hadn't realised that they were on sale because there was something wrong with them. But again he just said that he was really sorry but he couldn't give me a refund.
CI Oh, what a …
CA I know.
CI So what's happening now?
CA To be honest, I don't know. Jim's suggested that I call a lawyer or something, but I'm not sure I want to go that far.
CI Oh, I'm sorry. That really is bad, isn't it?
CA I know, I know. So what would you recommend I do?
CI Well, how about …

Unit 9

▶ 9.1

1
When I was in London last summer I went to a superb concert during the BBC Proms, which is a festival of classical music at the Royal Albert Hall. It's great to hear a symphony or a concerto when it's performed by an orchestra of professional musicians who are playing live. They played symphonies by Mahler and Beethoven and there was also a huge choir of 80 people that sang Mozart's Requiem. At the end of the concert everyone in the audience stood up and gave the performers a standing ovation which lasted for over five minutes.

2
I've just heard on the radio that the band have been in the recording studio for the last month. They're making a new album of jazz, soul and blues songs, which they're bringing out in September. I've just listened to an amazing playlist of their old songs on the Internet. It's got about 30 tracks on it and most of them are old songs of theirs from the 80s and 90s.

▶ 9.2

1 Radio stations which have a lot of adverts are really annoying.
2 The band's fourth album, which they recorded in 2010, was their best so far.
3 The pianist, whose brother is also a musician, gave a superb performance.
4 In the article it says that people who eat healthily usually live longer.
5 Tickets for last year's festival, which my sister went to, cost €250!
6 I think operas which last more than three hours are really boring.

▶ 9.3

PAM Hi, Mel. Listen. Ian and I were thinking of going out for a meal this weekend. Would you guys like to come with us?
MEL Yes, that's a great idea. Where were you planning to go?
P We thought about going to that new Chinese restaurant in town. It's meant to be really good.
M Hang on a second. I'll just ask Tony … Sorry, Pam, but Tony isn't a big fan of Chinese food.
P OK, never mind. We could go somewhere else.
M Oh, I know. How about going to that new Italian restaurant near the station?
P Mmm, that sounds interesting.
M Yes, it's supposed to be excellent, and very good value for money.
P Yes, I'm sure Ian would like it. He loves pizzas and pasta.
M Good. Shall I book a table for Saturday evening?
P Yes, that would be perfect for us. Why don't we get a table for 8 o'clock?
M Yes, OK. I'll book one.

▶ 9.4

1 Sorry, but Sean isn't a big fan of science fiction films. What other films are on?
2 The new novel by JK Rowling, who wrote the Harry Potter books, is supposed to be really good.
3 The new animated film from Pixar has had great reviews in the papers.
4 A There's a documentary about the Roman occupation of Britain on TV tonight.
   B Really? That sounds interesting.
5 I'm not sure if my father would be interested in going to an exhibition of surrealist paintings.
6 This hotel was recommended by a friend of mine, who stayed here last year.
7 That's a great idea. I'm sure Andy would love it.
8 The new Greek restaurant near my house is meant to be very good.

▶ 9.5

1 A Did you go to the concert with Luke?
   B No, I went with Will.
2 A Did James go to Edinburgh by bus?
   B No, he went on the train.
3 A So, your friend's a famous actor?
   B No, she's a famous dancer.
4 A So, you're from Lecce, in the south of Italy?
   B No, I'm from Lecco, in the north of Italy.
5 A Are you meeting your friend Pam on Thursday?
   B No, I'm meeting my friend Sam, on Tuesday.

▶ 9.6

DAVE OK, so that's the pizzas ordered.
MELISSA You remembered to get a vegetarian one for Greg and Kate, didn't you?
D Yes, yes. I got a vegetarian special. Oh, and there's plenty to drink for everyone too.
M Great. OK, so what film do we choose? This is supposed to be movie night after all.
D Well, let's have a look. Have you got all of them on your computer?
M Yes. I've downloaded a few, so we've got a good variety to choose from. Do you want to have a look with me so we can pick something?
D Sure, thanks. OK, so let's have a look. What's this, *Blackfish*? Is that a horror movie?
M Oh, no, it's a documentary. You haven't heard of it, then?
D Nope.
M Well, it's about the way killer whales are looked after in places like Sea World and Ocean World and that sort of thing.
D Oh, yeah?
M Yeah. It's an amazing film.
D So you've seen it already?
M Yeah, but I don't mind seeing it again.
D Hmm. Sounds a bit serious though. I mean I like documentaries but I think it would be better to watch something fun. What do you think?
M Hmm, yes you've got a good point there. OK, well we don't have to watch that one. It was just an idea.
D Great. So what about a comedy? Have you got any good ones?
LUCY Well, there's this one. It's quite old now but it's got Jim Carrey in it and he's usually quite funny, isn't he?
D Jim Carrey?
L Yeah, you know, um … Well anyway, *Man on the Moon* is supposed to be really good. Amazing performances, beautiful photography and a great story. I mean, it sounds really interesting and it was highly recommended by Professor Thomas.
D You mean your film studies lecturer?
L Yes, that's the one.
D Err, sounds a bit serious again. It says here that it's the biography of a comic actor but I'm not sure that it's actually a comedy. Yeah, look – most of the film is about the problems he had and about how he had to deal with a terrible illness. I'm not a big fan of films that are more intelligent than the audience, do you know what I mean? … You two really hate me now, don't you?
L No! Not yet.
M But I might do in a minute if you don't choose a film. Everyone will be here soon.
D OK, OK, just a moment. Hang on while I … There's *Star Wars*.
M/L No!
M I'm not really a fan of science fiction. And neither is Ofelia, or Rachel, or …
L Or Greg or Kate. Or me.
D OK, OK. Wait a minute. Oh! Oh! I've found it! I've found it! This is the one!
L *The Lego Movie*? Isn't that a cartoon?
M It's meant to be for kids, isn't it?
D Well, it is an animated film, but it's not just for kids. It's a comedy. And it's got some great songs. It's supposed to be really funny.
M Well …
D Will Ferrell does one of the voices.
M OK, then.
L Oh, OK then. Oh, have you got the cash for the pizza guy? Or do you need some more?
D Yes, I went to the bank earlier and …

Unit 10

▶ 10.1

1 I would go to the gym more often.
2 A Would he apply for a job in London?
   B No, he wouldn't.
3 She wouldn't lend you any money.
4 You wouldn't enjoy that film – it's too scary.
5 A Would you like to go for a pizza?
   B Yes, I would.

▶ 10.2

This is the story of how I met my wife Jane. It all started when I was going to work by taxi and it suddenly broke down. If my taxi hadn't broken down, I would've got to the station on time. If I'd arrived at the station on time, I wouldn't have missed my train. If I hadn't missed the train, I wouldn't have had to wait an hour for the next one. If I hadn't had to wait for an hour, I wouldn't have gone to the café for a coffee. If I hadn't had a coffee, I wouldn't have met my friend Sarah – and if I hadn't met Sarah, she wouldn't have introduced me to her friend Jane. So Jane and I met because my taxi broke down that morning!

▶ 10.3

1 If I hadn't fallen over, I wouldn't have hurt my knee.
2 We wouldn't have missed the bus if you had got up on time.
3 Julia would have passed her exams if she had worked harder.
4 If they had saved some money each week, they might have had enough to buy a car.
5 She would never have married him if she had known what a strange person he is.

▶ 10.4

A How do you feel about the party tonight, then?
B Er, I'm feeling OK …
A Good. Is everything ready?
B Yes, but I'm worried that not many people will come.
A You've got nothing to worry about. You've invited lots of people.
B Yes, but what if only a few people come?
A That's definitely not going to happen. Everyone I've spoken to says they're coming.
B Oh, good. You don't think we'll run out of food?
A No, I'm sure it'll be fine. You've made a lot of food and most people will probably bring something.
B Oh, OK, that's good.

▶ 10.5

1 That reminds me, what time does the match start?
2 Anyway, as I was saying, I'm worried about my exam.
3 You've got nothing to worry about.
4 Speaking of music, did you see *The X Factor* last night?
5 You don't think it will be a bit boring?
6 She's definitely going to like the ring.
7 I'm afraid that something will go wrong.
8 By the way, have you met his new girlfriend?

▶ 10.6

1 A How much will an engagement ring cost?
   B About £500.
2 A How long has your sister known her boyfriend?
   B About four years.
3 A What time does the film start?
   B At half past eight.
4 A How often is there a train to York?
   B Every 45 minutes.
5 A How fast was the car going when the accident happened?
   B About 100 kilometres an hour.
6 A How much does it cost to fly to New York?
   B Around £600.

Audioscripts

▶ 10.7

PHIL Hi, Wendy! How's it going?

WENDY Mmm? Oh, hi Phil, it's you. Yeah, I'm doing OK. Not too bad.

P Hmm. You could try to sound more convincing when you say that!

W It's just … I had my interview this morning.

P Of course. How did it go?

W Awful. I want to be a doctor so much, but after that interview …

P Oh come on, I'm sure it wasn't that bad. You've got nothing to worry about with your marks.

W Thanks, I know. But I'm pretty sure they want more than just good grades. I mean, this is medical school. I read somewhere that for every place at university at least 10 people apply. There are so many people who are expecting me to get in to medical school. What do I do if I don't? I'd be so embarrassed.

P But you didn't just get good marks. You got the highest marks at school in every subject. If only I had grades like yours. And I'm sure you did your best. You always do! So anyway, what happened at your interview that you seem to think went so badly?

W Well, I was so nervous I could hardly speak. I must have sounded like a mouse.

P But they're expecting people to be nervous. Who was interviewing you?

W Oh, it was two senior doctors from the hospital plus a second-year medical student who's studying on the course now.

P Well, OK, but remember they've all done the same interview once. They must have understood how you were feeling.

W I don't know. Maybe. I'm still convinced that I did something wrong. Doctors have to be really confident, don't they? I mean they have to tell nurses what to do and they also have to make decisions that could mean life or death.

P Well, I suppose …

W And you can't be nervous when you're talking to a patient. I mean, can you imagine? If you were my patient and you said 'Oh, Doctor Wendy, do you think I'll be all right?' and then you'd hear me saying 'Oh, um, well, uh, I, uh, think you'll, um, be fine!'

P You don't sound like that.

W But –

P Listen to me, Wendy – you don't sound like that. I promise you. And anyway, what's the worst thing that can happen? OK, let's just imagine that you don't get a place at medical school this year –

W Oh!

P Just imagining! Anyway, what would you do?

W Um …

P OK, well I know what I'd do – I'd apply again next year and I'd take advantage of the time off to do something really interesting. In fact, I'd do something that I knew would help me in my interview next year.

W Like what?

P Well, you say you need more confidence, right? Well, do some research. Find out what you could do that will help you become more confident. I don't know, like, you could try acting. Yes, what about that? You could get a job during the day and then in the evenings you could take part in a play or something. And don't forget, that would only be if you didn't get a place on the medical course. Which you will, of course.

W Yeah, I suppose you're right. Thanks, that's really helpful. Actually, that reminds me, did you say there was something you wanted to ask me about?

P Ah, yes, I've got an interview at the Business School at the university next week and I wanted to ask you to give me some advice. I mean, I'm not sure what kind of questions they are going to ask me.

W Right, OK, well let's have a think …

Answer key

Unit 6
6A
1

a 2 mustn't 3 ought to 4 don't have to 5 can 6 must 7 can't
8 shouldn't

c 2b 3a 4e 5d 6c

2

a 2 d 3 f 4 b 5 a 6 e

3

a 2 out 3 up 4 around 5 up 6 around 7 back 8 away

4

a 2 <u>rush</u> hour 3 <u>washing</u> machine 4 <u>cycle</u> lane 5 <u>lunch</u>time
6 <u>cash</u> machine

6B
1

a 2 This is by far the most luxurious hotel I've ever stayed in. / This is the most luxurious hotel I've ever stayed in by far.
3 She plays tennis much better than I do.
4 Today isn't nearly as hot as it was yesterday.
5 These are the most expensive shoes I've ever bought.
6 This restaurant is far cheaper than the restaurant we normally go to. / The restaurant we normally go to is far cheaper than this restaurant.
7 That was the hardest exam I've taken in my life.
8 Yesterday evening she got home earlier than usual. / She got home earlier than usual yesterday evening.

c 2 London is much more expensive than Edinburgh.
3 They make the best pizzas in Rome.
4 Colin is cleverer than his brother.
5 That was the saddest film I've ever seen.
6 The exam wasn't nearly as hard as I expected.
7 I think this is the simplest recipe in the book.
8 At the moment the weather in France is a little warmer than in the UK.

2

a 2 cooked 3 raw 4 crunchy 5 creamy 6 sour 7 fresh 8 heavy

b 2 mash 3 chop, fry 4 Add 5 mix, serve 6 Heat up, stir

6C
1

a 2 were 3 recommend 4 definitely 5 would 6 idea 7 better 8 should
9 kidding 10 worth

c 2 wear 3 to take 4 going 5 booking 6 I'd 7 should 8 to change

2

a 2 bored 3 excited 4 excited 5 bored 6 excited

6D
1

a 1 A 2 B 3 A 4 A

b True: 1, 5, 6; False: 2, 3, 4

2

a 2 rather 3 a bit 4 rather small 5 extremely 6 completely 7 reasonably
8 terribly

3

a Suggested answer:

Last Saturday I took my girlfriend to Chez Pierre for her birthday. It's a new French restaurant in the city centre. The atmosphere was really relaxing and although there was classical and French music it wasn't very loud so it was easy to talk. The waiters were extremely friendly and the service was good. Our fish was absolutely delicious and the salad was very fresh and tasty. For dessert I had a lovely apple tart with cream and Anna had ice cream. All the portions were extremely generous and although the meal was rather expensive I would definitely recommend going there for a special occasion.

A friend of mine recommended the *Villa Borghese* restaurant to us. It's an Italian restaurant just by the beach and they serve mostly Italian food such as pizzas and pasta. Unfortunately, it was a bit disappointing. The restaurant was extremely noisy because there were lots of young children and loud pop music so it was rather difficult to talk. Because of this, the atmosphere wasn't very relaxing. We went on a Friday evening and the restaurant was completely full but there weren't enough waiters. The service was awful – we were there for nearly an hour before anyone took our order. We ordered pasta but it was rather overcooked and the sauce wasn't very tasty. Our meal was fairly cheap but the food wasn't very good so I definitely wouldn't go there again.

Reading and listening extension
1

a True: 1, 4; False: 2, 3

b 1 a 2 b 3 c 4 b 5 a 6 c

2

a 1 c 2 b 3 a 4 a

b 2 for quite a long time 3 21 4 chain 5 traditional English dishes
6 meat dish 7 turn right

Review and extension
1

2 I think this is the best Greek restaurant in London.
3 Last night we had to take a taxi because we'd missed the bus.
4 His house is nearer the university than yours.
5 You mustn't park outside that school.
6 He's taller than his older brother.
7 You mustn't feed the animals in the zoo – it's forbidden.
8 I think French is easier to learn than English.

2

2 Can I borrow your spoon so I can stir my coffee?
3 We had three hours to wait so we looked round the old town.
4 The best way to get around New York is to take the subway.
5 Squeeze the lemon and pour the juice over the fish.
6 If you put in too much sugar, it will be too sweet to drink.

3

2 f 3 c 4 b 5 a 6 e

Answer key

Unit 7

7A

1

a 2 e 3 a 4 c 5 f 6 d 7 b

b 2 might 3 could 4 must 5 must 6 might 7 can't 8 could 9 might not 10 may 11 might 12 might not 13 could 14 must

2

a Across: 6 neighbourhood 7 view 8 floor
Down: 1 location 3 balcony 4 basement 5 doorbell

b 2 rented, flat 3 landing, floor 4 front, locks 5 out of, into 6 ground, terrace

3

a Final /t/ or /d/: 3, 4, 6

7B

1

a 1 some 2 enough 3 too many 4 plenty 5 a few 6 no 7 enough 8 little

b 2 Unfortunately, there aren't any good restaurants near here. / Unfortunately, there are no good restaurants near here.
3 He won't pass his exams because he hasn't worked hard enough this year.
4 **A** Is there any milk left? / Is there much milk left?
  B Yes, we've got plenty.
5 There were too many people at the bus stop to get on the bus.
6 There are too few eggs in the fridge to make a Spanish omelette. / There aren't enough eggs in the fridge to make a Spanish omelette.
7 My father's too old to play tennis these days.
8 She made a lot of mistakes in her translation. / She made lots of mistakes in her translation.

2

a 2 about 3 for 4 about 5 on 6 about 7 with 8 in

b 2 cope with 3 apologised to 4 rely on 5 worried about 6 belongs to 7 complained about 8 argued with

7C

1

a 2 f 3 e 4 c 5 a 6 b

c 2 really 3 Sure 4 control 5 lovely 6 better

d 2 leave 3 **A** I could **B** I'll 4 **A** I used **B** Let 5 anything 6 could

2

a 2 b 3 b 4 a 5 a

7D

1

a c

b True: 3, 4; False: 1, 2, 5

2

a 2 There's a good shop at the end of my road. Alternatively / Otherwise / Apart from that, you could go to the huge supermarket which is just before you get to the motorway.
There's a good shop at the end of my road. Another option / Another possibility is to go to the huge supermarket which is just before you get to the motorway.
3 You can get a good view of London from the London Eye. Alternatively / Otherwise / Apart from that, you can go to the top of The Shard building.
You can get a good view of London from the London Eye. Another option / Another possibility is to go to the top of The Shard building.
4 I suggest you go to the beach early in the morning, before it gets too hot. Alternatively / Otherwise / Apart from that, you could go late in the afternoon.
I suggest you go to the beach early in the morning, before it gets too hot. Another option / Another possibility is to go late in the afternoon.
5 Why don't you go to that Italian restaurant opposite Covent Garden Underground Station? Alternatively / Otherwise / Apart from that, you could try that new Japanese restaurant near Leicester Square.
Why don't you go to that Italian restaurant opposite Covent Garden Underground Station? Another option / Another possibility is to try that new Japanese restaurant near Leicester Square.

3

a Suggested answer:

Hi Pascale

Thanks for babysitting for us this evening. Hope you get on well with the children and that everything goes well. Here are some suggestions for the evening.

Please make yourself at home and help yourself to hot drinks and a snack. There is some tea and coffee by the kettle. Otherwise, you can make some hot chocolate. It's in the cupboard on the right of the fridge. There are plenty of chocolate biscuits on the table. Alternatively, there's some delicious cheesecake in the fridge.

Can you give the children their dinner at around 7 o'clock? In the fridge there's some chicken soup and fish pie. You can cook this in the microwave. Another option is to make them some sandwiches. You'll find plenty of cheese in the fridge and there's also some apple juice.

After that, you could watch something on TV with them. They both love watching *The X Factor*. Otherwise you could watch one of their favourite DVDs with them, such as *Pirates of the Caribbean* or *Toy Story*. All the DVDs are on the bookcase next to the TV.

By the way, they usually go to bed at about 9 o'clock. You can read them a bedtime story. You'll find plenty of books on the bookcase in their bedroom. They both love the *Harry Potter* books. Another possibility is to start reading *The Lion, the Witch and the Wardrobe* with them. I think they might enjoy it.

Finally, if you have any problems, please phone me on my mobile (07700 900221). Alternatively, you can call my husband's/wife's mobile (07700 900834).

Hope you have a good evening and see you around 11.30.

Reading and listening extension

1

a A 6 B 1 C 5 D 3

b 9, 7, 8, 2, 4, 1, 5, 3, 10, 6

2

a 2 f 3 a 4 e 5 c 6 b

b 1 c 2 c 3 c 4 c 5 a 6 c 7 b 8 c

Review and extension

1

2 George isn't good enough at football to play for the school team.
3 She can't be the manager – she looks too young!
4 There's a lot of traffic / There's lots of traffic in the town centre during the rush hour.
5 They can't be doing their homework at this moment – it's nearly midnight!
6 The maths exam was too difficult for most of the people in my class.

2

2 She complained to the waiter about the dirty glass.
3 I can't afford to buy a flat at the moment so I'm going to rent a flat in the city centre.
4 Don't worry about the bill. I'll pay for the meal.
5 I live in a really nice neighbourhood – everyone's very friendly.
6 When he told me about the accident, I didn't believe him at first.

3

2 c 3 a 4 f 5 e 6 d

Unit 8

8A

1

a 2 She said I should wait behind the line until it was my turn.
3 When I met her last Friday she asked me if I was going to Harry's party the next day.
4 She told me (that) he might be about fifty years old.
5 He told me he was sorry but he couldn't come to my party that evening. / He said he was sorry but he couldn't come to my party that evening.
6 She asked me if I had seen my uncle when I was in New York last year. / She asked me whether I had seen my uncle when I was in New York last year. / She asked me if I had seen my uncle when I was in New York the year before. / She asked me whether I had seen my uncle when I was in New York the year before.
7 He told Anna he would see her next week. / He told Anna he would see her the following week.

b 2 He said that Martin had just sent him a text message.
3 He told me that he would phone me when he got back from work.
4 He asked me if I was going to buy my brother a present that afternoon. / He asked me whether I was going to buy my brother a present that afternoon.
5 She asked me why I couldn't lend her some money.
6 The examiner said that we had to stop writing immediately and give him / her our papers.
7 She told me she wanted me to take the flowers for my grandmother.

2

a 2 news 3 entertainment 4 spread 5 celebrity gossip 6 organisation 7 current 8 political

b Across: 6 presenter 7 breaking 8 posted
Down: 1 headline 2 article 3 reporter 5 business

8B

1

a 1 going 2 seeing 3 to get 4 to come 5 visiting 6 waiting 7 going, to see 8 paying

b 2 Don't forget to give me back my book when you've finished reading it.
3 He admitted stealing the old lady's handbag.
4 We hoped to find a good place to eat in one of the streets near the station.
5 He threatened to tell my parents what I had done.
6 It's really important to teach your children how to cross the road safely.
7 She didn't know which book to buy her brother for his birthday.
8 You promised to help me with my homework!

2

a 2 come 3 sale 4 afford 5 priced 6 bargain 7 value 8 back 9 refund

3

a 2 agreed 3 suggested 4 warned 5 refused 6 offered

8C

1

a 2 In my experience, Americans tend to be very friendly.
3 I don't normally like that kind of thing.
4 On the whole, I liked his new film.
5 Some of his songs can be rather depressing.
6 As a rule, Italian coffee is excellent.

2

a 2 couple, whole 3 stuff 4 sort

3

a/b /h/: whose, heaviest, husband, had
/w/: when, went, way, which
First letter silent: wrong, wrote, hours

8D

1

a d

b True: 1, 4; False: 2, 3, 5

2

a 2 I heard a story on the radio about an elephant which, apparently, sat on a car in a safari park.
3 The 12-year-old girl stole her father's motorbike and rode it for 40 km along the motorway before the police stopped her near Oxford. / The 12-year-old girl stole her father's motorbike and rode it for 40 km along the motorway but the police stopped her near Oxford.
4 The woman hit the teenager hard on his head with her umbrella. Then she used his mobile phone to call the police. / The woman hit the teenager hard on his head with her umbrella and then used his mobile phone to call the police. / The woman hit the teenager hard on his head with her umbrella before using his mobile phone to call the police. / The woman hit the teenager hard on his head with her umbrella and then called the police with his mobile phone. / The woman hit the teenager hard on his head with her umbrella before calling the police with his mobile phone.
5 Amanda escaped from the burning building by breaking a window with her shoe.
6 There was an incredible story on the news about a baby in China who fell from a fourth-floor window but she wasn't hurt because a man in the street caught her.

3

a **Suggested answer:**

Hi Martina

There was an incredible story on the Internet today about a car which crashed into a family's house in Manchester. Apparently, Richard and Judy Knowles and their children were watching TV when suddenly they heard a loud noise. The driver of the car had lost control of his car and had driven straight through the front door of the house before stopping two metres from the kitchen. Amazingly, no one in the house nor in the car was seriously hurt. It seems that the family of four and their dog were all in the living room at the time of the accident. When they realised what had happened, they immediately called the police, who arrived at the scene five minutes later. The front of the house was badly damaged but, fortunately, the driver of the car and his three passengers only suffered minor injuries. It took the fire service six hours to remove the vehicle from the house.

Reading and listening extension

1

a 1 c 2 c 3 b 4 b

b 2 Frankie 3 Neither 4 Frankie 5 Neither 6 Frankie 7 Mercedes 8 Frankie 9 Neither 10 Mercedes 11 Frankie 12 Mercedes

2

a True: 2, 3, 4, 7; False: 1, 5, 6, 8

b 1 b 2 a 3 a 4 b 5 c 6 b

Review and extension

1

2 They asked me if I was going to the football match. / They asked me whether I was going to the football match.
3 He has agreed to take us to the airport.
4 When I phoned him last night, he said he had just finished his exams.
5 She advised me not to tell anyone about our meeting.
6 Yesterday he said he would help me with my homework. / Yesterday he told me he would help me with my homework.
7 I'm really looking forward to seeing you on Sunday.

2

2 The new song by Rihanna is going to come out next week.
3 My sister likes reading the celebrity gossip pages in the Sunday paper.
4 He advised me to buy a new laptop because mine is over five years old.
5 I don't usually watch programmes about politics on TV.
6 She remembered to book a table at the restaurant. / She reminded me to book a table at the restaurant.
7 The main headline on the front page of my newspaper today is BARACK WINS U.S. ELECTION.

3

2 on 3 on 4 in 5 in 6 on 7 in 8 in

Answer key

Unit 9

9A

1

a 2 *Saving Private Ryan* was directed by Steven Spielberg in 1998.
3 The actors have been told to come back at 15.00.
4 1,000 films are made in Bollywood every year.
5 The movie *Avatar* was seen by 35 million people in its first two weeks. / The movie *Avatar* was seen in its first two weeks by 35 million people.
6 The prime minister is being interviewed on TV at this very moment. / The prime minister is being interviewed at this very moment on TV.
7 200,000 cars are produced by our new factory every year. / 200,000 cars are produced every year by our new factory.
8 CGI is being used to create the special effects.

b 2 Five different varieties of orange are grown in this region.
3 Students will be given a loan to pay for their university fees by the government. / Students will be given a loan by the government to pay for their university fees.
4 The special effects are being created with the latest animation software.
5 The actors have been asked to give some of their fees to charity.
6 The car was being driven really fast when the accident happened.
7 The pop star was asked about his new album by the journalist. / The pop star was asked by the journalist about his new album.
8 The president was given a big bunch of flowers by a little girl in a pink dress.

2

a 2 horror 3 thriller 4 science fiction 5 game show 6 documentary
7 animated 8 chat show 9 action 10 soap opera

b Across: 4 character 5 based on
Down: 1 director 3 scene 6 studio

9B

1

a 2 While you're in Italy you should visit the town of Verona, where there is a lovely Roman amphitheatre.
3 John Lennon, who was a member of the pop group The Beatles, was murdered in 1980.
4 Pelé, whose real name is Edson Arantes do Nascimento, was a famous Brazilian footballer.
5 Steven Spielberg was the director of the film *Saving Private Ryan*, which was about a group of American soldiers in the Second World War.
6 First we went to Paris, where we visited the Eiffel Tower, and then we took the train to Lyon.
7 In my view, Bruce Springsteen's best album is *The River*, which he recorded in 1980.
8 Bill Clinton, who was President of the USA from 1993 to 2001, is giving a talk at our university next month.

2

a 2 performed 3 orchestra 4 musicians 5 live 6 choir 7 audience
8 recording 9 album 10 playlist 11 tracks

3

a 2 performance 3 charity 4 development 5 happiness 6 creativity
7 celebration 8 culture

4

a 2 non-defining 3 non-defining 4 defining 5 non-defining 6 defining

9C

1

a 2 Would 3 come 4 that's 5 to go 6 thought 7 meant 8 Hang 9 of
10 else 11 going 12 sounds 13 supposed 14 would like 15 Shall
16 don't

c 2 supposed 3 reviews 4 B sounds 5 sure, interested 6 recommended
7 idea, love 8 meant

2

a 1 No, I went with Will.
2 No, he went on the train.
3 No, she's a famous dancer.
4 No, I'm from Lecco, in the north of Italy.
5 No, I'm meeting my friend Sam, on Tuesday.

9D

1

a b

b True: 1, 4, 5; False: 2, 3

2

a 2 Although 3 However 4 Despite 5 While 6 Although 7 Despite
8 In spite of

3

a Suggested answer:

Why I prefer reading a book

I love going to the cinema and I have seen a lot of films which are based on famous books. However, I normally prefer reading the original book to seeing the film version.

The first reason for enjoying the book more than the film is because a book usually takes several days or weeks to read whereas a film only lasts for two or three hours. So I can enjoy reading a book for much longer than watching a film. Furthermore, because most films are much shorter than books, the director has to cut a lot of the interesting details from the story. As a result, films only show the most important scenes of the story and don't usually tell the audience what the characters are thinking.

Another reason I prefer the book is that when you are reading a story you have to use your imagination. The reader imagines what the people and the places in the story look like and how the characters speak. However, this isn't possible when you watch a film because the director makes the decisions about the appearance of the characters and the scenes.

Finally, reading a book is a great way to relax and to enter the world that the author has created. You can read a book anywhere you like – in bed, on the beach or on a train as you travel to work. While it is true that these days you don't have to watch a film at the cinema or on TV, it is still much easier to take a book with you and read a chapter when you have nothing else to do for half an hour.

So, although it is much easier to watch the film adaptation of a novel than to read the original book, I prefer reading the book. It lasts longer and gives me more enjoyment, it allows you to use your imagination and it is a very good way to relax.

Reading and listening extension

1

a True: 2, 3, 5; False: 1, 4, 6

b 1 d 2 d 3 b 4 c 5 a

2

a 1 b 2 c 3 c 4 a

b 2 computer 3 documentary 4 serious 5 performances 6 comedy
7 animated

Review and extension

1

2 A new bridge is being built at the moment by a Chinese construction company.
3 I interviewed the actor that had just won an Oscar.
4 *Sunflowers* was painted by Vincent Van Gogh.
5 Where is the new James Bond film being made?
6 He's the player that used to be in our team.

2

2 The actor was annoyed because someone in the audience had forgotten to switch off his mobile phone.
3 My father's a professional musician who plays the clarinet in the London Philharmonic Orchestra.
4 In *Titanic*, Leonardo DiCaprio plays a character who falls in love with the daughter of an American millionaire.
5 When I was about sixteen I saw The Rolling Stones play live at a festival in Germany.
6 I'm not very keen on horror films like *Dracula*.

3

2 Have you seen my brother? He said he'd meet me here.
3 I don't see why you're so angry with us.
4 She always listens to pop music in her bedroom.
5 I'm seeing my grandparents next Sunday.
6 Sorry, this phone's terrible. I can't hear you very well.
7 I've finished this exercise. Please look at it for me.

Unit 10

10A

1

a 1 'd be able to / could   2 'd take, were   3 'd go, lived   4 spoke, 'd apply   5 'd like, knew   6 'd learn, didn't have   7 would buy, could / were able to   8 wouldn't be, beat

b 1 'll pay   2 trained, 'd be   3 don't lose, 'll be   4 'd be, had   5 didn't live, 'd visit   6 'll come, finish

2

a 1 score   2 lost   3 didn't win, missed   4 beat   5 have a go   6 track

3

a 2 essential for   3 interested in   4 good at   5 similar to   6 worried about   7 scared of

4

a 2 **A** W **B** S   3 S   4 S   5 **A** W **B** S

10B

1

a 1 hadn't fallen
2 wouldn't have been able to, I'd lost
3 wouldn't have married, she'd known
4 hadn't, mightn't have
5 wouldn't have, hadn't
6 hadn't read, wouldn't have found
7 would have won, hadn't missed
8 hadn't started, could have finished

b 2 would've got / would have got   3 'd arrived   4 wouldn't have missed   5 hadn't missed   6 wouldn't have had to   7 hadn't had to   8 wouldn't have gone   9 hadn't had   10 wouldn't have met   11 hadn't met   12 wouldn't have introduced

2

a 2 f   3 a   4 b   5 d   6 e

b 2 made   3 take   4 doing   5 made   6 take   7 doing

3

a 1 W   2 W, S   3 S, W

10C

1

a 2 feeling   3 worried   4 nothing   5 about   6 what if   7 definitely   8 happen   9 think   10 it'll

c 2 Anyway, as I was saying, I'm worried about my exam.
3 You've got nothing to worry about.
4 Speaking of music, did you see The X Factor last night?
5 You don't think it will be a bit boring?
6 She's definitely going to like the ring.
7 I'm afraid that something will go wrong.
8 By the way, have you met his new girlfriend?

2

a 2 U   3 U   4 S   5 U   6 S

10D

1

a a

b True: 2, 4; False: 1, 3, 5, 6

2

a 2 would   3 definitely   4 pretty   5 better   6 expect   7 should   8 suggesting

3

a Suggested answer:

Positive reply:

Hi Jane

That's brilliant news about your exams! Congratulations!

I think you should definitely accept your dad's offer of a job. I'm pretty sure you'd enjoy working in one of his hotels as a trainee manager. You'd probably become a hotel manager in a few years' time and that would be fantastic. Also, I think it would be better to take a job now instead of going to university for three years. It might be hard to find a job when you finish in three years' time. I think this could be an excellent opportunity for you, so, if I were you, I'd go for it.

Let me know what you decide to do.

Speak soon

Careful reply:

Hi Jane

That's brilliant news about your exams! Congratulations!

I'm not sure what I think about your dad's offer. I can see that it would be exciting to train as a hotel manager but, if I were you, I'd think about it very carefully before making a decision.

I expect you'd enjoy working in one of your dad's hotels, but you also need to think about your career. Maybe it would be better to go to university and get a degree before you start working in a permanent job? If you take a degree in Business Studies, you'll be able to apply for jobs in lots of different areas of business after you graduate. On the other hand, if you start working in the hotel industry now, you might find that it's hard to get into another area in the future. I'm just suggesting that it might be better to go to university first and then decide what you want to do after you graduate.

Let me know if you want to meet up and talk about it.

Speak soon

Reading and listening extension

1

a 2 Luis   3 Dean, Luis   4 Stevo, Micky   5 Pilar

b True: 1, 4, 5, 6, 7; False: 2, 3, 8

2

a 1 Wendy   2 Wendy   3 Phil   4 Wendy   5 Phil   6 Phil

b 1 b   2 a   3 a   4 a   5 a   6 c

Review and extension

1

2 If there hadn't been an accident, we wouldn't have missed our flight.
3 If I were you, I'd wait until the shop has a sale to buy a jacket.
4 She wouldn't have failed her exam if she had studied harder.
5 If she were nicer, she'd make more friends.
6 We would have caught the train on time if we had left the house earlier.
7 I'd buy a new car if I had more money.
8 If it hadn't rained yesterday, we would have played tennis.

2

2 I'm doing some research into how children spend their pocket money.
3 In the final set Roger Federer beat Rafael Nadal 6 – 2.
4 I'm terribly sorry, Madam, for making a mistake with your bill.
5 My cousin's really good at languages – she speaks German, French and Russian.
6 Samantha's very worried about her exams.
7 He made a lot of money when he worked in the City of London, but now he's a teacher.
8 We've been working for two hours now, so let's take / have a short break and have a coffee.

3

2 stole   3 miss   4 rises   5 lend   6 currently

Answer key

Video exercises

Unit 6
a 2 exciting 3 interesting 4 public transport looks like
b 2 d 3 a 4 c
c 2 d 3 h 4 g 5 a 6 b 7 f 8 e
d 2 a 3 c 4 c
e 2 d 3 a 4 b

Unit 7
a 2 lives 3 people 4 parks for children
b 2 c 3 a 4 b
c 2 a 3 d 4 b
d 2 b 3 b 4 a

Unit 8
a 2 b 3 a 4 c 5 b
b 2 on the train 3 shopping 4 the *Independent* 5 occasionally
c 2 b 3 a 4 e 5 d
d 2 entertainment 3 international 4 local 5 people
e 2 c 3 a 4 a 5 b

Unit 9
a 2 c 3 a 4 b 5 b
b 2 b 3 d 4 a
c 2 several years ago 3 the whole family 4 happy
d 2 d 3 c 4 a

Unit 10
a 2 c 3 a 4 c 5 c
b 2 d 3 a 4 e 5 b
c 2 daughter 3 respects 4 is not interested in 5 for the bus
d 2 d 3 b 4 a 5 c

Acknowledgements

The authors and publishers acknowledge the following sources of copyright material and are grateful for the permissions granted. While every effort has been made, it has not always been possible to identify the sources of all the material used, or to trace all copyright holders. If any omissions are brought to our notice, we will be happy to include the appropriate acknowledgements on reprinting and in the next update to the digital edition, as applicable.

The publisher has used its best endeavours to ensure that the URLs for external websites referred to in this book are correct and active at the time of going to press. However, the publisher has no responsibility for the websites and can make no guarantee that a site will remain live or that the content is or will remain appropriate.

The publishers are grateful to the following for permission to reproduce copyright photographs and material:

Key: L = left, C = centre, R = right, T = top, B = bottom

p.34(TR): Getty Images/Doug Menuez; p.34(BL): Shutterstock/SK Kim; p.35(CL): Shutterstock/ariadna de raadt; p.35(BR): Shutterstock/Yellowj; p.36(B): Shutterstock/Viacheslav Lopatin; p.36(TR): Shutterstock/antb; p.37(T): Shutterstock/posztos; p.38(CR): Shutterstock/RioPatuca; p.40(CL): Shutterstock/Tyler Olson; p.41(TL): Shutterstock/Adam Gregor; p.41(TR): Alamy/Blend Images/Jade; p.42(TR): Alamy/Inmagine; p.42(BR): Shutterstock/Diego Cervo; p.43(C): Getty Images/Karl Blackwel; p.43(BR): Getty Images/Ekaterina Monakhova; p.44(C): Shutterstock/Darren Brode; p.46(T): Shutterstock/Kiko Calderon ESP; p.47(CL): Shutterstock/Takacs Szabolcs; p.47(TR): Getty Images/Jupiterimages; p.48(BL): Getty Images/Yellow Dog Productions; p.48(TR): Alamy/Geof Kirby; p.49(TR): Alamy/imageBROKER/Martin Schrampf; p.50(CR): Shutterstock/Lopolo; p.50(BR): Shutterstock/Blend Images; p.50(TR): Shuttertsock/wellphoto; p.51(B): Shutterstock/ronstik; p.52(TL): Kobal/Lucasfilm/20th Century Fox; p.52(TR): Getty Images/ABC/Lorenzo Bevilaqua; p.53(TR): Shutterstock/Igor Bulgarin; p.54(TR): Shutterstock/cdrin; p.54(B): Ronald Grant Archive/Walt Disney Pictures/Pixar Animation Studios; p.55(TL): Shutterstock/Air Images; p.55(BR): Shutterstock/Goodluz; p.56(B): Shutterstock/gualtiero boffi; p.57(TL): Shutterstock/stocksolutions; p.58(TL): Shutterstock/MIMOHE; p.58(TR): Shutterstock/arek_malang; p.58(CR): Getty Images/AFP/PAUL ELLIS; p.59(TL): Shutterstock/CHEN WS; p.59(BL): Alamy/P.D. Amedzro; p.59(TR): Shutterstock/Viacheslav Lopatin; p.60(BL): Alamy/Wild Places Photography/Chris Howes; p.60(TR): Alamy/AF archive/A.F. ARCHIVE; p.61(CR): Shutterstock/marchello74; p.62(B): Shutterstock/Rob Hainer.

Video stills by Rob Maidment and Sharp Focus Productions: p.69, 71.

Filming in King's College by kind permission of the Provost and Scholars of King's College, Cambridge.

Illustrations by Ben Swift p. 49.